Hermogenes, *On Issues*

HERMOGENES

On Issues

Strategies of Argument in Later Greek
Rhetoric

MALCOLM HEATH

CLARENDON PRESS · OXFORD
1995

Oxford University Press, Walton Street, Oxford OX2 6DP

Oxford New York
Athens Auckland Bangkok Bombay
Calcutta Cape Town Dar es Salaam Delhi
Florence Hong Kong Istanbul Karachi
Kuala Lumpur Madras Madrid Melbourne
Mexico City Nairobi Paris Singapore
Taipei Tokyo Toronto
and associated companies in
Berlin Ibadan

Oxford is a trade mark of Oxford University Press

Published in the United States
by Oxford University Press Inc., New York

British Library Cataloguing in Publication Data
Data available

Library of Congress Cataloging in Publication Data
Hermogenes on issues : strategies of argument in Later Greek
rhetoric / Malcolm Heath.
Includes bibliographical references.
1. Hermogenes, 2nd cent.—Criticism and interpretation.
2. Persuasion (Rhetoric) 3. Rhetoric, Ancient. I. Title.
PA3998.H8H43 1995   808.53—dc20   94–40972
ISBN 0–19–814982–4

1 3 5 7 9 10 8 6 4 2

Typeset by Hope Services (Abingdon) Ltd.
Printed in Great Britain on acid-free paper by
Biddles Ltd., Guildford and King's Lynn

Preface

> It's funny how many of the best ideas are just an old idea back-to-front. You see there have already been several programs written that help you to arrive at decisions by properly ordering and analysing all the relevant facts so that they then point naturally towards the right decision. The drawback with these is that the decision which all the properly ordered and analysed facts point to is not necessarily the one you want . . . Well, Gordon's great insight was to design a program which allowed you to specify in advance what decision you wished to reach, and only then to give it all the facts. The program's task . . . was simply to construct a plausible series of logical-sounding steps to connect the premises with the conclusion.
>
> (Douglas Adams, *Dirk Gently's Holistic Detective Agency*
> (London 1987), 55)

The ancient world did not have computer programs, but it did have rhetoric, which was (one might say) just such a device as Douglas Adams describes: if you know what case you have to argue, then the theory of invention offers systematic guidance as to how that case may plausibly be argued.

My interest in this aspect of later Greek rhetorical theory and declamatory practice was first stimulated by Kennedy 1983 and Russell 1983. When I tried to go beyond these works and explore the primary sources, I found the lack of more detailed introductory aids frustrating; this book is meant to be something like the one that I would then have found useful. My primary aim is to make the theory of issues, a fundamental but complex and neglected component of mature Greek rhetoric, accessible to those who do not read Greek, and to those who do read Greek but are (as I was) baffled by the rhetoricians' formidable and often cryptically deployed apparatus of technical terms.

If I owe the initial stimulus to the work of Kennedy and Russell, the greatest debt I incurred in the writing of this book is to the students (nineteen from Leeds and one from Thessaloniki) who took part in an experimental course on practical rhetoric which I taught in 1991/2, using a draft of the translation of Hermogenes as a set text. The intricate technicalities of ancient rhetorical theory are often dismissed (even by scholars who have a specialist interest in the subject) as sterile, mechanical, and pedantic. Such criticisms were not unknown even in antiquity; conceivably they are right. But how then are we to account for the cultural dominance of rhetoric in the ancient world? Why did rhetoric continue for so long to be central to ancient education? And why were classical patterns of rhetorical education revived in western Europe during the Renaissance? It is at least worth considering the possibility that we have missed something important. One obvious point is that such criticisms are generally made from an external viewpoint. We approach rhetorical theory as observers, and are disappointed to find a rather dull set of classifications and rules. But rhetoric was in essence a practical discipline, and we cannot expect its theoretical base to make proper sense when divorced from practice. What, then, if we were to adopt an internal perspective—the point of view of someone who tries to master rhetorical theory in order to apply it as a practical tool? The discipline of applying issue-theory myself, and of trying to teach students to apply it, forced me to confront many problems which I might otherwise have evaded, and brought to light many solutions which I might otherwise have overlooked. This opportunity to test and develop my understanding of the theory through its practical application laid the foundations of the present book.

M.H.

University of Leeds
May 1994

Contents

vii

CONTENTS

Note to the Reader

Much of the material covered in this book is unfamiliar even to specialists in ancient rhetoric, and I have therefore expanded the conventional indexes of names and technical terms into a brief prosopography and glossary. Readers baffled by unexplained references in the text will (I hope) find some enlightenment there.

An asterisk prefixed to a bare reference indicates that there is a relevant note (or series of notes) in the commentary on that passage of Hermogenes in Chapter 3; when prefixed to the name of any other ancient author the asterisk means that the text in question is one of the examples included in Chapter 4. Cross-references within the prosopography and glossary are also indicated by an asterisk prefixed to a term or name.

1   Prolegomena

I.I INTRODUCTION

Rhetoric is concerned with the persuasive use of language. In a broad sense, any skilled use of language to persuade or influence others could be counted as rhetoric; but in a stricter sense rhetoric is the consciously skilled use of language to persuade. The rhetoricians' claim is that they speak or write well because their speech and writing is based on an explicit understanding of the general principles which govern the effective use of language. It is possible to speak or write well through innate talent, or because one has simply acquired a knack of effective communication through practice; but (according to the rhetorician) conscious technique can supplement or enhance that unreflective eloquence.

In the modern world rhetoric has acquired a bad name; the characteristic modern use of the word is dismissive, so that we talk disparagingly of 'empty rhetoric' and 'rhetorical tricks'.[1] This modern prejudice makes it hard for us to appreciate the prestige and influence which rhetoric enjoyed in antiquity. It had its ancient detractors; but they were detracting from an institution central to their culture. The culturally dominant position of rhetoric is reflected above all in the place it had in ancient education. In Greece from the fourth century BC through to Byzantine times, and in the Roman world from the end of the second century BC onwards, rhetoric became a key component of the post-elementary curriculum. Every member of the educated male élite received in

---

[1] In *Collins COBUILD English Language Dictionary* (London 1987), based on a 20-million-word corpus of contemporary English texts, the entry for 'rhetoric' begins: 'Rhetoric is . . . speech or writing that is presented in a forceful and dramatic way which appears to be clever and important; often used showing disapproval. EG *She simply ignored his bluster as empty rhetoric . . . The liberalism of their rulers was a rhetoric masking vicious exploitation . . .*'. Note 'appears to be'; rhetoric is habitually invoked to make an antithesis between style and substance, as in this comment on a British politician: 'He has been criticised in the past for too much rhetoric and not enough substance' (presenter on BBC Radio 4's *PM* news programme, 4 October 1991).

adolescence a systematic training in the persuasive use of language; the assumptions and habits which this training inculcated were the common currency of their cultural, social, and political life. To understand these people, we must understand their rhetoric.

At the heart of ancient rhetoric in its mature form was a body of theory (the theory of στάσις, or issue)[2] which sought to classify the different kinds of dispute with which speakers have to deal, and to develop effective strategies of argument for handling each kind. The present book aims to provide an introduction to this branch of rhetoric in the highly developed form which it achieved through the work of Greek rhetoricians of the second century AD.

The core of the book (Chapter 2) is a translation of the fullest surviving systematic treatment of the theory, Hermogenes *On Issues*. The accompanying commentary (Chapter 3) aims to elucidate Hermogenes' text, and especially to understand the rationale of his detailed recommendations for the handling of each issue. I have also tried to give some idea of the diversity of opinions about many of the problems discussed by Hermogenes which existed within the tradition in which he worked. Hermogenes' treatise acquired an authoritative standing in late antiquity (which indeed is the reason for its survival), but in his own day Hermogenes was one rhetorician among many, and not the most influential; it is important, therefore, to balance our awareness of Hermogenes as an individual with a sense of the larger tradition of which he was part. Nevertheless, the primary concern of this book is systematic rather than historical. In general, I am interested more in the intelligibility and internal coherence of Hermogenes' system (and of the closely related systems of his colleagues and rivals) as a set of model argumentative strategies than in the development of issue-theory over time. So, for example, I have little to say here about the evolution of Hermogenean issue-theory from the significantly different Hellenistic systems attested in Cicero.

The impression most likely to arise from a first reading of Hermogenes and his commentators is that ancient rhetorical theorists were preoccupied with a pedantic and arbitrary shuffling of terms. This patronizing notion should be resisted. The rhetoricians were intelligent professionals, charged with teaching young people effective ways of coping with certain kinds of practical problem. The formidable abstraction and complexity of the theory they developed may reflect the

---

[2] This rendering of the term derives from Thomas Wilson's *Arte of Rhetorique*, first published in 1553; see the facsimile of the 1560 reprint, ed. G. H. Mair (Oxford 1909), 88 f.

intrinsic difficulty of the problems and the seriousness with which they were taken, and not simply an academic obsession with trivia. When we read rhetorical theory we should not forget that the theories were meant to be applied in practice; nor, when we read works written by the rhetorically trained, should we forget the sophisticated system of theory that informed their writing. To help bridge the gap between theory and application, I have given in Chapter 4 a selection of ancient rhetorical exercises and analyses in which issue-theory can be seen at work.

By way of orientation, Chapter 1 offers a brief overview of ancient rhetoric, the rhetorical curriculum, and the place of issue-theory within it.[3] Naturally this overview makes no pretence to being either comprehensive or authoritative. No single system of rhetorical theory enjoyed undisputed authority in the ancient world, since different rhetoricians had different views on many aspects of the subject. I have therefore selected from the diverse resources which the tradition makes available those elements which seemed most useful for the purpose in hand (and this is precisely what any ancient teacher of rhetoric had to do).

1.2 WHAT IS RHETORIC?

The use of language is a distinguishing feature of humankind in general; but human beings are also distinguished from each other by their effectiveness in using this shared capacity. This fact prompts a series of questions. Why are some speakers more effective than others? Why are certain approaches effective in certain situations? What underlying rationale is manifested in the observable patterns of effective speech? Most important, can we grasp that rationale in such a way as to make us more effective speakers than we are by natural talent or acquired habit? The rhetorician seeks to understand the phenomena of persuasion and to derive from that understanding an ordered set of techniques for identifying, organizing, and presenting to maximum effect the resources for discursive persuasion inherent in any given situation.[4]

---

[3] The best introduction to the material covered in this book is Russell 1983. For a concise general overview of classical rhetoric see Kennedy 1980, 3–119, 161–72; see also Kennedy's history of classical rhetoric in three volumes (1963, 1972, 1983), of which the last (and best) volume is particularly relevant. There is also a convenient overview of rhetorical doctrine in Clark 1957, 67–143.

[4] The optimum definition of rhetoric was a question much discussed by experts in antiquity; various definitions are collected in Quintilian 2. 15; cf. Martin 1974, 2–6. A

Rhetoric claims to understand and make explicit the underlying principles of persuasion, and thus to be an art or methodical expertise (in Greek, τέχνη).[5] We should note the limited nature of this claim. A discipline such as mathematics deals with matters that are necessary and invariant; the answer to a given mathematical problem will be the same in whatever circumstances it is solved. Rhetoric deals with matters that are contingent and occasion-dependent; the answer to a rhetorical problem will vary according to the circumstances. Since concrete situations are infinitely variable it is not possible to anticipate and prescribe for every possible situation; therefore no system of rhetoric can be exhaustive. The rhetoricians did not imagine that powers of persuasion could be reduced to an intelligible technique; they were aware that innate talent and acquired habit continue to be crucial to the success even of a trained speaker. The rhetorical theorist is concerned with general principles, but the speaker is always concerned in the last analysis with what is appropriate in the particular situation. The particular is indefinite; it cannot be exhaustively characterized by any finite set of generalized propositions. Therefore the principles which rhetoric teaches cannot be applied mechanically. A speaker has to consider not only what rhetorical theory recommends for a situation of this kind, but also what is best in this particular, and in some respects unique, situation.[6]

This means that there is an irreducible place for judgement as well as for the application of explicit principles. So rhetoric may claim to supplement and enhance, but not to replace, a natural talent or acquired knack of effective speaking; talent may indeed be the decisive element, since it will make the difference between the competent and the brilliant orator. But there are no grounds in this for dismissing the rhetorician's

typical example might be that expounded in Nicolaus *Prog.* 2. 11–3. 13 Felten: rhetoric is 'a faculty of discovering and expressing in an orderly way the possible means of persuasion in any discourse' (see Kennedy 1983, 68).

[5] See e.g. Aristotle *Rhet.* 1354ª6–11; Quintilian 2. 17. The concept of rhetoric as τέχνη was the first target of Plato's critique of rhetoric. In the *Gorgias* rhetoric is seen as just a knack, devoid of rational understanding (462b–466a); a genuine art of rhetoric would be indistinguishable from Socrates' own practice of philosophy (503a, 504d–e). For a later critique see Sextus Empiricus *Adv. Math.* 2.

[6] Quintilian 2. 13. 2: 'If the whole of rhetoric could be thus embodied in one compact code, it would be an easy task of little compass: but most rules are liable to be altered by the nature of the case, circumstances of time and place, and by hard necessity itself. Consequently the all-important gift for an orator is a wise adaptability since he is called upon to meet the most varied emergencies' (tr. H. E. Butler). Cf. e.g. Isocrates *Antidosis* 183 f.; Dionysius of Halicarnassus *On Composition* 12 (45. 6–21); and see n. 63 below.

systematic understanding of principle as superfluous. Untutored genius may excel tutored mediocrity: tutored genius will excel both.[7]

Rhetoricians could claim, therefore, that their art perfected the distinctively human capacity for rational discourse, and was for this reason an indispensable adjunct of civilized existence.[8] But so positive an image of rhetoric did not prevail at once; at first it was received with suspicion, and indeed hostility.[9] This is understandable. A community which resolves political and judicial disagreements through public discussion is likely to be dismayed by the discovery that the decisions which it reaches through discussion may reflect not the superior rationality of the policy adopted or the superior justice of the verdict reached, but simply the superior technique of one of the speakers. Ancient critics of rhetoric often characterized it as essentially manipulative: clever experts devise ways of deceiving gullible audiences.

This picture is not wholly convincing. Audiences are not passive lumps; they are composed of intelligent individuals, capable of responding to the speaker's arguments with critical suspicion. Moreover, judicial and deliberative oratory typically takes place in an adversarial context; each of the adversaries will encourage the audience's instinct to view the other's arguments critically. The more devious, deceitful, and manipulative a speaker's case, the more likely it is that the audience will see through it, with or without the opponent's prompting. The context in which rhetoric operates therefore places a premium on good arguments; and the more widely disseminated rhetoric is, the greater that premium. An audience (or opponent) trained in rhetoric will understand the techniques of the persuasive use of language, and so be better able to respond to them critically. One might argue then that rhetoric is as much an antidote to the (presumably no less pernicious) manipulative potential of natural eloquence; and the more widely rhetoric is disseminated, the less likely it is to function manipulatively.

The crucial factor in the transformation of rhetoric from subversive intruder to a fundamental element in ancient culture was its success in

---

[7] So Quintilian 2. 17. 11–13; cf. 2. 11 f., 19.

[8] Cicero *Inv.* 1. 5: 'Men, although lower and weaker than animals in many respects, excel them most by having the power of speech. Therefore that man appears to me to have won a splendid possession who excels men themselves in that ability by which men excel beasts. And if, as it happens, this is not brought about by nature alone nor by practice, but is also acquired from some systematic instruction, it is not out of place to see what those say who have left us some directions for the study of oratory' (tr. H. M. Hubbell). Cf. Isocrates *Nicocles* 5–9; Cicero *De Or.* 1. 32; Quintilian 2. 16. 11–19.

[9] For popular suspicion of the products of rhetorical training in 4th-cent. Athens see Ober 1989, 165–77.

the educational market-place. If the principles governing the effective use of language to persuade can be made explicit, then they can be taught; and if they can be taught there is a strong incentive to learn them. In the ancient world the maintenance and improvement of one's social and political position was deeply dependent on the ability to speak effectively. In consequence, rhetoric became the core component of post-elementary education in the Greek world from the fourth century BC onwards; and it was part of the cultural package which the Romans in turn took over from their Hellenistic Greek neighbours. Thereafter, to belong to the (admittedly restricted) class of highly educated persons was to have received a systematic training in the techniques of persuasive argument.

The social and cultural significance of this training naturally varied in its long history. A wealthy Athenian citizen of the fourth century BC might reasonably have regarded a training in rhetoric as a key practical requirement; he would know that, in the conditions of Athenian democracy, his political influence depended on the effectiveness with which he spoke in the assembly, and that the security of his property, and indeed of his life, might depend on the effectiveness with which he spoke in the law-courts.[10] For his counterpart in the fourth century AD things were rather different. Political power in the late Roman empire was vested in a military autocrat and mediated by a rapidly expanding bureaucracy.[11] In these circumstances, a more efficient way to protect your property might be to enter the civil service or become an advocate, and so secure tax immunities; and the essential subjects for these professions were not rhetoric but Latin and law.[12] Thus Libanius, who held an official chair of rhetoric in Antioch in Syria in the fourth century AD, complains in his autobiography about the way in which these more practical and remunerative subjects had begun to draw people away from the schools of rhetoric.[13] By this stage, rhetoric had been forced back on an appeal to cultural rather than material values to defend itself. This was perfectly legitimate. Rhetorical education involved courses of supervised reading in classical literature (embracing poets, historians, and philoso-

---

[10] Ober 1989, 104–51.

[11] A. H. M. Jones 1964; Brown 1971. For the intellectual and social background to rhetoric in the imperial period see Anderson 1989, 1993; Bowersock 1969, 1974; Bowie 1982; Brown 1992.

[12] Liebeschuetz 1972, 174–86.

[13] For the declining prestige of rhetoric see Libanius Or. 1. 154, 214, and 234, 2. 43 f.; Liebeschuetz 1972, 242–55.

phers as well as orators)[14] and the imitation of these models; the rhetoricians could therefore justly claim that rhetoric was a primary vector of classical culture to their contemporaries. Modern experience suggests that such claims are not always compellingly persuasive in practice.

We should not, however, overestimate the rhetoricians' loss of standing and custom. Even if the advanced study of rhetoric was losing ground, it can still be taken for granted that Libanius' uncultured bureaucrats had been through the basic course in rhetoric in their early to middle teens. Rhetorical training was a universal given within the literate élite, and remained a basic presupposition of social, political, and cultural activity.[15]

I.3 RHETORIC IN OUTLINE

Rhetoric is concerned with the whole process of persuasion in language, from the speaker's first thoughts about the subject in hand to the actual delivery of the speech. This process can be analysed in various ways. One popular scheme identified five distinct phases.[16] First the speaker identifies the argumentative and other resources available to him; then he organizes them; then he puts them into words; he commits the speech thus composed to memory; and finally he delivers it.

A technical term for the first phase is invention. The Latin word *inventio*, like its Greek equivalent εὕρεσις, means 'discovery'; the rhetorician does not make things up, but identifies the resources for persuasion which exist objectively in the subject and situation. Some rhetoricians distinguished invention from a subsequent phase of assessment and selection.[17] Typically a speaker will aim to generate a superabundance from which to select an effective combination of mutually supporting material. To make such a selection, however, the speaker must already have an eye on the way the material will be organized; invention and disposition (the second phase of the five-part scheme) are therefore closely interlinked. Together they comprise that part of rhetoric concerned with

---

[14] The most important surviving prescription is in Quintilian 10. 1; there are comparable prescriptions in Greek sources, notably Dionysius of Halicarnassus *On Imitation*, Dio Chrysostom *Or.* 18, and Hermogenes *Id.* 2. 10–12 (on which see Rutherford 1992).

[15] Liebeschuetz 1972, 242, 252–5; Brown 1992, 30 f., 35–70.

[16] Thus e.g. Quintilian 3. 3. 1–10, with a survey of some alternative schemes.

[17] See Quintilian 3. 3. 5, 9 (= Hermagoras fr. 1), 6. 5. 1; Zeno 320. 6–8; Dionysius of Halicarnassus *Lys.* 15 (25. 24–26. 2), *Isocr.* 4 (60. 12 f.), 12 (71. 15); Cicero *Or.* 47–9, *De Or.* 2. 307–9; [Augustine] 137. 8 f.

content (what in Greek could be called the πραγματικὸς τόπος, the practical department).[18]

The verbal department of rhetoric (the λεκτικὸς τόπος) is concerned with diction, word-order, rhythm, figures of speech, and so forth. It is hardly surprising that ancient rhetoricians paid a great deal of attention to this aspect of their craft; speakers want to present their arguments well. But first they must have arguments to present, and preferably good arguments since their aim is to convince a possibly sceptical audience in the face of an opponent who will delight in pulling bad or specious arguments to pieces.[19] Despite its interest in style, therefore, ancient rhetoric was also and inevitably concerned at root with matters of substance—that is, with the techniques by which the means of persuasion are identified, critically assessed, and effectively ordered. The present book is about one fundamental aspect of rhetorical invention.

It may be helpful to approach invention by identifying first of all the components of the situation in which rhetoric is applied: a speaker addresses an audience on a given subject against a certain opponent. These components of the situation and their interrelations can all present the speaker with opportunities to exploit and problems to overcome. For example, is the audience prejudiced against the speaker, or in favour of the opponent? Is the audience indifferent to the subject? Is the audience already committed to a particular view of the subject? Is it a complex subject that the audience will find hard to understand? Is the subject one in which the speaker is a recognized expert? Is it one in which he or she might be suspected of having a vested interest? Such factors have an obvious bearing on the effect one's speech will have, and have therefore to be taken into account in the preparation of one's case.

When a case is being prepared there are several aims which have to be kept in view. A speaker has of course to inform (or, if need be, to misinform)[20] the audience about the subject in hand. But the audience's role is not simply to assimilate information; we typically want them to act on that information, if only by casting their vote in our favour at the end of

---

[18] Dionysius of Halicarnassus *Lys.* 15 (25. 8–10), *Isocr.* 4 (60. 9), *Dem.* 51 (240. 20–2), *Thuc.* 34 (381. 11–14); for the division of rhetoric into content and words cf. e.g. Cicero *Part.* 3, Quintilian 3. 3. 1, 3. 5. 1. On the 'contamination' of invention and disposition in Hellenistic rhetoric see Wisse 1989, 77 f., 83–92.

[19] e.g. Cicero *Inv.* 1. 45: 'It will be necessary to keep a sharp watch that this kind of argument [sc. *conclusio*] cannot be refuted in any way, so that the proof may not contain only a form of argument and a mere appearance of a necessary conclusion, but rather may rest on rigorous reasoning' (tr. H. M. Hubbell).

[20] The issues raised by this possibility are discussed by Quintilian, 2. 17. 19–21, 26–9.

a trial or debate; so we have also to motivate them. But we will not be able to communicate either information or motivation effectively if the audience is bored or alienated; so we also need to attract them. These three tasks can be seen as loosely correlated with the main kinds of persuasive resource available to us. To persuade the audience that the view of the subject we wish to convey is correct we will have to deploy rational argument. To incite the audience to act on that view of the subject we will seek to arouse the audience's emotions. To attract the audience to our side we will want to project an impression of our own character that will inspire confidence.[21]

This correlation of tasks and persuasive resources has a bearing also on the typical structure of a speech. Of course, all the speaker's aims must be kept in view at all times, so that the various resources will be distributed throughout a speech; but it is legitimate to see different emphases as characteristic of different parts. It is particularly important to put the audience into a receptive mood at the outset, to ensure that they listen to our presentation of the subject with attention and sympathy; techniques for attracting the audience to our side will therefore tend to concentrate in the opening part of the speech.[22] On the other hand, there is little point in trying to incite the audience until we have established the view of the subject on which we want them to act; emotive devices will therefore tend to concentrate in the concluding part.[23] In a judicial speech especially, the presentation of the subject in hand is likely to involve two relatively distinct things: a certain version of the facts must be set before the audience; and it must be shown that this version is correct, and that the correct inferences have been drawn from the facts. This gives a four-part scheme: prologue, narrative, proof, epilogue.[24] More elaborate

[21] Resources: Aristotle *Rhet.* 1356ᵃ1–20; Dionysius of Halicarnassus *Lys.* 19 (30. 21–31. 2); Minucianus 340. 6 f. Spengel–Hammer; Neocles *ap.* Anon. Seguerianus 198; Quintilian 5. 8. 3. A binary classification of resources as practical or emotional is found in Cicero *Brutus* 89; Anon. Seguerianus 203; *RG* 4. 417. 12–26; Quintilian 6. 1. 1 (and see n. 24 below). On the orator's three tasks: Cicero *De Or.* 2. 115, *Brutus* 185; Quintilian 3. 5. 2. Cf. Fortenbaugh 1988, Wisse 1989.

[22] On the prologue: Cicero *Inv.* 1. 20–6; Quintilian 4. 1; Anon. Seguerianus 1–39; Apsines 217. 2–242. 11; [Hermogenes] *Inv.* 93. 4–108. 17.

[23] On the epilogue: Cicero *Inv.* 1. 98–109; Quintilian 6. 1 f.; Anon. Seguerianus 198–253; Apsines 296. 13–329. 23.

[24] Aristotle *Rhet.* 1414ᵇ7–9; Theodectes *ap. PS* 32. 6–9, 216. 1–4; [Dionysius] 367. 18–21; Anon. Seguerianus 1; Zeno 320. 14–16; and cf. Cicero *Part.* 4, Apsines 297. 2–6: 'Every speech is divided into two elements (I am speaking of the judicial speech here), the practical and the emotional. Narrative and proof are subsumed under the practical, proem and epilogue under the emotional.' Historians of rhetoric in late antiquity attributed the

systems are common. In particular, the proof could be divided into two parts (by distinguishing the confirmation of one's own view from the refutation of the opponent's) or three (by prefixing a 'partition', setting out what one thinks are the questions at issue), giving a five- or six-part scheme.[25] But the underlying concept of a speech's typical structure is not altered by these refinements.

Just as different parts of a speech may emphasize different components of the rhetorician's repertoire, so different subjects require a different emphasis in their treatment; thus the correlated tasks and resources of a speaker also provided ancient rhetoricians with one of their systems for classifying speeches. A fourfold scheme distinguishes 'practical' themes, which invite a treatment oriented primarily towards objective facts and therefore dependent largely on the resource of argument, from those which invite a treatment based primarily on character or on emotion, while allowing also for 'mixed' themes.[26] Themes could also be classified in terms of the problems they pose in managing the audience's response. An ideal subject would be honourable, weighty, plausible, and readily intelligible; where a theme has a discreditable aspect, or is trivial or paradoxical or hard to follow, special care must be taken (especially in the proem) to make the audience sympathetic and attentive.[27]

More familiar is the classification of themes according to their context and function as judicial, deliberative, and epideictic.[28] The typical context of judicial oratory is (as the name implies) a court of law; it aims to reach a verdict on some past act. Deliberative oratory is concerned with the future, commending one or another course of action. Epideictic oratory is, essentially, everything else; it is therefore not easy to define. It aims to persuade, in the sense of commanding the audience's assent

fourfold scheme to the supposed 5th-cent. 'founder' of the art, Corax: *PS* 67. 3–7, 125. 22–126. 15, 189. 13–17 (variants in 25. 11–26. 6 cf. 270. 7–24; 52. 3–20); see Cole 1991.

[25] Five parts: Cicero *Or.* 122; Quintilian 3. 9. 1–5. Six parts: *Rhet. ad Herennium* 1. 4; Cicero *Inv.* 1. 19; Sulpicius Victor 322. 4–9 substitutes this for the fourfold scheme of his main source, Zeno.

[26] This is Aquila's version of the scheme (Syrianus 2. 43. 13–23). Substitutes for the practical species are found in Zeno (316. 3–22: judicial, but omitting the mixed form) and in the scholia to Hermogenes, attributed to Dionysius (*RG* 4. 190. 12–18: panegyric and deliberative) and Minucianus (Syrianus 2. 42. 11–43. 12, *RG* 7. 165. 17–24: panegyric and judicial; *RG* 4. 182. 8–183. 14: judicial only); cf. also Fortunatianus 88 f.

[27] See Quintilian 4. 1. 40 f.; Cicero *Inv.* 1. 20; *Rhet. ad Herennium* 1. 5; Zeno 316. 23–317. 31; [Augustine] 147. 18–151. 4 (= Hermagoras fr. 23a).

[28] e.g. Aristotle *Rhet.* 1358ᵃ36–ᵇ8; *Rhet. ad Herennium* 1. 2; Cicero *Inv.* 1. 7; Quintilian 3. 4.

and/or admiration, but no immediate action is demanded of them; thus, for example, praise of the deceased at a funeral or of the honorand at some ceremonial occasion would be instances of epideictic. Epideictic oratory was treated in a special way in ancient rhetoric; the primary concern of this book will be with the judicial and deliberative branches of rhetoric.

These classifications had a practical point; a speaker will need to approach different kinds of theme in different ways. Classifying one's speech was therefore a crucial foundation for invention; some theorists identified a preliminary phase in which the theme was analysed in these terms.[29] The theory of issues played a central role in this preliminary analysis. But before considering this topic more closely we should set it in context by looking at the rhetorical curriculum.

1.4 THE RHETORICAL CURRICULUM

Education in the ancient world was primarily a matter of private rather than of state provision; since that provision seems to have varied from time to time and place to place generalizations about the typical pattern of ancient education are hazardous.[30] For our present purposes, little need be said about the early stages. After acquiring the rudiments of literacy, either at home or with an elementary teacher, a Greek son of wealthy parents in late antiquity would have attended the school of a 'grammar' teacher (γραμματικός), working on topics such as grammar, correctness of style and language, and metre. Literary texts, especially poetry, were studied closely. The language, content, moral import, and literary aspects of the text were expounded; careful attention was given to correct reading aloud (not easy in the ancient world, where written texts had neither word-division nor punctuation); rote memorization was stressed. After some years with the grammarian, the boy would progress to the teacher of rhetoric (ῥήτωρ); in the Greek-speaking world

---

[29] For this analytical phase (νόησις) see Zeno 315. 5–319. 35, giving a tripartite scheme together with invention and disposition, which subsumes (320. 29 f.) the verbal expression and delivery as well as the organization of material; cf. PS 60. 21–61. 12, 69. 1–6, 175. 16–177. 7, 199. 25–202. 8; [Augustine] 137. 4–6.

[30] Kaster 1983 has shown that the conventional account of a three-stage educational system, with a clear demarcation between the primary and secondary teacher (γραμματιστής and γραμματικός) is an over-simplification. In general, the best synoptic treatment of ancient education is Bonner 1977; also relevant is Clark 1957. Walden 1909 contains much useful material (despite its misleading title).

the courses in grammar and rhetoric overlapped, and the pupil would continue to attend the grammarian's school for a while.[31] Some talented students, especially those aiming for a rhetorical career of their own, would go on to do further advanced work in rhetoric, perhaps travelling to a major academic centre like Athens for this purpose. For example, in AD 362/3, having already studied rhetoric in his home city Sardis, Eunapius went to Athens for advanced work under the sophist Prohaeresius; he was then aged 15, and stayed in Athens for four years.[32]

So the ancient rhetoricians were above all teachers. Naturally the sneer that 'those who can, do: those who can't, teach' was current in antiquity; it can be found, for example, in Cicero.[33] But Cicero, who received extensive tuition from Greek rhetors, himself constitutes evidence to the other side's advantage; those who can, have been taught. In any case, the choice of a professor of rhetoric as ambassador, as advocate, or as speaker on a ceremonial occasion was commonplace, and many sophists did speak in the courts;[34] those who taught, therefore, could, and often did. But although this sneer at teachers of rhetoric is unconvincing, the pairing of teaching and doing conveys an important point. What the rhetoricians taught was a practical skill. The criterion of their success was not whether their pupils went away with a systematic abstract understanding of the principles of persuasion, but whether they had acquired the ability to apply those principles concretely—that is, whether they could in

[31] In Roman schools especially the grammar teacher increasingly took over the preliminary exercises in rhetoric, postponing the pupil's progress to the rhetoric school: Quintilian 2. 1. On the grammarians see Kaster 1988.

[32] Eunapius 493; Penella 1990, 1–5. Libanius likewise was a student in Athens for four years, but his early career was unusual (*Or.* 1. 5–8; cf. Booth 1983). His enthusiasm for rhetoric was kindled when he was 14 or 15, when he had completed the grammarian's standard curriculum and after he had started working with a rhetor; to make up for his earlier slackness he studied for five more years in his native Antioch, concentrating on memorization of the classics rather than on rhetoric *per se*.

[33] e.g. *De Or.* 2. 75 (the speaker is Catulus, not Cicero *propria persona*): 'Nor do I need any Greek professor to chant at me a series of hackneyed axioms, when he himself never had a glimpse of a law-court or judicial proceedings' (tr. H. Rackham). Note also the youthful Cicero's snide assessment of Hermagoras (perhaps reflecting the professional jealousy of Cicero's own teacher): 'for an orator it is a very slight thing to talk about his art, as he has done; by far the most important thing is to speak in accordance with the principles of his art, which we all see he was wholly incapable of doing' (*Inv.* 1. 8, tr. H. M. Hubbell). According to Sextus Empiricus (*Adv. Math.* 2. 18) in open court the sophists are 'more mute than fish'; cf. Quintilian 10. 5. 18; Philostratus 614.

[34] Thus Philostratus attests to forensic activity on the part of Nicetes (511), Scopelian (516, 519), Polemo (524 f.), Theodotus (567), Ptolemy of Naucratis (595), Apollonius of Athens (600), and Damianus (606); and it is a matter of remark when a sophist active in his own city, such as Nicetes (511) or Antiochus (568), preferred not to address the local assembly. See further Bowersock 1969, 43–58; Bowie 1982; Russell 1983, 12 f.

fact speak persuasively. Hence the main focus of rhetorical education was on practical exercises. We can distinguish two stages.

(a) Preliminary Exercises

The first stage was based on a series of exercises in composition called 'preliminary exercises' (γυμνάσματα or προγυμνάσματα).[35] These ranged from the very simple to the moderately sophisticated; as the student progressed through them techniques and concepts which would be fundamental in more advanced work were gradually introduced. The sequence and recommended treatment of these exercises varies between different rhetoricians; my outline here follows the treatise of the fourth-century rhetor Aphthonius.[36]

The sequence begins with the retelling of a *fable*, a simple exercise providing continuity with the kinds of material a child had met at earlier stages of his education. The second exercise was *narration*. Narrative was part of the typical structure of a judicial speech; the ability to present a clear, concise, and plausible account of events was therefore a basic requirement. The student would be introduced here to the six elements of circumstance (who? what? when? where? how? why?), which will be important in the construction both of narrative and of arguments in advanced exercises.[37]

The third exercise was the *anecdote* (χρεία); in it the student was given some wise saying and required to develop it as the theme of a moral essay; for example, one theme understandably popular with teachers of rhetoric was the saying attributed to Isocrates that 'the root of education

---

[35] Modern discussions of the preliminary exercises include Kennedy 1983, 53–70; Bonner 1977, 250–76; Clark 1957, 177–212; Hock and O'Neill 1986, 9–22 (on the terminology 12–15); Anderson 1993, 47–53.

[36] Aphthonius is translated in Matsen *et al.* 1990, 267–88 (a revision of Nadeau 1952); the brief treatise falsely attributed to Hermogenes is translated in C. S. Baldwin 1928, 23–8. Both include illustrative treatments of each exercise (but the translation of the examples in Aphthonius is extremely unreliable: Matsen's revision of Nadeau concentrates on the theoretical sections, leaving the examples substantially untouched). More expansive and polished examples can be found in the works of Libanius, unfortunately untranslated. Pseudo-Hermogenes is in substantial agreement with Aphthonius, as is Nicolaus of Myra; the treatise of the 1st-cent. rhetor Theon stands in a significantly different tradition. Only the prefaces of Nicolaus and Theon are available in translation (Matsen *et al.* 1990, 254–65). Quintilian includes a survey of the preliminary exercises in his account of rhetorical education (2. 4).

[37] See [Hermogenes] *Inv.* 140. 10–147. 15; Quintilian 5. 10 (the term 'circumstance' appears at 104), cf. 3. 5. 17 f.; [Augustine] 141. 8–142. 14 (= Hermagoras fr. 7).

is bitter, its fruit sweet'.[38] The fourth exercise, *maxim*, was essentially the same; the theoretical distinction is that maxims are not explicitly attributed, but in fact their source was usually known.[39] In these exercises the student was expected to follow a standardized pattern in developing his theme; thus in anecdote one should:

first praise the figure to whom the saying is attributed;
then paraphrase the saying;
then uphold the saying in various ways:
• by showing why it is true;
• by pointing to its converse;
• by adducing analogies;
• by giving examples; and finally:
• by citing other authorities for the same principle;
conclude the treatment with an exhortation.

This procedure may seem mechanical. But ancient rhetoricians could have maintained with some justification that the standard structure is recommended because it is a good one—arguably the best, and certainly better than a student might devise off the top of his head. The headings do not tell the student what arguments to use; but they do tell him where to look for arguments. This means that the student does not have to work out from scratch how to treat each theme set to him; he knows already how to treat a theme of this kind, and can address himself immediately to determining the most effective arguments for this individual theme. Having a general framework ready in advance means that effort can be concentrated on the specifics of the particular problem in hand. Of course, there will be cases where the general framework is best modified or abandoned; but the student who has experience in working within the framework is likely to be a better judge of such occasions. The principle that a theme can be divided into a standardized sequence of heads is basic to issue-theory; here too, therefore, the student is being gently introduced to something that he will need to master in a more sophisticated form in advanced exercises.

The purpose of these two exercises was not, of course, for the student to express an opinion on the prescribed theme. Aphthonius illustrates

---

[38] Aphthonius and pseudo-Hermogenes both use this theme for their example; we also have a more elaborate treatment by Libanius which shows how the standard scheme for this exercise could be handled with extraordinary wit and elegance (8. 82–97 Foerster; summary in Bonner 1977, 259 f.). On χρεία in general see Hock and O'Neill 1986.

[39] There is an early example of maxim in *Rhet. ad Herennium* 4. 57.

maxim by developing some lines of Theognis on the disadvantages of poverty; he would have wanted his students to be able to elaborate a maxim in praise of poverty with equal facility. Rhetoric is able to argue both sides of a case;[40] hence some of the later and more explicitly argumentative exercises come in antithetical pairs.

The next two exercises provide the first antithetical pair by taking the student back to narrative: he is required to offer a *refutation* or *confirmation* of some story. As in anecdote and maxim the student is supplied with standard sources of arguments: he will consider whether the story can be faulted as contradictory, implausible, immoral, and so forth. But these heads do not determine the structure of the composition; one should follow the order of events in the story. This can be done in two ways. Aphthonius' example of refutation sets the story out as a whole and then gives the criticisms *en masse*; his confirmation tells the same story piecemeal, defending each step of the story before moving on to the next. The student is thus offered two models for organizing material.[41]

The seventh exercise is the *common topic*. The student elaborates on generalizations applicable to any instance of a given category; for example, the common topics against adulterers or tyrants provide material for attacks on any particular adulterer or tyrant.[42] It is essentially an exercise in amplification, that is in the techniques of increasing the perceived importance of some fact that is taken as given.[43] Amplification will be required as a regular element in the advanced exercises, especially in the epilogue where the incitement of emotion comes to the fore; a prosecutor will need to persuade the jury not only that the defendant is guilty of (for example) murder, but also that murder is a serious crime and deserves to be treated severely. To help handle common topics the student was taught a checklist of criteria by which an action can be assessed: is it legal? just? honourable? advantageous? feasible? what will its consequences be? These so-called heads of purpose will have a number of applications in more advanced exercises.[44]

[40] e.g. Quintilian 2. 17. 30–6; Sextus Empiricus *Adv. Math.* 2. 47.

[41] Cf. Aristotle *Rhet.* 1416ᵇ16–26; *Rhet. ad Alexandrum* 1438ᵇ14–29; Alexander son of Numenius *ap.* Anon. Seguerianus 129–33.

[42] Here for the first time we encounter the imaginary context in which the themes for advanced exercises are generally set. It is a democracy, but chronically unstable, so that actual or planned tyranny is frequent, and tyrannicide is a correspondingly common occurrence; rich and poor are in chronic political enmity; adultery (or worse) is frequent. For an entertaining and informative account see Russell 1983, 21–39.

[43] On amplification see e.g. *Rhet. ad Herennium* 2. 47–9; Cicero *Inv.* 1. 100–5, *Part.* 52 f.; Quintilian 8. 4; cf. Martin 1974, 153–8.

[44] On the heads of purpose see Apsines 291. 3–296. 12; [Dionysius] 370. 20–371. 1.

From the general we move to the individual, *encomium* and *invective* being antithetically paired. These exercises have complex ramifications. Encomium is the foundation for the whole epideictic branch of oratory; but it also enters into judicial reasoning about motive and intention. An advocate who wishes to argue that an alleged crime is out of keeping with the character of the accused will exploit the heads of encomium to show what an admirable person his client is. Sometimes a paradoxical theme was set for encomium, requiring the praise of an archetypal villain; Libanius, for example, has an encomium of Thersites. This is not just a display of wit and ingenuity. In extracting from Homer's very unflattering portrayal of Thersites the basis for its complete inversion, Libanius provides a brilliant demonstration of how to overcome prejudice and elicit favourable points from evidence that is *prima facie* damning. These are important skills for a judicial speaker.[45] Encomium and invective teach the student how to present a given subject in a good or bad light; the tenth exercise, *comparison*, combines these skills. Aphthonius' example compares Hector and Achilles, and concludes that they were equals; since by common consent Achilles was the greatest of the heroes at Troy, this conclusion is a way of tendentiously enhancing Hector's standing.

The eleventh exercise, *characterization*, requires the student to imagine what some specified individual would say in a given situation. Direct quotation is an effective way of making a report or narrative vivid, and can be used in particular to make explicit the reasoning or traits of character alleged to underlie an action; we will see this technique used to powerful effect in some of the illustrative advanced exercises translated in Chapter 4. In the twelfth exercise, *description*, the student is supposed to place a scene vividly before the imagination; this, like characterization, is a useful skill for the speaker who wants to make maximum impact on the audience.

In the next exercise, *thesis*, the student is required to argue for or against some general proposition. This has direct application in more advanced exercises, and is in fact a standard head in the division of some issues. A judicial speaker will often need to show that the act in question

---

[45] Libanius 8. 243–51; cf. Homer *Iliad* 2. 211–77. Libanius points out, for example, that Thersites deserves credit because he joined the army and fought effectively (no one disputes his claim to have taken prisoners at 2. 231) despite his physical infirmities; that he deserves more credit than Nestor for his courageous outspokenness towards Agamemnon; and that Odysseus tacitly concedes the truth and justice of his contentions when he responds with violence rather than reasoned argument. For Thersites as a theme of encomium see also Aulus Gellius 17. 12. 2 (Favorinus).

falls in a class of actions which are to be praised or punished as a class; for example, if the defendant is charged with tax evasion one will want to show that tax evasion is in general a bad thing.[46] Aphthonius introduces in this exercise the concepts of counterposition and solution; one may 'counterpose' an argument by putting it into the mouth of the opposing speaker, and then 'solve' the counterposed argument. This technique is used extensively in advanced exercises.

The fourteenth and last of the preliminary exercises is the *proposal of a law*, in which the student speaks in favour of or against a law. This is almost a deliberative theme; all that is lacking is a specification of the circumstances—who proposes the law, where, when, why? But in judicial oratory, too, a speaker will often have to interpret a law, and the kinds of reasoning that enter into legislative debate are equally relevant to debates about the intention with which an existing law was enacted.

(b) Advanced Exercises

The student who has reached the end of the series of preliminary exercises is very close to the advanced exercises. In thesis he has argued for or against a proposition expressed in general terms; similarly in the proposal of a law he has argued for or against a law without any particular circumstances being specified. In the advanced exercises a set of hypothetical circumstances is specified, and the student is asked to speak to that hypothesis as one might in a genuine judicial or deliberative context. 'Should one fortify a city?' is a thesis; one may turn it into a hypothesis thus: 'When Xerxes invades Greece the Spartans deliberate whether to fortify their city.'[47] The student would take the role of a Spartan speaking for or (more likely) against this proposal; he would have to consider fortification not now in the abstract, but in the light of an assessment of the Persian threat, the prospects for Greek resistance, and the traditions and character of the Spartans. The Greeks called this kind of exercise

---

[46] On generalizing in judicial oratory see Cicero *Orator* 45 f., *De Or.* 2. 132–41, 3. 120, *Part.* 61; Quintilian 3. 5. 9–13.

[47] For this example see Aphthonius 42. 1–5; Philostratus 514, 584 (= Aristides fr. 105 Behr); and compare Seneca *Suas.* 2. The absence of particular circumstances was the conventional way of distinguishing thesis from hypothesis, but is not a wholly satisfactory criterion; Zeno 314 f. observes that the thesis 'Should Socrates marry?' and the hypothesis 'Socrates deliberates whether to marry' are not differentiated by circumstance, but by their ends, speculative and practical respectively (cf. Quintilian 3. 5. 11). On thesis and hypothesis see further Throm 1932, Matthes 1958, 123–32, Calboli Montefusco 1986, 42–50.

μελέτη, which means 'practice' or 'exercise'; modern writers usually refer to it as 'declamation' after the (not wholly satisfactory) Roman term.[48]

Declamation was not just an educational experience for adolescents. Many continued to declaim in adulthood and to take a connoisseur's interest in the practice. Professional rhetoricians gave public performances to large and enthusiastic audiences; often they would display their virtuosity by speaking impromptu to themes proposed by the audience. Given the intense rivalry between them, these public displays often had a sharply competitive edge.[49] Rhetoricians also composed and circulated carefully polished written treatments of declamation-themes. Thus declamation, as well being an educational tool, was a hobby, a public entertainment, a competitive sport, and a literary genre.

The preliminary exercises prepared the student for the advanced exercises in various ways. Of course they helped the student to acquire a general facility in invention and expression. More particularly, as we noted in connection with anecdote and maxim, they taught the student how to use a standard set of heads in developing a theme; this concept is crucial to issue-theory. In addition, they gave the student an opportunity to practise one by one a number of elements that he would later have to combine and co-ordinate; the building-blocks which make up the lists of recommended heads in issue-theory often are (or are similar to) material covered in the preliminary exercises, so that in handling the advanced exercises the student is frequently referred back to material he has already mastered at this early stage.

I.5 ISSUES AND THEIR DIVISION

The preliminary exercises accustomed students to treating a theme by using a set of standard heads. The transition to more advanced work in epideictic oratory must have been undemanding (the preliminary exercise encomium is, indeed, an epideictic speech in miniature). It is rela-

---

[48] There is an excellent account of the advanced rhetorical exercises in Russell 1983; see also Bonner 1977, 277–327; Clark 1957, 213–61; Berry and Heath (forthcoming). On Roman declamation Bonner 1949, although in some respects outdated, is still useful; Fairweather 1981 provides a detailed study of Seneca, our main source for Latin declamation in the early empire. Winterbottom 1982 discusses the relationship between school exercises and the demands of genuine speaking.

[49] Cf. Russell 1983, 74–86; anecdotes in Seneca, Philostratus, and Eunapius provide ample illustration. On the contexts and occasions of declamation see also Anderson 1989, 89–104.

tively easy to classify the situations in which an epideictic speech might be required, and to specify the set of heads appropriate to each—what topics one should cover when, for example, welcoming a visiting dignitary or celebrating a wedding.[50]

Judicial and deliberative oratory pose more complex problems. The situations which they actually or (in declamation) hypothetically address are infinitely diverse, and it is correspondingly hard to devise a principle of classification which will be of real use to the intending speaker. If, for example, one tried to determine the heads of argument appropriate to murder trials one is unlikely to get beyond the common topic against murder; and this gives the speaker no purchase on the specifics of the case in hand. The theory of issue (in Greek στάσις, rendered in Latin as *status* or *constitutio*) was developed to meet this need.

Reflections on the different kinds of issue that arise in legal oratory can be found already in the fourth century BC;[51] but their systematic classification seems to have begun in the second century BC. The most important second-century contributor to issue-theory was Hermagoras of Temnos. Rival systems were proposed by various contemporaries, and Hermagoras' own system was criticized by some for an unnecessary innovation;[52] so we should not infer that he created issue-theory from scratch. But he clearly made a decisive advance, and his system was by far the most influential. Unfortunately, only fragments of Hermagoras' work have been preserved; our knowledge of the subsequent evolution of Hellenistic issue-theory is derived primarily from two Latin handbooks (both dependent, directly or indirectly, on Greek sources) dating from early in the first century BC, the young Cicero's *On Invention* and the anonymous *Rhetorica ad Herennium*.[53] In the first century AD Quintilian reviewed many different versions of the theory in his comprehensive

---

[50] See especially the two treatises on epideictic oratory attributed to Menander Rhetor, translated with commentary in Russell and Wilson 1981.

[51] Aristotle *Rhet.* 1373ᵇ38–1374ᵃ17, 1417ᵇ21–7 (cf. Quintilian 3. 6. 49; Thompson 1972); *Rhet. ad Alexandrum* 1427ᵃ23–30.

[52] For Hermagoras' innovation and its critics see Cicero *Inv.* 1. 16, Quintilian 3. 6. 60; cf. on Hermogenes *36. 7–43. 14, *42. 5–43. 8. Of the contemporary systems, that of Athenaeus (Quintilian 3. 6. 47 f.) is of particular interest since it seems to have had an indirect influence on the Homer scholia (Heath 1993).

[53] Cicero *Inv.* 1. 10–19, 2. 12–end; *Rhet. ad Herennium* 1. 18–27, 2. 2–26. Cicero presents an explicitly modified version of Hermagoras' system of issues (cf. Quintilian 3. 6. 56–61, 11. 18; Heath 1994*b*, 117–21); the radically different system of the *Rhet. ad Herennium* stands in the tradition established by M. Antonius (cf. 1. 8 with Quintilian 3. 6. 45). Cicero also touches on issues in later works: *De Or.* 1. 139 f., 2. 104–13; *Part.* 98–108; *Top.* 93–6.

survey of rhetoric.[54] The theory was brought to full maturity by Greek rhetoricians during the second century AD, and it is with their work that this book is mainly concerned.[55]

The distinguishing feature of this mature stage of the tradition was the promotion of what had previously been subdivisions of issues to being issues in their own right; this created a system of thirteen issues, which later achieved canonical status.[56] The system of thirteen issues was not known to Quintilian; no theory covered in his survey recognizes more than eight issues (3. 6. 55). Nor were the thirteen issues known to Greek rhetoricians at the beginning of the second century; the younger Hermagoras is reported to have recognized seven issues, Lollianus five.[57] We do not know who established the thirteen-issue system. Some ancient sources identify Minucianus as its earliest exponent; but this claim to precedence is questionable if (as seems likely) the Latin writer Sulpicius Victor preserves in substance the treatise of the second-century Greek rhetor Zeno; for here we find the mature system in a form which seems to antedate Minucianus' work.[58] But there is no doubt that Minucianus was for some time the system's most influential exponent. In later antiquity, however, Minucianus' work was overtaken in popularity by that of his younger contemporary Hermogenes, whose treatise *On Issues*[59] is in consequence the fullest surviving systematic treatment of the subject. For the views of Minucianus and of later rhetoricians, we are mainly dependent on the fragmentary information preserved by Hermogenes' ancient commentators; in addition, we have instructive examples of the application of issue-theory to declamation themes in Sopater's *Division of Questions*.

How, then, does issue-theory work? Suppose that I am charged with assault; there are various points which might become the focus of dispute. I might deny that I had hit the other party; or, if I admit to hitting

[54] Quintilian 3. 6; see Adamietz 1966 ad loc.; Holtsmark 1968; Nadeau 1959. Quintilian's substantive treatment is in 7. 2–10.

[55] For brief expositions see Russell 1983, 40–73; Kennedy 1983, 73–86. Much material is collected in Calboli Montefusco 1986.

[56] For their canonical status cf. Eunapius 490–2: when the prefect Anatolius visited Athens in the 340s he sent in advance a declamation theme for the sophists to prepare; when they failed to agree on its issue he remarked sarcastically that if there had been more than thirteen of them they would have needed to invent some additional issues. But for a later addition to the canonical thirteen see the note to Hermogenes *79. 18 f.

[57] See *RG* 5. 8. 18–20 (with Gloeckner 1901, 52 f.), 79. 10–15; *PS* 60. 13 f.

[58] Minucianus' priority: *RG* 5. 8. 21 f. (note λέγεται); *PS* 60. 14 f., Syrianus 2. 55. 1–3. On the reasons for doubting the claim see Heath 1994a.

[59] I have, for convenience, retained the traditional title; but the original title may well have been *On Division* (see on *28. 7–14).

him, I might deny that doing so constitutes assault; or, conceding that an assault had been committed, I might argue about the degree of blame attaching to it. These options constitute respectively the issues of conjecture, definition, and quality: did it happen? how is what happened to be categorized? how is what happened to be evaluated? In the last case, where the issue is one of quality, there are several further options: I might deny that assaulting him was in any way wrong; or, conceding that there was a *prima facie* wrong, I might argue that it was justified by its outcome; or, if it cannot be justified in that way, I might try to shift the blame to the victim, or to a third party, or to circumstances. If all else fails, I might challenge the procedural validity of the charge. Failing that, I have no defence to offer: there is no issue.[60]

Identifying the issue of a case is the first step; next one proceeds to the division, and it is here that the standard heads come in. Each issue comes with a prepackaged outline of the most effective strategy for handling it. Thus in a deliberative context the standard list of heads of purpose will guide you towards the kinds of consideration that are likely to be relevant in arguing for or against a proposed course of action. Or, to take a judicial example, once you have decided that the defence will best be conducted by attempting to shift the blame to a third party, the division of this issue will show you how to proceed by a series of plausible steps from the initial concession that a wrong has been done to the triumphant conclusion that you have done nothing wrong.[61] First you demonstrate the innocence of your intentions; then you effect the transfer of blame to someone or something else; next you minimize the wrong done in comparison to the constraint you were under; then in the light of that comparison you recharacterize your action in such a way that you no longer appear to have done anything wrong after all. So a student who claims that he failed to submit an essay on time because of the constant demands of his elderly, bedridden landlady for assistance and companionship could argue along these lines: it was not the result of idleness (*intent*); it is all because of my old landlady (*transference*); my obligation to be kind to the elderly and infirm outweighs the obligation to produce the essay (*relative importance*); so my default is more dutiful than negligent (*forcible definition*).

Of course, this strategy will only result in acquittal if the speaker can

---

[60] A further refinement is that in qualitative disputes the focus of the argument may be either logical (i.e. concerned with the inherent properties of the allegedly criminal actions) or legal (i.e. concerned with the interpretation of some verbal instrument).

[61] See Hermogenes 72. 2–74. 15.

at the same time succeed in countering his opponent's inversion of the same strategy. In an adversarial setting one's own problem involves the opponent's problem as a term of its own analysis. So the theorists' lists of standard heads could be set out as if defining the structure of a dialogue, prescribing every move and countermove. (In reality, of course, the arguments would not be presented dialogically: the speech for the defence would be a reply to a prosecution speech that had tried to anticipate and pre-empt its arguments.) So issue-theory would also suggest various lines of argument for the prosecutor of my defaulting student to explore. Was the student really motivated by concern for the old woman, or was this just a convenient cover for his disinclination to write essays (*alternative intent*)? If it was really her welfare that concerned him why didn't he call in friends, neighbours, voluntary agencies, and the social services (*objection*, based on person)? He was, after all, under no obligation to attend to all her needs himself, but he was obliged to write the essay himself; so clearly the latter had a prior claim on his own direct involvement (*relative importance*). Therefore his so-called kindness towards her was really a way of evading his true responsibilities (*forcible definition*). If it were otherwise, why was it his academic work that was sacrificed, and not some other and less important activity (*second objection*)?[62]

Like the standardized sequence of headings recommended for the preliminary exercises such as anecdote, the division of an issue provides the speaker with a framework to guide and stimulate his invention. But it must be stressed that the division of each issue is not a rigid structure to which slavish adherence is required; it is a set of recommended argumentative tools and a recommended order for applying those tools. But which of them are actually used must be a matter for judgement in the particular circumstances; likewise, there may be good reasons for departing from the standard order in particular cases.[63]

---

[62] Both sides could back up their forcible definition by means of a *thesis*, i.e. by developing the case for the underlying premise in general terms. This is one illustration of the way in which the preliminary exercises provided piecemeal training in techniques that would subsequently be combined in the handling of advanced exercises.

[63] On the exercise of judgement see p. 4 above; for its role in the application of issue-theory see Hermogenes' remarks at *30. 3–9, *44. 1–20, *78. 10–21; note too the vigorous comments of Menander on the relation of theory and practice (sch. Dem. 19. 101 (228)). On the need for flexibility in the order of the heads of argument see [Dionysius] *On Mistakes in Declamation* 363. 11–20; this principle is an application of the broader distinction between natural and artificial order, or τάξις and οἰκονομία: *Rhet. ad Herennium* 3. 16 f.; Cicero *De Or.* 2. 307–9; Quintilian 3. 3. 8, 7. 10. 11–13; Zeno 320. 9–20. Only the school of Apollodorus made rigid adherence to a prescribed order a matter of principle

Furthermore, thinking through the circumstances of a case in relation to the standard division of its issue provides the speaker with no more than the outline of a speech; much more work remains to be done. Further levels of the theory of invention give guidance on the articulation of the arguments;[64] and advice was also available on the management of the speaker's relationship with the audience: how to project a confidence-winning character; how to foment helpful emotions, such as outrage or pity; how to identify the audience's prejudices and encourage or deflect them as required.[65] Thus my hypothetical defaulting student, if pleading before a jury of academic staff, might fear an unsympathetic hearing; by drawing attention to this prospect (while of course asserting his complete confidence in their sense of justice, so as not to give offence) he would hope to prompt a compensatory reaction in his favour. He would insinuate that the prosecutor's attempts to subject his excuses to rational appraisal are merely callous, while presenting himself (with becoming modesty) as a selfless humanitarian and conjuring up a pitiful image of the old lady's plight. Even this does not complete the task, for the material generated by invention must be organized and expressed effectively before this outline becomes a finished exercise.

Issue-theory is therefore only a part of the equipment needed by a rhetorician—and not the most advanced and demanding part.[66] But identifying the issue and working through its division provides a firm underlying structure of argument, without which all subsequent elaborations would be ineffective. Phrynichus, an otherwise unknown sophist of the late third or early fourth century AD, dismissed issue-theory as drivel ($\phi\lambda\upsilon\alpha\rho\acute{\iota}\alpha$) and taught his pupils to speak through unstructured improvisation; but his case is reported as a ridiculous curiosity.[67] Even

(Anon. Seguerianus 26–9, 113, 124); this position is criticized for treating rhetoric as if it were a science ($\grave{\epsilon}\pi\iota\sigma\tau\acute{\eta}\mu\eta$) rather than an art ($\tau\acute{\epsilon}\chi\nu\eta$): thus Alexander son of Numenius, *ap.* Anon. Seguerianus 30–2 (cf. Grube 1959). But less talented teachers will presumably have tended in practice towards a mechanical application of theoretical precepts.

[64] See e.g. Cicero *Inv.* 1. 34–96; Quintilian 5.

[65] These points are handled especially in discussions of the proem and epilogue; see nn. 22 and 23 above.

[66] Phoenix of Thessaly was thought better suited to teaching beginners because he set out the facts 'naked', without stylistic elaboration (Philostratus 604). The implication is that the leading sophists in their work with advanced students could take for granted an acquaintance with the principles of invention and disposition, and would concentrate on expression; thus Philostratus (527) thinks it noteworthy that Lollianus gave classes in theory ($\tau\grave{\alpha}\varsigma$ $\sigma\upsilon\nu\upsilon\sigma\acute{\iota}\alpha\varsigma$ $o\grave{\upsilon}$ $\mu\epsilon\lambda\epsilon\tau\eta\rho\grave{\alpha}\varsigma$ $\mu\acute{o}\nu o\nu$ $\grave{\alpha}\lambda\lambda\grave{\alpha}$ $\kappa\alpha\grave{\iota}$ $\delta\iota\delta\alpha\sigma\kappa\alpha\lambda\iota\kappa\grave{\alpha}\varsigma$ $\pi\alpha\rho\acute{\epsilon}\chi\omega\nu$).

[67] *PS* 364. 14–367. 12 ($\pi o\lambda\grave{\upsilon}\nu$ $\tau\grave{\eta}\nu$ $\gamma\acute{\epsilon}\lambda\omega\tau\alpha$ $\check{\omega}\phi\lambda\eta\sigma\epsilon\nu$); Syrianus 2. 3. 23–5. 14 identifies Evagoras as the source; see B. Keil 1907*b*, 550. Himerius (74. 4) seems to treat this rhetor with more respect; but he is concerned with his striking formulation of the commonplace

Cicero's Antonius, although he is generally unenthusiastic about the precepts of Greek teachers, recognizes that it is useful for students to have a point of reference and a source of arguments available as soon as a case is put before them.[68] Hermogenes reasonably contends (35. 2–14) that an understanding of issues and their division is an essential prerequisite for rhetorical expertise.

1.6 INTRODUCTION TO HERMOGENES *ON ISSUES*

Despite the importance of issue-theory, Hermogenes *On Issues* has not engaged the enthusiasm of translators or commentators in recent years. To my knowledge, there has only been one previous English translation of the treatise, and that is difficult of access and somewhat unreliable.[69] The competition among commentators is even less intense; the most recent commentary known to me was published in 1614.[70]

The lack of scholarly attention[71] to this text is due in part, of course, to its forbidding and unattractive nature. Only extensive exposure to Sopater's *Division of Questions* could make Hermogenes appear an easy or enjoyable read. In preparing the translation I have tried in some degree to mitigate the text's unreadability; if as a consequence I have sometimes treated Hermogenes' idioms a little high-handedly,

that constant practice is necessary to the formation of an orator, rather than with his rejection of theory. Even in their fragmentary form Himerius' declamations show signs of adhering to the conventional divisions; e.g. in *Or.* 3, in which the speaker is prosecuting Epicurus for impiety and the issue is counterplea (cf. on Hermogenes *65. 18–20), note the reply to part of right (3. 8, cf. *65. 14–22), and the amplification (3. 11, cf. *66. 13–67. 1) leading to a reply to the counterplea proper (3. 14, cf. *67. 1–3). Cf. Schenkeveld 1991, 493 f.

[68] Cicero *De Or.* 2. 117, 162; cf. *Brutus* 263, 271 ('the precepts of Hermagoras, which though they do not supply the richer embellishments of oratory, yet furnish outlines of argument ready made and applicable to every type of case'). Cf., in a very different context, Alexander of Aphrodisias *In Top.* 27. 21–4.

[69] Nadeau 1964. For Hermogenes' treatise on types of style we now have the excellent translation by Cecil Wootten (1987).

[70] Laurentius 1614; in the previous century J. Sturm's lectures had been published in two distinct versions by pupils (Sturmius 1570, 1575). This observation from J. Cocinus' preface to Sturmius 1570 is apposite: 'Sunt enim quidam, qui nec certo ordine legunt artium atque disciplinarum scriptores: neque iustum tempus in doctrina ipsorum cognoscenda collocant: verum si quasi de primo limine salutatos non intelligunt: statim impudenter et calumniose eos reprehendunt atque vituperant: tamquam sint obscuri, inutiles, inepti.'

[71] Other kinds of secondary literature are not quite so scarce. Particular mention should be made of Gloeckner 1901, which is fundamental, and the relevant parts of Russell 1983. Calboli Montefusco 1986 offers a fuller collection of evidence for each issue than I have attempted to provide, especially with reference to the Latin sources, and readers are tacitly referred to it *passim*.

readers will I hope be forgiving—some may think I should have gone further.[72]

Hermogenes begins the treatise with a brief preface on the nature and subject-matter of rhetoric (28. 3–29. 6). He then discusses two fundamental elements of judicial and deliberative themes, person and act; the classification of kinds of person and act which he produces is meant to show how different categories of person and act supply the speaker with different resources for argument (29. 7–31. 18). Next he identifies four conditions which must be satisfied if a theme is to be valid (i.e. if it is to be capable of sustaining the kinds of argument in which the student of rhetoric is to be trained); on the basis of these conditions he identifies a number of classes of theme which have no issue, and are therefore technically invalid (31. 19–34. 15). At this point Hermogenes summarily dismisses the further preliminary topics which appeared in other rhetoricians' treatises on issues (*34. 16–35. 14) and turns to the theory of issues proper. He starts with a systematic overview of all the different issues, designed to show how the issue of a proposed theme can be identified through a series of binary decisions (34. 16–43. 14).

The rest of the treatise is devoted to discussion of the individual issues in turn. Hermogenes usually begins by listing the heads appropriate to a standard form of the issue in question; he then discusses the heads in order, illustrating their use by sketching out appropriate lines of argument for one or more specimen themes. If the issue has variant forms he will briefly explain their treatment after he has gone through the headings for the simplest form.

At first sight the list of heads which Hermogenes gives for any issue may look wholly arbitrary. Closer scrutiny reveals sequences of heads which recur in the same or similar order in several different issues; reflection on the various ways in which these sequences are combined and modified can usually elicit a coherent argumentative strategy from the apparent chaos. In the commentary I have tried to show how the heads proposed for each issue can be broken down into a number of phases, each of which has an identifiable rationale; it must be emphasized that

---

[72] The treatment of technical terms has posed particular problems. I have tried to find English equivalents in every case (readers are warned that my renderings often differ from those in Russell 1983; e.g. Russell's 'plea' corresponds to my 'counterplea', his 'counterplea' to my 'objection'). The results are not always wholly satisfactory; but transliteration would have produced passages like this (59. 11–15): 'The *diairesis* of *horos* is: *probolē; horos; anthorismos; sullogismos; gnōmē nomothetou; pēlikotēs; pros ti;* one of the *antitheseis* (in some cases); if this is relevant, *metalēpsis* and *antilēpsis* will be found to follow immediately; then *poiotēs* and *gnōmē*.'

these analyses are an interpretative and expository device, designed to bring out the underlying rationale of Hermogenes' divisions, and do not correspond to the way in which Hermogenes himself presents the material.

The fact that the same heads (and the same or similar sequences of heads) recur in many different issues should come as no surprise. The division of an issue provides the speaker with a set of tools (p. 22). The total number of different tools (i.e. the different kinds of argument available) is relatively small; what distinguishes the issues from each other is the selection made from the tool-set, and the order in which the tools are used. In other words, the division of an issue points the speaker toward a strategy for deploying resources drawn from a relatively limited pool.

This fact explains a number of potentially irritating and confusing features of Hermogenes' presentation. One is the way his treatment of the heads becomes increasingly sparse as the treatise progresses. This is largely because the heads in question have already been mentioned and illustrated in earlier issues; the reader is assumed to be able to make the connection. I have tried to supply relevant cross-references in the commentary. Another point is that the name of each issue is also (in most cases) the name of a head used in that and in other issues. Where this occurs, the name of the head is basic, the name of the issue derivative; the issue is named after the head which forms the crux of its argumentative structure, and which in other issues may play a supporting role (*42. 5–43. 8). There is an obvious potential for confusion where the same term may designate a head and an issue;[73] that potential is increased when the same term has other technical (and indeed non-technical) uses, as is the case with 'counterposition'. The glossary may help readers to find a way through these problems.

The heads are forms of argument, and Hermogenes' recommendations therefore apply primarily to the part of the speech concerned with argument (he does also discuss the treatment of epilogues, which can be seen as an exploitation of the position established by argument). It is assumed that a student tackling an exercise will be able to supply a suitable introduction and narrative; the treatise is concerned only with how the position set out in the introduction and narrative can be secured by argument. There were other rhetorical handbooks based on the parts of

---

[73] e.g. Kennedy 1983, 85.

a speech, but they presuppose a familiarity with issue-theory;[74] the material covered in this treatise is therefore, as Hermogenes claims (35. 2–6), fundamental to an understanding of ancient rhetoric.

[74] See Apsines 276. 10, 291. 4 f.; Anon. Seguerianus 216; [Hermogenes] *Inv.* 129. 17–19, 131. 3–11, 132. 2–4, 137. 6 f., 162. 3–6.

2   Translation

There are many important elements which constitute rhetoric as an art. These have of course been grasped from the beginning and set in order 5 by practice over time, and their practical usefulness, both in deliberative and in judicial contexts and everywhere else, is manifest. But the most important, in my view, is that concerned with division and with demonstration. By this I do not mean the division of kinds into classes, or of wholes into parts; that is another major component of rhetoric, but is not 10 my immediate concern. The present discussion deals with the division of political questions into what are known as heads. This subject is almost identical with the theory of invention, except that it does not include all the elements of invention.

15 29   First of all, we must state what is meant by a *political question*. It is a rational dispute on a particular matter, based on the established laws or customs of any given people, concerned with what is considered just, honourable, advantageous, or all or some of these things together. It is 5 not the function of rhetoric to investigate what is really and universally just, honourable, etc.

PERSONS AND ACTS

Such a dispute must be concerned with persons and with acts. There is of course a very great variety of these. An understanding of this variety 10 makes it easy to grasp the divisions of questions into heads, and the number of divisions which are possible in general.

As to *persons*, some can provide a basis for argument, and some cannot, but are place-holders for person. Those which can provide a basis for argument are, in descending order of argumentative force:

(i) *determinate proper names*; e.g. Pericles, Demosthenes, etc.;   15
(ii) *relative terms*; e.g. father, son, slave, master;
(iii) *prejudicial terms*; e.g. dissolutes, adulterers, flatterers;
(iv) *characterizing terms*; e.g. farmers, gluttons, etc.;
(v) *terms combining two appellatives*; e.g. rich youth: neither term has   20
much force on its own, but when combined each provides grounds for
judgement;
(vi) *terms combining person and act*; e.g.:- An adolescent who uses cos-   30
metics is prosecuted for prostitution;
(vii) *simple appellative terms*; e.g. general, politician.

Clearly, these may occur in questions both singly and in multiple
combinations; for example, Demosthenes was of course a father, a politi-   5
cian, an ambassador, and indeed even a soldier. This is the reason why
determinate proper names have greater force. But one should assess the
force of each individually, and use it as occasion allows.

These are the persons which provide a basis for argument. One should   10
adhere to the topics of encomium and use whichever are relevant. Those
which do not provide a basis for argument are:

(i) *the indeterminate*; e.g. someone;
(ii) *the wholly equivalent*; e.g. if two rich young men were to bring
charges against each other for some reason: whatever one could say   15
against one party will also count against the other.

There is a variety of *acts*, as well as of persons (starting again with
those which afford the strongest basis for argument):

(i) *acts for which someone is charged as himself the agent*; e.g.:- A man is
apprehended burying a recently slain corpse in a remote place; he is   20
charged with homicide;
(ii) *when the matter for judgement is directly referred to a person other than
the agent*; e.g.:- The enemy erect a statue of a triple-hero; he is charged
with treason;   31
(iii) *intermediate cases*; e.g.:- Pericles records expenditure of fifty talents
for 'necessary expedients'; Archidamus is charged with receiving bribes.
The fifty talents are in no way referred directly to Archidamus, but in the   5
light of other circumstances provide a basis for argument as if they were
so referred.

An exactly similar case is this:- The father of a dissolute son goes
missing; the son is charged with homicide. I realize that in some people's

10 view there is no act to be judged in this case. But I doubt whether anyone would supply an explanation and what is known as a 'gloss' where
there is no act to be judged; and the dissolute son will, in my view, have
something to say in his own defence. In my view, it is only an *equivalent*
act which provides no basis for judgement; e.g.:- A poor man and a rich
man both have beautiful wives, and each simultaneously apprehends the
15 other coming out of his house; they bring reciprocal charges of adultery
against each other. In this case the persons differ, and so provide a basis
for argument, but the acts do not because they are equivalent.

VALID AND INVALID QUESTIONS

32 Next we may infer from these points which questions have issue and can
be divided, and which do not. Questions *have issue* if:

(i) they involve either both a person and an act to be judged, or at least
one of these;
(ii) there are persuasive arguments on both sides which are different and
have probative force;
5 (iii) the verdict (which lies with the jury) is neither self-evident nor
prejudiced, but can be brought to a conclusion.

If any one of these conditions is not satisfied, the question *lacks issue*.
10 Questions which lack issue are to be classified as follows:

(i) *one-sided*, i.e. forceful arguments do not exist on both sides; e.g.:- A
brothel-keeper admits ten young men who come in a revel to his house,
catches them in a prepared trap, and kills them; he is charged with homicide;
15 (ii) *wholly equivalent*; e.g.:- Two rich young men both have beautiful
wives, and each simultaneously apprehends the other coming out of his
house; they bring reciprocal charges of adultery against each other.
(iii) *reversible*; e.g.:- One man demands the repayment of a loan with
interest, while the other claims that it was a deposit on which no inter-
20 est is owed; the assembly meanwhile decrees a cancellation of debts; the
first man demands that the money be repaid as a deposit, while the other
33 claims that it was a debt, and therefore no longer owing. Here the proofs
do not differ and have no force, since each party falls foul of his own
arguments;
(iv) *insoluble*, i.e. no resolution or conclusion can be reached; e.g.:-

Alexander is warned in a dream not to trust dreams; he takes advice.   5
Whatever advice one gives will lead to the opposite result;
(v) *implausible*; e.g. an invented case in which Socrates is a brothel-
keeper or Aristides acts unjustly;
(vi) *impossible*; e.g. a suggestion that Siphnos or Maroneia is debating the   10
conquest of Greece, or that Apollo tells a lie;
(vii) *disreputable*; e.g.:- A man hires out his own wife as a prostitute, and
sues a client who fails to pay the fee;
(viii) *uncircumstantial*; e.g.:- A man disinherits his son for no cause.   15

These would not be valid questions. There are other classes of question which are close to those lacking issue, but which are nevertheless
used as themes for exercises:

(i) *ill-balanced*; e.g.:- Critias takes refuge at the statues of Harmodius
and Aristogeiton; the Athenians consider whether to have him dragged   34
away. This is not one-sided, but is ill-balanced;
(ii) *flawed in invention*; e.g.:- On the receipt of Nicias' letter someone
proposes that Cleon be appointed general. Or:- Mardonius, retreating
after his defeat, is required to make a defence before the king. The   5
invention is mistaken in essentially the same way in each case—Cleon
died before the Sicilian expedition, Mardonius before the Persian fugi-
tives reached home;
(iii) *prejudiced*; e.g.:- A woman shows her husband how to gain access to   10
a tyrant, which no one else has been able to discover; he goes up and
assassinates the tyrant, and charges his wife with adultery. It is unlikely
that anyone will vote against the woman responsible for the killing of the
tyrant, even if it is shown that she did commit adultery.

This classification is not necessarily exhaustive.   15

SYNOPSIS OF THE ISSUES

We must now discuss the division of questions which do have issue.
There is no point discussing the class of problems and their mode at present; the reason for learning classes and modes is to ensure that we use   20
appropriate styles of discourse when treating problems in exercise—i.e.
judicial subjects in a judicial style, deliberative subjects in a deliberative
style, and epideictic subjects in an epideictic style, and each in a style   35
suitably adapted to the subject-matter. But it is of course impossible for

anyone who has not yet studied the pure division of questions into their so-called heads, or who is unfamiliar with what are known as the issues of problems, to have a sound grasp of the things I have just mentioned. So it is completely senseless to teach the theory of types of style before these other subjects, especially since if we were to try to say anything about types of style at this point the discussion of the incidental material would be longer than that of our main subject. The theory of styles of discourse and their respective use is the subject of a separate and far from trivial treatise—in fact, a very important and advanced one. So for the present we should confine our discussion to division into heads.

Correct division is made possible by an understanding of the variety of persons and acts, and their force, and also of what is known as the *issue* of the question. The question of the origin of the term 'issue' (whether it is derived from the fact that the opposing parties 'take issue' with each other, or whatever) is one I leave for others to argue out. But leaving aside whether this is a common or indeed contingent name for all questions, to help us understand this subject I will first set it out here systematically, and then begin the division of heads with conjecture—inevitably, as will become clear; then I will discuss the others in turn. The systematic presentation is as follows.

For any given question, assuming it has issue, one must first consider whether the matter to be judged is or is not clear.

If the matter is unclear, the issue is one of *conjecture*. Conjecture is a proof of the existence of an act that is unclear from a sign that is clear; e.g.:- A man is apprehended burying a recently slain corpse in a remote place; he is charged with homicide. On the basis of the burial, which is clear, we investigate an act that is unclear, i.e. who committed the homicide?

If the matter to be judged is clear, one must next consider whether it is complete or incomplete. By 'incomplete' I mean that when some deficiency is supplied a description is immediately available, and the act contains no further scope for enquiry. In such a case, the issue is one of *definition*. The issue of definition is an enquiry into the description of an act that is partially performed and partially deficient with regard to the completeness of its description. E.g.:- A man steals private property from a temple; the legal penalty for temple-robbery is death, while the legal penalty for theft is twofold repayment; the man is prosecuted as a temple-robber, but claims to be a thief. If one adds that the property is sacred, the man is clearly a temple-robber, and the act contains no further scope for enquiry.

If the matter to be judged is clear and complete, the issue of the   15
enquiry is one of the quality of the act, e.g. whether it is just, lawful,
advantageous, or one of their opposites. The generic name for this is
quality, but it may involve enquiry either into an act or into a verbal
instrument. If it is concerned with a verbal instrument, the issue is legal;
if it is concerned with an act, it is logical.

The *logical* issue can be divided in two: the enquiry may be concerned   38
with a future act, or with a past act. If it is concerned with a future act,
the issue is *practical*; for a practical dispute is one concerned with a future   5
act—whether this should or should not happen, whether or not to grant
this; e.g.:- The Athenians deliberate whether they should bury the
Persian dead at Marathon.

If the act being judged has already been performed, the generic term
(analogous to 'quality' above) is *juridical*. Again, this can be divided in   10
two as well: the defendant either will or will not concede that the act was
a wrong and in some respect forbidden. If he denies altogether that the
act was forbidden, the issue is *counterplea*; for counterplea arises out of
the prosecution of some act not generally held to be actionable as if it   15
were actionable; e.g.:- A farmer disinherits his son for studying philosophy.

If the defendant concedes that the act in question was a wrong, the
generic name is *counterposition*. This is divided as follows. The defendant
will either accept all responsibility for what happened himself, or will   20
transfer it to some external factor. If he accepts responsibility himself he
makes a *counterstatement*; a counterstatement arises when the defendant,
while conceding that he has done some wrong, sets against that some
other benefit achieved as a result of that same wrong. If he transfers   39
responsibility to some external factor, it may be to the actual victim, or
to a third party. If to the victim, it is a *counteraccusation*; a counteraccusation arises when the defendant admits that he has done some wrong,
but in turn accuses the victim of deserving to suffer what he did. If   5
responsibility is transferred to a third party, a division can again be made:
the defendant, while admitting that he has done some wrong, transfers
responsibility either to an act or person capable of being held to account,
which is a *transference*, or to one not capable of being held to account,   10
but wholly unaccountable, which is a plea of *mitigation*. An example of
transference:- An ambassador is to set out within thirty days on receipt
of 1,000 drachmas from the treasurer for travelling expenses; he does not
receive them, and for this reason does not set out; he is brought to trial.
An example of a plea of mitigation:- The ten generals who fail to recover   15

the bodies after a sea-battle because of a storm, and are brought to trial. (If anyone is inclined to dispute these definitions—I mean, of transference and mitigation—I will discuss them in greater detail in the section on counterposition.)

20 The logical issues can be recognized from these points; I now turn to *legal* issues.

The enquiry must be concerned with a verbal instrument; by 'verbal
40 instrument' I mean laws, wills, decrees, correspondence, definite proclamations, and in short everything given verbal expression. Such an enquiry may be concerned with one verbal instrument or several (by 'several' I mean to include instruments divided into two sections, where each
5 of the two parties is seen to rest its case on one of the sections). If the enquiry is concerned with a single instrument (either about its single intent, or with one of its sections), the issue is one of *letter and intent*; let-
10 ter and intent occurs when one party (usually the prosecution) advances the letter of the law while the other appeals to its intent; e.g.:- It is a capital offence for an alien to ascend the city walls; during a siege an alien ascends the city wall and fights heroically; he is prosecuted under the
15 law. Alternatively, one may compare an act with the letter by equating what is not made explicit in the law with what is made explicit; this is an *assimilation*, assimilation being the comparison of an act not made explicit in writing with what is explicit, where someone equates what is not explicit with what is. E.g.:- The son of a (female) prostitute may not speak in the assembly; an injunction is sought to prevent the son of a man who has prostituted himself from speaking.

20 If the enquiry is concerned with two or more verbal instruments, or
41 one divided into two sections, the issue is a *conflict of law*. A conflict of law arises when two or more verbal instruments, or one divided into two parts, which are not inherently contradictory come into conflict because of special circumstances. In general, this is a double enquiry into letter
5 and intent; e.g.:- A disinherited son shall not have a share in his father's property; a man who remains on board a ship abandoned during a storm shall become the owner of the ship; a disinherited son remains on board a ship abandoned during a storm, but his title is contested on the grounds that the ship belonged to his father. An example of conflict of
10 laws arising from the division of one instrument:- A victim of rape may choose either marriage or the death of the rapist; a man rapes two young women at the same time; one chooses to marry him, the other chooses his death.

The meaning of *ambiguity* is clear from the term. Ambiguity is a dis-

pute concerning a verbal instrument arising from accentuation or syllab-   15
ification. From accentuation, e.g.:- If a prostitute wears gold ornaments,
dēmosia estō; a prostitute is arrested wearing gold ornaments; she claims
that the gold ornaments become public property (reading the law with
the accent *dēmósia*), but the prosecution maintains that it is not the gold
ornaments but the woman herself who becomes public property (read-   20
ing with the accent *dēmosía*). Concerning syllabification, e.g.:- A man
has two sons, Leon and Pantaleon; in his will he writes 'I name as heir   42
to my property *pantaleōn*'; each lays claim to the whole property, one
reading *Pantaleōn* as a single word ('Pantaleon'), the other dividing *panta*
and *Leōn* ('in its entirety, Leon').

That is how to recognize these issues; but *objection* is different, and   5
arises when the enquiry is about whether the case should be allowed to
come to trial. In objection you will not, in the first instance, enquire
whether something exists (as in conjecture), or what the thing which
occurred was (as in definition), or the quality of the thing (as in the oth-   10
ers), but simply whether there should be an enquiry about any of these
points; it is a procedural exception. It has two species: one is documentary, and the enquiry is based on a verbal instrument; the other is non-
documentary. The *documentary* type seeks to restrain the primary case by
means of a procedural exception based on a verbal instrument, on which   15
the enquiry focuses; e.g.:- The same charge shall not be tried twice; a
man is tried for homicide, and acquitted; later, when he consults an oracle, the god replies 'I do not give oracles to murderers'; he is charged
again. The issue of the first argument is letter and intent; there then follows a conjectural argument as to whether he had committed homicide.

The *non-documentary* type likewise seeks to restrain the primary case   20
by means of a procedural exception based on a verbal instrument, but the
enquiry here is not concerned with the instrument, but with one of the
circumstances of the act—i.e. place, time, person, cause, manner. We   43
concede the act as such, but find fault with one of these by way of objection; e.g.:- Both an adulterer and an adulteress may be summarily killed;
a man kills the adulterer alone, but subsequently discovers his wife weep-   5
ing at the adulterer's tomb and kills her; he is charged with homicide. It
is of course the time and place with which we find fault in this case.

This is how we recognize the so-called issues. We must now discuss   10
the division of each. It should be understood that what will be said about
conjecture (which will necessarily be discussed first) will apply to almost
everything that follows; the discussion will naturally therefore be comparatively extensive.

15

When conjecture has both person and act subject to judgement it is divided thus: exception (in some cases); demand for evidence; motive;
20 capacity; sequence of events; counterplea; objection; transposition of cause; persuasive defence; common quality.

44   *Exception* arises in four ways:

(i) from deficiency; e.g.:- The father of a dissolute son goes missing; the son is charged with homicide. He will demand that it first be proved whether the father has been killed;
5 (ii) from excess; e.g.:- Ten young men swear not to marry; they are charged with living immorally. Each of them will demand to be tried separately;
(iii) because one should not be brought to trial for another's acts; e.g.:- The triple-hero charged with treason, because the enemy have erected his statue;
10 (iv) with regard to time; e.g.:- A coward's son fights heroically; the father charges his wife with adultery. She claims that she should not be tried after such a long elapse of time.

If the exception is based on a verbal instrument, it is powerful and there is a complete procedural exception; otherwise it is weak, but gives
15 some measure of assistance to the user. An example of one based on a verbal instrument, which as I say is a complete objection and procedural exception:- A man tried for homicide is acquitted; subsequently he consults an oracle, and the god replies 'I do not give oracles to murderers'; he is brought to trial again. But 'the law forbids a second trial on the same charge'; so he enters an exception, and the first question is legal, based on the exception.

45   *Demand for evidence*: this is twofold: either there are or there are not witnesses.

(i) E.g.:- A girl's mother told her daughter's suitor that the girl would die sooner than be married to him; the girl died with symptoms of poison-
5 ing; when the father interrogates the servant-women he learns nothing more about the poisoning, but is told of his wife's adultery with the suitor; he charges the wife with poisoning. Here there are witnesses, i.e.
10 the servant-women. She will not, therefore, demand witnesses, but will attack them, arguing that they are untrustworthy, since 'slaves are by nature hostile to their masters'; and 'since we accept that even free peo-

ple are not always trustworthy, we should hardly trust slaves'; one could find more points. One should also oppose witnesses to witnesses, and examine which are more trustworthy (as Demosthenes does in *Against Conon*). This should generally be your technical principle regarding witnesses: either attack them on the grounds that they give evidence out of partiality or enmity, or because of personal relationships, or for private gain, or because they are untrustworthy because of their age. 20

(ii) If there are no witnesses, the defendant will demand them, using the following points: person (e.g. who gave it?), act (what did he give?), place 46 (where?), manner (how?), time (when?), cause (why?); he will use all of these, or those which are relevant. The prosecutor will argue that proof from facts is more trustworthy than that from witnesses: 'For facts can- 5 not be persuaded, and do not seek to ingratiate themselves with anyone by what they say, as witnesses often do; but as they are in reality, so they appear under examination.'

Motive and *capacity* arise from the attributes of the person, i.e. the top- ics of encomium. When the person is determinate, more or less all of the 10 topics will be relevant; otherwise, we will use those consistent with the arguments we discover. E.g. a rich young man: here you have his age and his fortune as bases for arguments, and their concomitants. The topics of encomium are of course as follows: birth, rearing, education, age, 15 physical and spiritual nature, occupations, achievements (which is the strongest head), fortune (e.g. rich, poor, etc.). These weigh on both sides when forming the base of an argument in either part (i.e. both in motive and in capacity), but some carry more weight in one than in the other; 20 e.g. fortune is more apposite in capacity, just as age is in motive. Seeing that this is so, one should elaborate these points wherever one of them seems more apposite.

One should examine the motive and capacity not only of those per- 47 sons brought to trial, but of all those given in the problem. E.g. the pros- ecutor of the rich youth who maintains disinherited sons and is charged with conspiring to establish a tyranny is stronger when the quality of dis- inherited sons is examined. So in all conjectures one should consider all 5 the persons about whom a judgement can be formed.

Sequence of events generally belongs to the prosecutor; it arises, and can be amplified, from the same points as the demand for evidence (i.e. who? 10 what? where? how? when? why?).

If this belongs to the prosecutor only, all the remaining heads except objection belong to the defendant, if there is the opportunity to use them

15 all. But if the sequence of events is common (and a conjecture of this kind is occasionally found), the remaining heads too will be common to both. An example of conjecture with common sequence of events:- A charge of conspiring to establish a tyranny lay against a certain man; his brother, having fought heroically, asked as his reward that the indict-
20 ment be struck out; this was granted; the man did establish a tyranny; the brother overthrows him, and is charged with complicity. The prosecutor will exploit the striking out of the indictment and the circumstances surrounding that, while the defendant will exploit the killing and the cir-
48 cumstances surrounding that; and each party must refute the arguments of the other.

It is not possible for the sequence of events to belong to the defendant alone.

Counterplea is not always relevant. If one is brought to trial on the
5 basis of one's own acts counterplea will certainly be relevant; but if on the basis of other people's acts, it will not. It runs along the lines: 'This is permissible, and not forbidden.' Example:- A rich youth maintains all disinherited sons, and is charged with conspiring to establish a tyranny. He will argue that it is permissible to maintain any people one wants.

10 *Objection* is always opposed to counterplea, not just in conjecture but wherever it is found. If one of the opposed parties uses either one of these (I mean, counterplea and objection), the other will certainly use the
15 other. Objection may be by refutation or by counter-representation. Refutation is forcible—one will deny that the act is in fact permissible— while the counter-representation proves that even if it is permissible, it is not permissible in this way and on these conditions. E.g.:- An adoles-
20 cent who uses cosmetics is charged with prostitution. The prosecutor will insist forcibly that it is not permissible for males to wear cosmetics and then that, even if it is permissible, it is not permitted in this way and
49 on these conditions. It is not easy to say which should be used first (refutation or counter-representation); the order varies according to the nature of the facts. One should beware that in certain cases denying from
5 the outset that something is permissible may be extremely arrogant; it can be stronger placed second, and one should proceed in whichever way the requirements of the case demand.

Transposition of cause arises in relation to the sequence of events. That is based on words, acts, or feelings:

(i) If it is based on words, the transposition of cause is introduced
10 according to letter and intent; e.g.:- A rich young man comes in a noc-

turnal revel to the prison and shouts out 'Cheer up, prisoners—it won't be long before you are freed'; he is charged with conspiring to establish a tyranny. Here he admits the utterance, but demands consideration of the intent of his utterance.

(ii) If the sequence of events is based on acts, the transposition of cause 15 is argued in the manner of a thesis. E.g.:- A man is apprehended burying a recently slain corpse in a remote place, and is charged with homicide. He will run through a thesis, claiming that it is honourable to inter the unburied.

(iii) If it is based on feelings, the transposition of cause arises in the man- 20 ner of a plea of mitigation. E.g.:- A rich young man constantly looks at the acropolis and weeps; he is charged with conspiring to establish a tyranny. He says: 'It was out of pity for the victims of tyranny that I was in such a state.'

One should realize that all these are found in all conjectures, but each 50 is elaborated in the appropriate one.

If the trial arises out of what others have done the transposition of cause will be speculative and (in a sense) self-contradictory. E.g.:- The 5 enemy erect a statue of a triple-hero; he is charged with treason. He will say that they erected it out of admiration for him, or to set an example to their own people, or to appease him, or wanting to excite envy against him. Not all of these can be true, and this is why I say that speculative 10 glosses should be found in a conjecture of this kind. If a man is brought to trial because of his own acts, he will say either one thing, or several things which are at least consistent; e.g.:- A man begging at night is charged with robbery. He will say that he did it at night because he was 15 ashamed, and because he does not want to make himself unpopular by begging from those he meets during the day, and because people are more generous then, being relaxed in attitude, and so forth. These are many reasons, but they are not mutually inconsistent.

The *persuasive defence* is an inversion of the sequence of events. The 20 points which the one party uses as indications that something is the case, the other party will use as indications that it is not the case. E.g.: 'Where 51 you look and cry, you will establish yourself as tyrant': 'But if I had been intending to be a tyrant, I would not have looked and so exposed my intentions.'

This head is omitted in some cases. It is omitted whenever the indi- 5 cations on the basis of which the case is brought are necessary concomitants of the act about which judgement is being made; e.g. it is necessary for someone conspiring to establish a tyranny to prepare arms. Consider, then:- Pericles' house is struck by lightning, and a thousand suits of armour are found; he is charged with conspiring to establish a tyranny. He cannot say here: 'If I had been intending to be a tyrant, I would not have prepared arms.' In these cases the prosecutor will sometimes argue out the sequence of events in the manner of a definition, as in the case of the adolescent using cosmetics and charged with prosecution; the prosecutor will argue forcibly that using cosmetics is prostitution in itself. Here too the plausible defence is omitted, but in its place one should introduce into the corresponding head the argument that the facts are not convertible. This is the only point on which one can insist here; e.g.: 'Those who intend to be tyrants prepare arms, but it does not follow that those who prepare arms are conspiring to establish a tyranny; for it is possible to prepare arms for some other purpose.' And: 'Male prostitutes use cosmetics, but it does not follow that men who use cosmetics are necessarily also prostitutes; for it is possible to use cosmetics for some other reason.' And he will say, obviously, all the things that are found also in the transposition of cause.

Common quality are epilogues and second speeches. They arise in all questions, not just in conjecture. Prosecutors, after their proofs, run through the charge in the manner of a common topic (e.g. against a tyrant, a brothel-keeper, or whatever the charge may be) and summarize each of the relevant points, as Demosthenes does, e.g.: 'I want to draw together the charges; I have shown that he has made no true statement' etc.; defendants too summarize the points in a similar way, but make a different use of them, appealing for pity and stirring up emotion. Here the presentation of children, wives, relatives, and so forth is useful; the prosecutor will of course rebut these things by an argument from advantage. The so-called heads of purpose are common to both sides here, i.e. legality, justice, advantage, feasibility, honour.

In general, epilogues are developed from the same topics as prologues, and have the same force. Both are introduced for the sake of emotion (e.g. fear, anger, pity, envy, etc.). They differ in that prologues prepare for the acceptance or rejection of a given emotion, while in epilogues the heads are used to intensify or moderate it, and to enhance what is already complete. Epilogues and prologues also differ in that epilogues are rhythmically free, and advance each of the arguments discovered at some length, not briefly as in the prologues; but this will be discussed in more detail in my treatment of the prologue.

This is the division of a *complete, simple* conjecture. But some conjec-

tures are incomplete, and also there are double conjectures, complete and   54
incomplete, in which we will use a double division as well. We must now
discuss these.

An *incomplete* case based only on *acts* has issue; this is when the person provides no grounds for judgement and the act is single. E.g.:- A   5
man is apprehended burying a recently slain corpse in a remote place; he
is charged with homicide. This does not have motive and capacity, but
is divided under all the other heads, just as in a complete case.   10

An *incomplete, simple* conjecture based only on person cannot arise in
my view; this will be very clear, I think, if one considers what was said a
little while ago about acts which provide grounds for judgement. Some
have posited as an example of an incomplete simple case, claiming that
only the person is being judged:- The father of a dissolutes son goes
missing; the son is charged with homicide. First I will ask them whether   15
there is no sequence of events here. There is: the disappearance of the
father; this is a matter not of person but of act. And will we not require
a transposition of cause from him? This too—otherwise, what will the   20
defence be? So how can there be a case if there is no act? Further, will he
not use the persuasive defence? He will, in my view. So how is such a case
incomplete? However, the facts here have less force than in the case of   55
the man burying the recently slain corpse. For in all conjectures the
sequence of events has less force when someone is brought to trial
because of what others have done, especially when it is not directly   5
referred to him, as in the case of Archidamus being tried for receiving
bribes because Pericles recorded in his accounts an expenditure of fifty
talents for 'necessary expedients'. So there cannot be a simple conjecture
based only on persons, in my view, although there can be a double one.   10
But first we must discuss the complete double conjecture.

A *complete double* case arises when there are two persons and two acts
which provide grounds for judgement; e.g.:- Aeschines and Demosthenes, on returning from the embassy to Philip, bring reciprocal
charges of receiving bribes against each other, since the one   15
(Demosthenes) is found burying gold, the other (Aeschines) is found to
have composed a defence on a charge of ambassadorial corruption. Here
the demand for evidence is omitted, since it is equally balanced; but the
other heads should be used in two ways by both sides; e.g.: 'I would not   20
have wished to act corruptly as ambassador for such-and-such a reason,
but you would have done for such-and-such a reason,' and likewise in the
other heads we shall develop arguments by opposing one thing to
another. Dividing and presenting one's defence through all the heads in   56

one section, and in another presenting one's accusation under the same heads lacks competitive energy and is extremely tedious; so one should interlink them.

5   A *double, incomplete* case based on *acts* is when only the acts provide grounds for judgement; e.g.:- Two politicians go on an embassy to a tyrant and on their return bring reciprocal charges of receiving bribes against each other, since the one is found burying gold, and the other is found to have composed a defence on a charge of ambassadorial corrup-

10 tion. Here the persons are equivalent, and so provide no basis for argument; the acts differ, and so do provide a basis for argument. Again, therefore, motive and capacity are omitted, but the case will be divided into the other heads just like the complete double case by opposed arguments.

15   A *double* conjecture based only on *persons* arises when only the persons provide grounds for judgement; e.g.:- A hero dies with symptoms of poisoning; he had a stepmother and a captive concubine, who bring reciprocal charges against each other. Here only motive and capacity are the bases of argument, these being by nature characteristic of person, and all

20 the other heads are equally balanced.

    There are in addition to these three other classes of double conjecture, which we call *conjunct*: incident, pre-confirmatory, and co-confirmatory.

25   *Incident* conjecture arises when the transposition of cause raises a whole question, and it is necessary to give that too a complete division.

57   E.g.:- A man convicted of treason is to be held under arrest by the general until he reveals his accomplices; a general convicted of treason is held in the house of a fellow-general, who kills him, alleging that he had found him with his wife; the second general is charged with complicity.

5 Here after the sequence of events the defendant uses the transposition of cause that 'I killed an adulterer'; so a second question is encountered: is it probable that he committed adultery while a prisoner and is it probable that the wife would give herself to such a man? After the division of

10 this question, the defendant will come back again to the persuasive defence of the original conjecture.

    Pre-confirmatory conjecture arises when in advance of the main question the truth or falsity of some other fact requires prior confirmation by conjecture. E.g.:- A rich general arrested the three sons of his poor

15 enemy as traitors; he executed two, who made no confession under torture, and the third, who confessed to treason before torture; the father takes no action, and the general charges him with complicity. Each side

20 has something to establish first: the rich man that they were traitors, the

poor man that they were not; then, granting by concession that they were 58
traitors, the poor man will offer a defence on his own behalf.

Co-confirmatory conjecture arises when the indications of the act are
established through each other. E.g.:- Prisoners are to be released for the
Thesmophoria; a man who suspects his servant of adultery with his wife 5
places him under restraint during an absence abroad; the servant is freed
by the wife for the Thesmophoria and absconds; subsequently the man
is found murdered, and the wife is charged with complicity. The man's
having been killed by the servant is established by the adultery; the adul- 10
tery is established by the servant's having killed him; in general, they are
mutually supporting—in conjunction, of course, with the other points
(the man's suspicion, the wife's freeing him, and so forth). This differs
from pre-confirmatory conjecture, because there the questions are sepa- 15
rate from each other, but here they are all established by means of each
other.

In addition to these there is conjecture *based on intention*, which is
argued purely on intention, the act and person both being clear; e.g.:- A 20
stepmother wounded her son and killed her stepson, apparently mad;
she recovers and is charged with homicide. A conjecture of this kind differs from a plea of mitigation, because there the factor to which respon- 59
sibility is transferred is agreed upon (e.g. pity, torture, etc.), while here
the question is whether she was or was not mad.

It might be possible to discover other classes of conjecture, but there 5
is no point going into endless detail. In my view, whatever other kind
there may be will be found to be some kind of combination of these;
clearly, the division in those cases will not be difficult for anyone who has
examined these kinds.

DEFINITION 10

The division of definition is: presentation; definition; counterdefinition;
assimilation; legislator's intention; importance; relative importance; one
of the counterpositions (in some cases); if this is relevant, objection and
counterplea will be found to follow immediately; then quality and inten- 15
tion.

The *presentation* is actually the sequence of events.

The *definition* distinguishes the act, and arises from the things passed
over in the sequence of events. E.g.:- A philosopher persuades a tyrant
to abdicate and claims the reward. The presentation: 'I put an end to the 60

tyranny, and should receive a reward.' (Clearly, he will amplify this statement from the concomitants of the sequence of events.) The definition
5   from what is passed over: 'This is not tyrannicide'—which is defined as
the thing which is passed over, i.e. killing him.

The *counterdefinition* is in turn based on what has been done, e.g.: 'No,
it is putting an end to the tyranny.'

The *assimilation* draws both together; it is of course the person claiming the reward who will argue that these do not differ from each other.
10   In general, assimilation in all cases opposes definition in just the same
way that we have said counterplea opposes objection; whichever of them
one party uses, the other party will certainly use the other.

Legislator's intention will be argued out by both sides for their own
advantage.

15   *Importance* will show that what has occurred is important.

Relative importance: that it is in fact a greater thing to put an end to
tyranny without slaughter and riot and disorder than with them.

The *counterposition* is not relevant in this example, but is often found
20   in other questions; e.g.:- A man finds a eunuch with his wife and kills
61   him as an adulterer; he is charged with homicide. After the question who
is an adulterer has been concluded through the points already mentioned, he will make the counteraccusation that he deserved to die.
Necessarily the *objection* will follow, i.e. that he should have brought the
5   man to trial and accused him; and once the objection has been found,
there will also be a *counterplea*, that it was legitimate.

Quality is based on the concomitants of person: if the person is determinate, obviously from all the topics of encomium; if indeterminate,
10   then if it is one of the persons which can be judged (e.g. father, or one of
those mentioned already in the section on person) we will consider the
concomitants in our speech; if wholly indeterminate, we will base on the
act in this case a conjectural argument about what he was in the past and
15   will be in the future if acquitted or convicted (for we will argue about
quality on both sides).

Intention will likewise be used as a basis for argument by both parties:
with what intention did he do such-and-such, and with what intention
does he accuse or oppose, and so forth.

The *common quality* will be argued out here in conjunction with qual-
20   ity of person and intention.

As there are several classes of conjecture, so too of definition. The one
62   already discussed is *simple*, the others are *double*.

First is that called *counterdescription*, when the defendant opposes one description to another. E.g.:- A man steals private property from a temple, and is brought to trial as a temple-robber; he claims to be a thief, and requests the penalty of twofold repayment. Just as with double conjectures, you will divide this by doubling the heads and opposing head to head; e.g.: 'You are a temple-robber, not a thief; for theft is such-and-such, and temple-robbery is such-and-such,' and so on for the rest. The defendant will use the argument in a similar way, but inverting it.

Second is that named *by inclusion*, when the defendant offers a counterdescription and the prosecutor says that he is liable under both descriptions. This is quite similar to counterdescription; we will explain the difference by giving an appropriate example:- A man serving as ambassador places his daughter in the care of the general; he rapes her; on his return, the father charges him with harming the public interest; the general offers to pay the 10,000 drachma fine laid down for a rapist. Here when the defendant says 'I am a rapist, but have not harmed the public interest,' the prosecutor says that he is liable to both charges (i.e. both for rape and for harming the public interest), since if he denies that the other committed rape, of course he acquits him of harming the public interest; if there is no rape, of course there is no crime against the public interest either. For this reason, the two are interlinked; for it is not possible to bring an accusation of harming the public interest if he acquits him of rape. Demosthenes did this in *Against Meidias*; when Meidias maintains that there was an assault and a private wrong rather than a crime against the public interest respecting the festival, Demosthenes draws the two together (the assault and the crime with respect to the festival), to avoid undermining the crime with respect to the festival by dismissing the assault; for unless the assault is established in advance, the crime with respect to the festival does not stand up either. But in counterdescription the speaker rejects one description (e.g.: 'You are not a thief, but a temple-robber'). The difference is that there the act attends on the charge by nature (e.g. a temple-robber must of necessity be a thief, since a temple-robber is of course a thief of sacred property); but being a rapist does not follow on harming the public interest, since it is possible to harm the public interest in other ways. So here the prosecutor will include both in his speech, there he distinguishes one from the other. So this case has this head in its division over and above counterdescription, and the division is of course different as compared to counterdescription for this reason.

Third is the double *according to person*. It arises when an act has been performed as a whole by two persons, or in some other way has to do

45

with two persons. E.g.:- Sons succeed to priesthoods; a man who has a son fights heroically and requests to take over the priesthood of another man, who also has a son; this is granted; both men die, and the sons con-
10 test the priesthood. The question is, who is the son of the priest? The original state of affairs favours one (i.e. being born in the priesthood), the final one the other (i.e. his father died while still being priest). You will divide this in much the same way, opposing head to head.

15 Fourth is the *incident*, when (as in conjecture) another whole question arises in the middle of the heads. E.g.:- An uninitiated man sees the mysteries in a dream; he tells someone what he saw, and asks whether it is so; the man he asks agrees, and is brought to trial for revealing the
20 mysteries. The question is, what is it to reveal the mysteries? This proceeds as far as relative importance; then another question arises—who is the uninitiate? And you will divide this too into all the heads as far as relative importance, then you make the remaining heads common to both questions.

65 The fifth class is that called *dual definition*, which arises when the question concerns two descriptions applied to one person that are not counterdescriptions; e.g.:- A priest must be pure and of pure parentage;
5 a man kills his father as an adulterer, and is excluded from the priesthood. The question is, who is pure and who is of pure parentage? One must first go through one completely under all the heads, then commence the other from the beginning.

So much for definition.

COUNTERPLEA

10 The division of counterplea is: presentation; parts of right; person; definition, with its concomitants as far as relative importance; counterplea as such; objection; counterposition; second objection; thesis; quality and intention.

Presentation is as in definition.

15 *Part of right* is the same as the counterplea, but differs in that here it is placed straightforwardly at the beginning without argument, in the place of an exception, but there it is handled differently. E.g.:- A painter paints a shipwreck and displays it at the harbour; no one puts into port;
20 he is charged with harming the public interest. The presentation is obvious; the part of right is that it is inappropriate to be brought to trial for things which no law forbids.

46

Person: 'Even if that is appropriate, nevertheless private citizens   **66**
should not be tried for harming the public interest, but politicians,
ambassadors, generals, and the like. These people would have the capacity to harm the public interest, since they perform public duties, but
private citizens cannot.'

Definition: 'Indictments for harming the public interest have other   5
grounds, for example, for betraying ships, walls, allies, and things of that
sort.'

The *assimilation* necessarily follows: 'Both these things and the others
are a crime against the public interest, and there is no difference. There
are many ways of committing a crime, and the fact that someone has not   10
committed a crime in all of them will not give him immunity; he is to be
punished even if he commits a crime in one way.' This point will, of
course, be developed.

Each side will use *legislator's intention*, if relevant, for its own advantage.

Importance: that what occurred is serious.

Relative importance: that it is more serious than what is cited in
defence, e.g. that causing a shortage of all necessities because none of the   15
merchants puts into port is more serious than betraying ships or walls. In
these (i.e. importance and relative importance) the sequence of events
necessarily arises.   **67**

The reply to this, as we learned in conjecture, is the *counterplea*: 'It is
permissible and no law forbids it.' Then the objection, by refutation if
there is opportunity: 'It is not in fact permissible'; and by counter-
representation: 'Even if it is permissible, it is not so on these conditions   5
and in this way.'

The *counterposition* in this case is a counterstatement, e.g.: 'I acted on
behalf of mariners, so that they should know the harm they would probably come to if they sailed at the wrong time, and so take care.'

Second objection: 'You should have offered your advice in a different
way.' And if the prosecutor uses an objection, the defendant too will   10
again use a *counterplea*, e.g.: 'Each gives advice as he is able, and is not
forbidden to do so; the politician by his speeches, the painter by his art.'

The *thesis* is consequent; the thesis in this instance is that everyone
should be useful to the community as he is able. The prosecutor will also   15
use it sometimes, inverting it; e.g. that one should not abuse arts to the
detriment of the common good.

We have learned in definition how *quality* and *intention* are argued.

We have made these comments not as a division—many points have   20
been passed over—but just so as to indicate the nature of the heads.

There are several kinds of counterplea also. Two of them are simple,
68 and (principally) two double, although certain combinations occur so
that more can be found; but anyone who has learned only the classes just
mentioned can avoid errors in the division of those too, so we will discuss only these.

5   Of the *simple*, one involves judgement based on the *act* itself; e.g.:-
Alcibiades, having been recalled from exile after the battle of Cyzicus,
has the events of the Sicilian expedition portrayed on drinking-cups, and
is charged with harming the public interest. This is divided only into the
previously mentioned heads as relevant.

10   Another involves judgement based on the act itself and some other
contingency, as in the case of the painter who paints a shipwreck, and is
brought to trial when no one puts into port. Also in this case:- After the
battle of Chaeroneia Philip sends a message offering a choice between
15   recovering the two thousand prisoners or the thousand dead; Demosthenes argues successfully for the choice of the thousand; Philip executes
the prisoners; Demosthenes is charged with harming the public interest.
In counterpleas of this kind there is a special head besides those already
20   mentioned, the *exception*; this can be placed before the other heads, or in
the middle of them, or in general in whatever way is advantageous. It is:
'On what grounds are you bringing me to trial? If for the things done
69   subsequently, it is not right to hold someone accountable for what
others do, not even if they are close relatives, still less when they are enemies and not related in any way. But if for the advice I gave or what I did
at the outset, you should have spoken against me or resisted me at the
5   time. And if you did oppose and were defeated, you are now attacking
and accusing not only me, but also those who voted for me, or failed to
restrain me. But if you did not oppose and did not restrain, either you
had something better to say or do but passed it over at the time, in which
case you stand convicted of being an enemy of the common good; or else
10   you had nothing to say against me and are equally liable as me for the
same ignorance of subsequent events and what occurred without anyone
anticipating them. You deserve to suffer a penalty, if you think that I do.'
Also, in counterpleas of this kind, before the relevant counterposition
15   one should certainly use the head of *mitigation*; e.g.: 'No one knows the
future; so I too cannot be held to account for my ignorance.' Someone
expert in the whole art of rhetoric will treat this as is appropriate; knowl-
20   edge of division, which is this treatise's only subject-matter, is not
enough—knowledge of treatment is also needed.
So much for simple counterpleas.

Of *double* counterpleas, one is by combination, the other by distinc-   70
tion. By *combination*, when there are two charges and neither charge can
stand separately, but only in combination with the other. E.g.:-   5
Someone opposes everyone's proposals but offers none of his own; he is
charged with harming the public interest. Here it is obvious that there
are two counterpleas, since it is permissible both to speak and to refrain
from speaking; also that there are likewise two counterpositions, e.g. 'I
oppose; for it is right to oppose what speakers say in error,' and 'I do not   10
speak; there is no need to speak about matters which are not pressing.'
But a distinctive feature of this class is the need for defendants to make
a distinction and speak separately about each, and for prosecutors to link
the two together.

A double counterplea by *distinction* arises when there are two charges   15
which can be judged separately from each other; e.g.:- A man has frequently changed wives and adopted many children; he is charged with
living immorally. Here, similarly, the prosecutor will interlink the
charges and the defendant will distinguish them. However, it is clear   20
that the prosecution links together for the sake of amplification two
things which could in fact be judged separately, while the defendant distinguishes them for the sake of diminution; but in the previous instance,
this occurs not simply for the sake of amplification or diminution, but
because the act cannot be subjected to judgement otherwise than by   71
being introduced in this way.

I said that there can be further classes of counterplea. For example,
this kind differs from those previously mentioned; e.g.:- Two men who
had charged each other with adultery drop the charges and exchange   5
wives; they are charged with living immorally. First of all, there are two
persons being judged; then there are four counterpleas, the same for each
of them; e.g. it is permissible to bring a charge, and again to drop a
charge; it is permissible to marry whoever one chooses, and to divorce   10
one's existing wife; none of these things is forbidden, and the prosecutor
must refute each of them. The approach on both sides, for the prosecutor and the defendant, is clear from what has already been said.

There are other kinds of counterplea, which it would be pointless to   15
discuss here; every counterplea can be divided by anyone who follows
correctly what has already been said.

All counterpositions are divided: presentation; definition (in some cases), with its concomitants as far as relative importance; intent; counterposition as such—whichever shares the name of the question's issue (i.e. counterstatement, counteraccusation, transference, mitigation); alternative intent; objection; relative importance; forcible definition; thesis; second objection; counterplea; quality and intention.

The *presentation* is obviously from the events that have occurred.

We will use *definition* when it is relevant, just as we have already explained in counterplea; after the amplification of course comes sequence of events, in reply to which the defendant will use *intent*. As an example:- A hero killed his son for prostituting himself, and is charged with homicide. Definition is not relevant. After the presentation the prosecutor will place the sequence of events, since definition is not relevant. In reply to that, the defendant will use intent, asserting that the argument should be based not just on what was done, but also on the intention with which it was done: first, that he was not hostile to or scheming against the son; secondly, that he acted reluctantly, but out of necessity.

Then the *counterposition*; in this case a counteraccusation is relevant— he deserved it; and he will develop the common topic against a male prostitute (in every counteraccusation the counterposition takes the form of a common topic). He will also say something by way of counterstatement, that he did this on behalf of the victim himself. In general, all counterpositions are—by and large—interlinked with each other, and not only with each other but also with the other issues.

The *alternative intent* belongs to the prosecutor, that it was not for this purpose but for some other. It should be realized that even if this head is not very appropriate in the present case, in others it is found both extremely appropriate and very useful.

Objection: he should have done it in some other way than this.

Relative importance belongs to both parties, trying to show in opposition to each other whether the benefit or the crime is more important.

Forcible definition likewise belongs to both parties. This head will be easier to recognize in the following question:- During a famine under siege, the general unsuccessfully advocates giving battle by sortie; he then secretly cuts through a section of the wall; there is a victorious sortie; the general is subsequently charged with harming the public interest.

The forcible definition, then, is that this is not in fact a victory, so much as the capture and overthrow of the city. And, correspondingly, on the defendant's side, that this is not in fact to have cut through the wall, so much as to have restored it when breached.

The *thesis* follows consequentially: 'A general should, in whatever way opportunity allows, serve the city, even if the citizens are sometimes opposed because of ignorance of the best course of action, and he should do a small amount of damage instead of a great amount.' This is common to all counterpositions.

The *second objection* in turn belongs to the prosecutor: 'He should have discussed this matter with the assembly and the army officers.'

The *counterplea*: 'I was a general, and empowered to act,' or 'As a father, I was permitted to take decisions about my son.' In general, we will use the relevant heads as occasion allows.

We have learned how *quality* and *intention* arise in definition.

Some of those who have, under the title of the art of rhetoric, written on the part concerned with division have tried to say that there are classes of counterstatement, and indeed of the other counterpositional issues. They did not aim to show us any difference in their division, as we have done in counterplea and the others; that would perhaps have been worthwhile. Their point is that one class is private, another public, another mixed, and so forth. This is the same mistake as in discussions of classes and modes. For this is useful to those considering private and public discourse; but I doubt whether there is any call for someone who is still unfamiliar with division to know these things. To someone who lacks this knowledge, what would be the use of the distinction of questions into private and public?

Some have not differentiated mitigation from transference in terms of accountability and non-accountability; they have simply said that arguments transferring the crime to some external factor are all transference (e.g. a storm, torture, or something else of that nature), and defined only arguments transferring the crime to the individual's own internal state as belonging to mitigation (e.g. pity, sleep, etc.). This may be satisfactory— there is no difference except in the use of the term 'mitigation', which one would often find good use for even in cases of transference; and, conversely, in what are agreed to be mitigations one will use transference. This is not, in my view, a matter of division, but of knowing how to use opportunities and how to treat ideas correctly.

PRACTICAL

5 The practical issue is divided: legality; justice; advantage; feasibility; honour; consequence.

It may be documentary or non-documentary. The *documentary* is that in which the question is based on a verbal instrument, e.g.:- The law prescribes that a declaration of war should be debated over three days; when
10 Philip occupies Elateia Demosthenes proposes an immediate sortie. The *non-documentary* is that not based on a verbal instrument; e.g.:- After the Pylos campaign Cleon requests the title 'Pythian'.

Legality in the documentary class falls under one of the legal issues, and is divided accordingly; we will discuss legal issues in due course. In
15 the non-documentary class, custom should be treated as a basis for argument as if it had the force of law; e.g.: 'Your request is unprecedented; no one has ever made a request of this nature or magnitude before.' We will handle this by refutation and counter-representation. Counter-representation: e.g.:- After the Pylos campaign Cleon requests the title
20 'Pythian': 'Your request is unprecedented': 'Indeed it is—my achievements are unprecedented as well.' Refutation: 'But actually it is not unprecedented; in fact, Pericles received the title "Olympian".' The
77 occasion will show which should be used first (refutation or counter-representation), as we laid down in conjecture.

Justice falls under one of the juridical issues, and is divided into heads
5 accordingly, as opportunity allows.

Advantage is twofold: usefulness and necessity. E.g.: 'Accepting Olynthus as an ally is useful; or rather, it is necessary if we are to prevent Philip increasing his power at our expense by taking the city.' You will
10 argue this out in two ways: what will the result be if we adopt the course of action under consideration, and what will the result be if we do not? Each of these you will argue out in four ways, e.g.: 'If we choose this our existing advantages will remain and advantages which we do not now have will be gained in addition; conversely, we will dispense with our
15 existing disadvantages, and we will acquire no additional ones that we do not have at present. If we do not choose this, our existing advantages will be lost, and those which we do not have but stand to gain will not be gained; conversely, our existing disadvantages will remain, and others which we do not now have will be gained in addition.'
20 *Feasibility* you will subdivide, first of all showing that it is not difficult,
78 using refutation; then showing by counter-representation that even if it

is difficult, it is necessary, and that one must submit to toil and danger for worthwhile objectives, and also to avoid running into more serious difficulties; then, that it is in fact easy. If the subject is war or something 5 of that kind, consider feasibility on the basis of the attributes of the persons, as Demosthenes does in the *Second Olynthian*—Philip's condition (his despondency), the state of his foreign relations (e.g. the Thessalians, the Illyrians), finance, 'his mercenaries and guards infantry', and what follows. Corresponding to this was the examination of Athenian power; 10 the reason why Demosthenes passed it over can of course be shown by anyone who examines the speech in the light of theory. The division demands it, but there is no cause for surprise if it is passed over, since some of the other heads are omitted in accordance with nature there as 15 well, and we often make omissions, not only in the practical issue but everywhere else as well. Art shows the method of division, but art must be adapted to the nature of the facts as opportunity allows. The one is a matter of invention, the other a matter of judgement; in particular, we 20 will not use everything that invention generates in a speech—we should only say whatever we judge appropriate.

Honour is treated similarly to advantage. E.g.: 'What reputation that we now enjoy will remain, and what reputation that we currently do not enjoy will be acquired if we do adopt the course of action under consideration? What existing disgrace shall we set aside and what disgrace not 79 currently existing, but anticipated, shall we avoid acquiring? Conversely, if we do not adopt this course of action, what existing shame will we fail to set aside, and what shame currently not existing will overtake us? What existing reputation will disappear, and what reputation not exist- 5 ing but potential will fail to be added?'

Consequence is handled hypothetically for both outcomes; e.g.: 'Whether we are victorious or not, it is to our advantage to give aid, and indeed even simply to vote to give aid.' As in the *Philippics*, e.g.: 'Even if 10 you do not in fact do as I think you ought, the resolution will not be one by any means to be taken lightly, by god; either he will hold back out of fear, knowing that you are prepared, or he will ignore it and be caught off guard'; and: 'Whether those who are seeking alliance with us are defeated without us or win without us, the result will in each case be 15 against our interests,' as in *On behalf of Megalopolis*.

OBJECTION

Objection can, in turn, be documentary or non-documentary.

20   The *documentary* class is a complete procedural exception, and the prior question is found to be about one of the legal issues, which we will
80   discuss in due course, as has been said. Sometimes the prior question is analysed according to definition. The question following the exception will be divided according to one of the other logical issues. E.g.:-
Anyone opposing a law must oppose within thirty days of it being
5   passed; it shall not be permissible thereafter. While the poor man is serving as ambassador, his rich enemy proposes a law excluding those with property of less than five talents from public office or speaking in the assembly; the poor man returns after the thirty days, and wishes to
10   oppose the law. The prior enquiry follows letter and intent: when and to whom does the law prescribe opposition within thirty days—not to ambassadors or those abroad, and so forth. The second enquiry follows
15   the practical issue, whether the proposal made is lawful, just, etc. Here too a second argument by way of exception is relevant, e.g.: 'Because you do not have property of five talents or more, you are not empowered to speak'; it is clear how he will counter this too from the nature of the facts: because the enquiry is still about whether the law needs judicial review it cannot be invoked as already valid.

81   The *non-documentary* class is divided: presentation; exception based on a verbal instrument; objection; assimilation; definition; counterposition; second objection; counterplea; thesis; quality and intention.

5   E.g.:- A man who has fought heroically asks for and is granted the death of a citizen; he is found to have killed him already, and is charged with homicide.

Presentation: 'You are a murderer.'

Exception: 'I will not give an account for someone handed over to me by the people to be killed.'

Objection: 'When he was killed he had not been handed over.' The
10   speaker objects, of course, to the element of time; he concedes the act, but seeks judgement on the circumstance of the act, inasmuch as that the people would not in fact have granted it had he been present and spoken in opposition.

Assimilation: 'It makes no difference whether at one time or another.'
15   (We are saying this not by way of a division, but to indicate the nature of the heads; there is a great deal to be said here by those making a division.)

Definition: 'It makes every difference.'

Counterposition: 'Seeing that the people voted against him, he deserved death.'

Second objection: 'You should have stated that you had killed him and that he deserved to be slaughtered, and asked for immunity.' 20

The *counterplea* follows on these points: 'I was free to ask for whatever I wanted, and you should not be laying down the manner in which I ought to have made my request.'

Thesis: is it right to permit these things? Or: is it right to put brave 82 men into the hands of malicious prosecutors?

Quality and *intention*, as in what precedes.

LETTER AND INTENT

The enquiry on the basis of letter and intent is divided: presentation of 5 the verbal instrument; intent; exclusion of further distinctions; legislator's intention; assimilation; definition; counterposition; objection; relative importance; forcible definition; thesis; second objection; counterplea; quality and intention.

The *presentation* is the actual occurrence contrary to the terms of the 10 document; e.g.:- It is a capital offence for an alien to ascend the city walls; in wartime a man ascended the walls and fought heroically; he is brought to trial under the law. The presentation is 'You ascended.'

Intent is the basis of two arguments, that of the legislator and that of the man held to account. Of the legislator, e.g. when he speaks of peo- 15 ple ascending the walls, when and on what condition and for what reason? Of the person subject to the verbal instrument, e.g.: 'One should not consider only whether I ascended the walls, but also my intention in doing so, and the fact that it was not with hostile intention.'

The *exclusion of further distinctions* belongs to the party appealing to the letter of the verbal instrument; e.g.: 'The legislator made none of 83 these further distinctions, but said straightforwardly that aliens should not ascend the walls.'

The *second intent* is common to both parties. The defendant uses it in meeting the exclusion of further distinctions; e.g.: 'The legislator 5 thought there was no need to make further distinctions about things that are obvious by enjoining that those with friendly intention should not be subject to the ban.' The prosecutor will say that he thought it absurd under any circumstances to allow aliens to ascend the walls.

Assimilation, that making or not making further distinctions makes no
10 difference to the document, which is clear even without that.

Definition: it makes a great difference in every way.

The *counterposition* is the actual occurrence, and the defendant will
have more advantage here.

Objection: e.g.: 'You should have done it in another way', and 'It was
possible for you to benefit the city, if you chose, without breaking the
law.'

15 *Relative importance*: as in counterpositionals, whether the benefit or
the crime is more important. It is common to both parties.

The rest of the heads will also be argued as in the counterpositionals.

CONFLICT OF LAW

20 Conflict of law is a kind of double letter and intent, as I defined it in the
84 systematic introduction of the issues. It shares most of the heads with
that issue—doubled, naturally—but it also has a distinctive element of
its own, as will become clear.

It is to be divided thus: presentation of the verbal instrument; intent;
5   alternative presentation of the verbal instrument; alternative intent. Of
the subsequent heads, some are generally omitted because they are
equally balanced; e.g. these are followed as in letter and intent by the
exclusion of further distinctions, second legislator's intent, assimilation,
10 and (in reply to that) definition; but these seem in a sense to be equally
balanced, since much the same can be said on both sides, and it is difficult to be able to use them. However, the heads after these are obvious,
i.e.: counterposition; objection; relative importance; forcible definition;
15 thesis; second objection; counterplea; then quality and intention.

A distinctive head over and above the division in letter and intent is
the question of which includes and which is included by the other, i.e.
which outcome will abrogate neither of the verbal instruments. This
20 head will be placed after relative importance.

85 All this will be clear from an example; e.g.:- A disinherited son shall
not have a share in his father's property; a man who remains on board a
ship abandoned during a storm shall become the owner of the ship; a disinherited son remains on board his father's ship when it is abandoned
during a storm, and is prohibited from taking possession.

5   *Presentation of the verbal instrument*: 'As a disinherited son, you have
no share in your father's property.'

Intent: 'He means, presumably, when someone makes a claim to inherit or succeed to any part of his father's property under the laws applying to children, not when the claim is made as a stranger standing in no relation.'

Then follows the *alternative presentation of the law*: 'Especially when the law explicitly grants title to the person who remains on board ship.'

The *alternative intent* is a reply to this: 'But it grants this subject to the proviso that the property is not that of the father, that it is a stranger's, that one is not disinherited, that one is not prohibited by law.'

Then there is the *exclusion of further distinctions*; whichever side uses this, the other side too will be able to use it, and it is equally balanced. One might in fact be able to treat it in a division; at present we are not dividing, but indicating the heads, and they are clear. Consequent on this head, *definition* and *assimilation* are also equally balanced.

However, the *second intent*, which is the intention of the legislator, is argued differently by each side with reference to both laws. E.g.: 'Why does the legislator exclude a disinherited son from his father's property?' The prosecutor will say, 'Because he thought someone hateful to his father unworthy to have a share in any of his property'; the defendant: 'No, the aim was to force them to earn their living by working for themselves and exposing themselves to dangers, and so cast off the idleness and self-indulgence which led to their disinheritance. This is what I have done by remaining on board ship.' Conversely, 'Why does he grant the ship to the man who remains on board?': 'So that mariners will be steadfast in the face of danger,' or whatever either side devises. (As I have often stressed, I am not giving a division here; I make these remarks to give an indication of the heads.)

The *counterposition* is double on both sides; e.g.: 'But you are disinherited,' and here there is an attack in the manner of a common topic. The other party: 'But I remained on the ship'; here there is something in the nature of a counterstatement, and a description of the circumstances of the storm.

The *objection* too is double: the disinherited son will say 'It would be unjust to exclude me from title to the ship, even if I were such a person; this is not the occasion for these charges'; the other party: 'You should have displayed your courage in other circumstances, not in these.'

The *relative importance*—which of the laws it is better to maintain— if there is opportunity to say that one law is old, the other recent; one enacted by Solon, if such is the case, the other by so-and-so; the one is common, the other private; the one is concerned with extremely serious

57

matters, the other with minor ones; that if the one is undermined, the community will suffer severe harm, but little or none if the other is undermined.

10   In addition to these there is also the head which is more distinctive to conflict of law, *which is inclusive and which is included*, i.e. which outcome will abrogate neither of the laws. The nature of this head is hard to discern in the present case; it will be clearer in the light of this question:- A
15   man raped two young women at the same time; one chooses marriage, the other the rapist's death. The one who demands his death will say that he will pay a penalty to both if he dies, but if he marries the other woman half of the law will be nullified.

    Forcible definition: that the ship belongs not, in fact, to the father but
88   to the storm; or that it is not the father's property, but no one else's either.

    The *thesis* and what follows, if relevant, are argued out as in counter-positionals.

ASSIMILATION

5   Assimilation is divided: presentation of the fact; letter; assimilation; definition; legislator's intention; importance; forcible definition; relative importance; counterposition (in some cases); if this is relevant then an objection will also be found, and counterplea will certainly follow; then quality and intention.

10   In general, except for the different order of the first heads, assimilation is divided as is definition.

    This will be clearer in the light of an example; e.g.:- It is illegal to ridicule anyone by name in comedy; someone introduces characters in a comedy with identifiable masks, and is brought to trial under the law as having ridiculed by name in comedy.

15   *Presentation of the fact*: 'You subject citizens to ridicule in comedy illegally.'

    Letter: 'But I named no one; that is what the law prohibits.'

    Assimilation: that there is no difference between the two.

    Definition: there is every difference.

    Legislator's intention is common: what was the legislator's aim in prohibiting this? The prosecutor will say: 'The aim was to abolish straight-
89   forward, unaccountable slander of any citizen on any charge these people like'; the defendant will say: 'This is not the reason; he wanted people to

be subject to reproof through comedy, and therefore did not ban comedy outright; but he did not want records left for subsequent generations, 5 or for contemporaries, containing abuse of any citizen. In the absence of names the reproof comes about by means of masks, but the record for subsequent time is removed as is the slander before others.'   10

Importance: as in definition, that what occurred is important.

Forcible definition: that this is in fact to ridicule by name in comedy.

Relative importance and subsequent heads are all argued out as in definition.

There are many classes of assimilation, all of which you will divide in 15 the same way; however, examples may be set down. They arise either on the basis of:

(i) the *equal*, like the one discussed above;

(ii) the *greater*, e.g.:- It is permissible to execute exiles who try to return; someone whips an exile who is trying to return, and is charged with unlawful punishment. He argues: 'Whoever grants the greater also 20 grants the lesser';

(iii) the *contrary*, e.g.:- A hero shall receive a reward; the general executes a deserter, and is charged with homicide. He will use a counteraccusa- 90 tion not on its own, but in conjunction with the points mentioned above.

(iv) the *lesser*, on the basis of its consequences; e.g.:- It is permissible to brand adulterers; someone kills an adulterer while branding him, and is charged with homicide. He argues: 'Whoever grants the antecedent also grants the consequences that ensue from it.'

5

AMBIGUITY

Ambiguity is divided: presentation of the verbal instrument; alternative presentation of the same instrument in accordance with the ambiguity; legislator's intent; inclusive and included; counterposition; objection; thesis; quality and intention.   10

One should be aware that if ambiguity is treated as a self-sufficient question, it is inevitably pedantic and correspondingly somewhat frigid in respect of division. But if it is part of a question, its division is useful. This is exhibited in all invented questions based on oracles and prophecies.   91

For consideration of the heads, take this question:- If a prostitute wears gold ornaments, *dēmosia estō*; a prostitute is arrested wearing gold

ornaments; someone maintains that she is public property (reading
5 *dēmosía estō*), but she denies that she is public property herself, claiming
that the ornaments are (reading *dēmósia estō*).

Presentation of the verbal instrument: 'The law requires that you are
public property.'

Alternative presentation in accordance with the ambiguity: 'Not me but
the gold ornaments.'

Legislator's intention is argued by both sides for their own advantage;
10 e.g.: 'The legislator took this to deserve punishment . . .'—one party will
say '. . . the severest punishment', but she will say: '. . . punishment, but
moderate, just as he assigned proportionate penalties for other crimes.'

Inclusive and included: that if the prostitute becomes public property,
15 so do the ornaments; but if only the ornaments become public property
the prostitute goes free.

92 The *counterposition* follows immediately; it is by way of counteraccusation, and the prosecutor goes through an argument against the prostitute in the manner of a common topic.

This is followed in turn by *objection*; e.g.: 'Granted that she is a pros-
5 titute, she enjoys the distinctive rights of this profession—not to be like
free women, nor to be subject to the same expectations.' And obviously
her advocate will appeal to pity at this point, advancing her poverty or
something of that sort.

Quality and *intention* as in the above. It so happens in this question
10 that the argument based on intention is extensive—whether she wore
the gold ornaments out of contempt for the law or simply out of ignorance.

3   Commentary

INTRODUCTION (28. 3–43. 14)

Preface (28. 3–29. 6)

28. 3–7 **There are many important elements:** Hermogenes' opening reference to rhetoric's status as an art (τέχνη, cf. p.4) alludes to the common definition of art as 'a system of cognitions ordered by practice for some goal advantageous in life' (in Greek 'constitute' and 'grasp' are cognates of 'system' and 'cognition'). Although Stoic in origin (*SVF* 1. 21, 2. 30 f.; Long and Sedley 1987, 1. 259), the formula came to enjoy far wider currency; Quintilian describes it as almost universally accepted (2. 17. 41). In Hermogenes its terms have lost the technical sense they had in Stoic philosophy, and the focus of interest has shifted from epistemology to history ('from the beginning . . . over time'). According to standard histories, rhetoric was established as an art in the fifth century by the Sicilians Corax and Tisias (see p. 9 f.), but an implicit grasp of its principles was attributed to earlier writers, especially Homer (e.g. Quintilian 10. 1. 46; cf. Radermacher 1951, 3–10; Kennedy 1957); in the second century AD Telephus of Pergamum even included issue-theory in his monograph on the 'seeds' of rhetoric in Homer (*PS* 189. 2–7).

28. 7–14 **the most important . . . is that concerned with division:** Although the traditional title of this treatise is *On Issues*, there is good reason to suspect that Hermogenes himself would have called it *On Division*; that, certainly, is how he regularly defines its subject-matter (see e.g. 29. 9–11, 34. 16, 35. 12–14, 36. 3, 43. 10 f., 43. 17 etc., 74. 16 f., 76. 1). The system of issues is not the main focus of the treatise, but is introduced (like the classification of person and act at *29. 7–11) as part of the prior knowledge required for correct division (35. 15–17).

By 'division', Hermogenes here means the analysis of a rhetorical problem into the relevant heads of argument. To justify his claim that this is the most important part of rhetoric Hermogenes contrasts it with two other fundamental concepts in rhetorical theory, the standard division of speeches into kinds (see p. 10 f.) and the division of a speech into its parts. The doctrine of the parts of a speech was seen as so basic that it came to be identified as Corax's decisive contribution to the establishment of rhetoric as an art (Ch. 1 n. 24). For Hermogenes' contention that division into heads is more important than the classification of speeches into kinds see *34. 16–35. 14. Hermogenes further emphasizes the importance of his subject by asserting its virtual equivalence to invention. The extravagance of this claim will become increasingly apparent. Hermogenes admits later that knowing how to divide a question is not enough (69. 16–20, 75. 21–76. 2). Moreover, in this treatise he does not divide questions, but merely indicates the nature of the heads into which they are to be divided (67. 19–21, 81. 13–16, *85. 16–86. 3, 86. 15–17); to divide a question would be to show how the heads thus abstractly defined relate to the particulars of the given case (as Sopater does in his *Division of Questions*). Hermogenes himself wrote a separate treatise *On Invention* (see on *53. 12 f.).

28. 15–29. 6 **what is meant by a political question:** Hermogenes defines the political questions with which rhetoric is concerned in terms of both content and perspective. They are:

(i) *particular*: this differentiates the circumstantially specific hypothesis from the thesis (cf. p. 16 f.);
(ii) *practical*: 'just, honourable, advantageous' are the main heads of purpose (see p. 21); rhetoric is concerned with human actions and purposes, and does not address theoretical issues (e.g. questions of cosmology);
(iii) *relative*: rhetoric is concerned with whether a given action is (e.g.) just according to the norms of a given community; by contrast philosophy would ask whether the action is just in a universal and absolute sense.

Rhetoric may, of course, raise general, theoretical, or universal questions (e.g. in the head called thesis: *67. 13–18; cf. Ch. 1 n. 46); but they are introduced to serve the case being made for one or other side of a particular, practical, and local dispute.

Persons and Acts (29. 7–31. 18)

29. 7–11 must be concerned with persons and with acts: Schouler 1990 gives a good account of Hermogenes' treatment of person and act. In general, the significance of the classification can be seen by substituting different categories into given themes and observing how this changes the resources available for argument; e.g. if Odysseus is found with a bloody sword beside the corpse of Ajax, then the known enmity between them, together with other mythological data about Odysseus' character and deeds, provides more extensive resources for argument on both sides than does the variant in which 'someone' is found beside an unspecified corpse (see note to *49. 16–19; cf. *RG* 4. 88. 5–13, 5. 39. 19–28 for the same experiment with Demosthenes). For applications of the classification see 44. 6–9, 46. 10–14, 48. 3–5, 56. 9 f., 61. 7–15.

29. 12 f. some can provide a basis for argument: Person and act are necessary components of all questions (29. 7 f.), since someone has to do something for a question to arise at all. Hermogenes explains below (53. 14–56. 20) that some themes are incomplete, i.e. deficient in respect of either person or act; this does not mean that an incomplete theme lacks person or act, but that either person (30. 12–16) or act (31. 12–18) provides the speaker with no resources for argument. See further *31. 6–11.

29. 13–16 determinate proper names have a richness of content lacking in the other categories listed, and so provide more extensive resources for argument, because their individual history extends beyond the circumstances stated in the declamation theme (as in the example of Demosthenes at 30. 5–8). With the other categories, once the stated circumstances have been fully exploited the speaker is thrown back on general presumptions about how a person of that kind might be expected to behave; but arguments based on generalizations are inherently vulnerable to counterexamples—it is easier to make a case for or against Demosthenes having taken a bribe than 'a certain orator' having done so. Cf. the contrast between historical and 'private' problems in [Hermogenes] *Inv.* 117. 2–118. 14.

29. 16 f. relative terms have greater argumentative force than the other general categories because in linking two persons they imply obligations or likely dispositions (*RG* 4. 93. 20–97. 7). E.g. if a son is found beside his father's corpse, their relationship can be exploited to make the alleged crime appear either incredible or exceptionally heinous; likewise, the hostility of slaves towards their masters can be assumed as a basis for argument (45. 10 f.).

29. 17 f. **prejudicial terms** have more argumentative potential than ordinary characterizing terms because of the scope they provide for invective.

29. 18 f. **characterizing terms** are those designating the stock characters familiar from New Comedy and often met with in declamation—misers, misanthropes, boorish farmers, etc.

Themes involving such persons emphasize character over argument (cf. p. 8 f.), sometimes to the extent of being technically invalid (cf. *31. 19–34. 15); e.g. the farmer who charges his wife with prostitution because she has gone into town has no real case, but gives the declaimer an opportunity to display his skill in evoking the man's boorish character. This is one of the examples mentioned by Hermogenes' commentators (RG 4. 101. 10–24, 103. 14–16; 5. 45. 14–46. 17); they also refer to the bad-tempered man who disinherits his son for laughing when he tripped over, and the envious man who seeks permission to commit suicide when his neighbour is suddenly enriched—the themes of Libanius' *Decl.* 27 and 31 respectively. Libanius handles this kind of theme with particular skill; see Russell 1983, 87–105.

29. 19–22 **terms combining two appellatives:** Rich men are conventionally ambitious, oppressive, and arrogant; young men are rash, high-spirited, and unstable (see e.g. RG 4. 341. 7–11, 346. 28–30; cf. Aristotle *Rhet.* 1389^a3-^b12, $1390^b32-1391^a19$). The intersection of these two sets of characteristics gives the speaker a firm basis for argument: see 46. 12–14, and note the frequent appearance of rich young men in this treatise, often in the role of aspirants to tyranny (30. 13 f., 32. 14–17, *47. 2–5, 48. 6–9, 49. 10–14, 49. 21–3).

29. 22–30. 2 **terms combining person and act:** This category was added by Hermogenes to the six recognized by Minucianus (Christophorus *ap.* Rabe 1895, 243). Introducing act into a classification of persons troubled some ancient rhetoricians (RG 4. 106. 9–14), but is perhaps defensible. The act in Hermogenes' example, because it is habitual, has implications about the youth's character, and is therefore relevant to arguments based on person; but it is not simply an aspect of his character, since there is also scope for arguments based on the nature of the act which are independent of the agent's character, e.g. that it is *per se* legal (see *48. 18–21 for the declamation theme in which this youth appears).

30. 2 f. **simple appellative terms** are argumentatively weak because they carry relatively little presumptive information with them; we cannot tell, independently of the circumstances of the case, whether (e.g.) a general is competent, loyal, etc.

30. 3–9 **Clearly, these may occur:** The richness of content characteristic of determinate individuals must be used selectively, in the light of the needs of the case in hand. The need for such an exercise of judgement is a recurrent theme in this treatise (see especially *78. 10–21).

30. 10–12 **the topics of encomium:** On encomium see p. 16, and Burgess 1902, 119–27. The standard encomiastic topics (which Hermogenes lists at 46. 9–18) are designed to provide comprehensive coverage of the attributes of the person being praised; they can therefore also serve to guide the declaimer in his handling of the aspects of a question which refer to person.

30. 12–16 **Those which do not provide a basis for argument:** See *29. 7–11.

30. 19–21 **someone is charged as himself the agent:** For the example see *49. 16–19.

30. 21–31. 1 **directly referred to a person other than the agent:** Persons charged as a consequence of another's acts appear at 44. 6–9, 48. 3–5, 50. 2–11, 55. 4; cf. 68. 22–69. 1. For the example see *44. 6–9.

31. 1–6 **intermediate cases:** This category of acts was an innovation of Hermogenes, entailed by his rejection of Minucianus' thesis that there could be simple questions based only on person (see *31. 6–11). The example (see 55. 6–8) conflates Archidamus' delays in the invasion of Attica in 431 BC (Thucydides 2. 18–23) with the story that Pericles had bribed the Spartan king Pleistoanax to abandon an invasion in 445 BC, entering the item in his official accounts as 'necessary expedients' (Thucydides 1. 114, Plutarch *Pericles* 22 f., Aristophanes *Clouds* 859). Pericles' act has no direct reference to Archidamus, but can sustain a case against him when taken in conjunction with the mismanagement of the campaign.

31. 6–11 **An exactly similar case:** Hermogenes here introduces the controversy over incomplete questions. An incomplete question lacks resources for argument based on either person or act (see *29. 12 f.). It is easy to see how a declamation theme might offer no resources for argument based on person (e.g. if 'someone' is accused), but rhetorical theorists hotly disputed whether there could be a case with a single

defendant (as distinct from the 'double' case at *31. 12–18) and no scope for argument based on act. Minucianus had offered the dissolute's missing father as an instance, but Hermogenes maintains that it involves an intermediate act: the father's disappearance has no direct reference to the son but does provide grounds for argument against him in the light of his known bad character. As well as countering the attack on his character, the son will 'gloss' (a common alternative name for the head which Hermogenes calls 'transposition of cause': cf. *49. 7–50. 19) the disappearance, i.e. he will try to show that explanations are available which do not incriminate him; so the case does not lack arguments based on act. For further discussion of this controversy see *54. 9–55. 8.

31. 12–18 **only an equivalent act:** Since the acts on both sides of this double question are identical, the argument is based solely on person; cf. *56. 4–13. Each party in a case of reciprocal accusation tries to establish its own innocence and the other's guilt. The opposition of poor man and rich man means that a different set of conventional assumptions underlies each side's argument; if both parties had been rich young men any argument applying to one would apply to the other, and the theme would be invalid (cf. 30. 14–16, 32. 14–17).

Valid and Invalid Questions (31. 19–34. 15)

31. 19–32. 9 **which questions have issue:** Hermogenes specifies a number of conditions which a declamation theme must satisfy if it is to be valid:

1. There is a person and/or act to be judged.
2. Both parties have resources of persuasion that:
   (*a*) differ from those of the other party, and:
   (*b*) have some probative force.
3. A verdict is:
   (*a*) not self-evident, but:
   (*b*) can in principle be reached.

If one or more of these conditions is not satisfied, the theme lacks issue (is ἀσύστατος) and is invalid.

32. 9–33. 16 **Questions which lack issue:** On invalid themes see Calboli Montefusco 1986, 12–28. For the concept in practice see Philostratus 595 f. (Philostratus rejects an allegation that Ptolemy of Naucratis had

failed to recognize an invalid theme), Aulus Gellius 9. 15. 5–8 (an insoluble theme is used to set a trap for an over-confident declaimer).

Hermogenes' classification is not easy to correlate with his stated criteria; ancient commentators proposed different solutions, not always consistent with Hermogenes' text (e.g. *RG* 4. 141. 11–142. 30, 143. 13–145. 8). A possible correlation is this. The *one-sided* case violates criterion (2). Cases that are *equivalent* or *reversible* violate (2a) in different ways. *Insoluble* cases clearly violate (3b). The *implausible* and *impossible* categories violate (2b), since there cannot be arguments with probative force in favour of a claim which is grossly implausible or impossible. The same may perhaps be said for the *disreputable* class; in Hermogenes' example, there is nothing to be said in support of the husband. *Uncircumstantial* cases violate criterion (1). This appears to leave no category corresponding to criterion (3a) except that of *prejudiced* cases, which Hermogenes oddly describes as only 'close to' lacking issue (*34. 8–14). However, it might be argued that a violation of all or part of (2) entails that the case is in breach either of criterion (3a), if it is one-sided, implausible, impossible, or disreputable, or of criterion (3b), if it is equivalent or reversible; similarly an uncircumstantial case as well as violating criterion (1) is bound also to lack persuasive arguments (2b) and to be irresolvable (3b). Since Hermogenes' criteria are concerned in part with the resources offered for argument and in part with the potential conclusion, it is not surprising they intersect in this way; but it cannot be said that the scheme is tidy. Moreover, some of the categories themselves overlap confusingly. It is not clear from the examples given what distinction is being made between implausible and impossible—e.g. between the proverbially just Aristides acting unjustly and the proverbially insignificant towns of Siphnos and Maroneia aspiring to world-domination; and one suspects that with the one-sided category a genus has been made co-ordinate with its species, since being implausible, impossible, or disreputable are ways of being one-sided (indeed, Hermogenes' example of one-sidedness might be classed as disreputable). The treatment of invalid themes is therefore unsatisfactory as a body of theory; this does not necessarily remove its pragmatic value, and the commentators prefer it to the more systematic approach of Minucianus (see *36. 7–9).

32. 11–13 **A brothel-keeper:** The example is derived from a valid theme (Seneca *Contr.* 10. 1. 13, Calpurnius Flaccus *Decl.* 40) in which the brothel-keeper warns a group of young men who have been bothering him not to come again; after they have fallen into his trap he is charged with harming the public interest.

Hermogenes' commentators observe that some scope for argument would be opened up, and the theme would become valid (as counteraccusation), if the brothel-keeper were replaced by a reputable person who might claim to have acted from a legitimate concern for public morals, such as a general or a philosopher (e.g. *RG* 4. 150. 10 f.; 5. 38. 4–12, 62. 25–63. 4; cf. Syrianus 2. 37. 26 f.). They also note how in Hermogenes' version the crime has been carefully exacerbated to enhance the one-sidedness of the example; note the number of victims, the triviality of their offence, the prepared trap (*RG* 5. 60. 1–7).

32. 14–17 **Two rich young men:** See *31. 12–18.

33. 3–7 **no resolution or conclusion can be reached:** A commentator (*RG* 7. 163. 5–10) compares the crocodile paradox: a woman was walking by the Nile when a crocodile seized her child; the crocodile promised to give the child back if she correctly predicted what he would do with it; she says that the crocodile will eat the child. If she is right the crocodile is bound to give the child back; in which case she is wrong, and the crocodile can eat it; in which case . . . The paradox was known to Lucian (*Vit. Auct.* 22).

33. 9–11 **Siphnos or Maroneia:** For the insignificance of these cities see Demosthenes 13. 34, 17. 23.

33. 11 **that Apollo tells a lie:** For the truthfulness of the Delphic oracle see Plato *Apology* 21b7 and (e.g.) Garvie on Aeschylus *Choephori* 559; but Philostratus 575 reports one declaimer (Alexander Peloplaton) making Pericles accuse Apollo of lying.

33. 11–14 **disreputable:** In Zeno (315. 19 f., 317. 15–23) 'disreputable' (ἄδοξον) designates both a mode, in which the theme is trivial (on mode cf. p. 10 and *34. 16–35. 14), and a species of invalidity, in which the theme is scandalous. On Zeno's view a theme is only invalidated as disreputable if both person and act are scandalous; where a scandalous act is compensated by a reputable person (or *vice versa*) we have a valid theme in the ambiguous (ἀμφίδοξον) mode (317. 7–14). Minucianus took a very different approach (*RG* 4. 163. 15–164. 7, 180. 23–181. 6, 188. 6–189. 12; Syrianus 2. 43. 23–44. 10). He did not regard disreputable themes as invalid. Where both person and act are disreputable (his example was a pimp charged with impiety for naming his prostitutes after the Muses) the theme is valid, the mode disreputable; but when the person is reputable and the act disreputable (or *vice versa*) the discrepancy between them renders the theme implausible and therefore invalid.

Disagreement over the classification of scandalous cases is attested also in Quintilian 4. 1. 40.

33. 15 A man disinherits his son: For disinheritance see *38. 15 f.

33. 19–34. 2 Critias takes refuge: The theme presupposes a right of asylum at the statues of Harmodius and Aristogeiton (on their cult in Athens see Fornara 1970, 155 f.). It is assumed that this legal right will carry little weight when the claimant is Critias, leader of the proverbially oppressive Thirty Tyrants who seized power in Athens in 404 BC: how can he (of all people) lay claim to protection from the tyrannicides (*RG* 4. 172. 24–9, 5. 72. 1–5)? Aristides treated this theme twice, once briefly in the manner of a common topic (reflecting its ill-balanced nature), once more elaborately and deliberately taking the weaker side in order to display his powers (frr. 115–17 Behr). Cf. the variant at *RG* 4. 801. 12–17:- It is a capital offence to violate asylum at the statues of Harmodius and Aristogeiton; someone kills Critias after he takes refuge at the statues; he is prosecuted.

34. 2 f. Nicias' letter: In 414 BC Nicias wrote to the Athenian assembly asking for the expeditionary force in Sicily to be recalled or reinforced, and for himself to be relieved of the command (Thucydides 7. 10–15). The idea of sending Cleon to take his place is inspired by the unexpected success which he won at Pylos in 425 BC after Nicias stood down in his favour (Thucydides 4. 27–39); but Cleon had died at the battle of Amphipolis in 422.

34. 3–5 Mardonius, retreating after his defeat: The Persian general Mardonius, having died at the battle of Plataea in 479 BC (Herodotus 9. 64), could not have been called upon to defend his role in the defeat.

As well as chronological blunders, confusing the customs and laws of different societies (e.g. basing a theme set in Sparta on Athenian laws) was held to be a flaw in invention (*RG* 4. 72. 6–73. 1).

34. 8–14 A woman shows her husband how to gain access to a tyrant: The case is mentioned in the preface to [Libanius] *Decl.* 43 (7. 438 f. Foerster; the reference is not to the case in Sopater 247. 8–252. 2, as Foerster ad loc. and Russell 1983, 60 n. 65 suggest).

Synopsis of the Issues (34. 16–43. 14)

34. 16–35. 14 There is no point discussing the class of problems and their mode: In this paragraph Hermogenes rejects a standard doctrine.

According to Zeno (316. 3–317. 31), once it has been established that a theme has issue, the next step in its analysis is to identify its class and mode; Minucianus is known to have taken a similar approach (*RG* 4. 182. 9–183. 26, 185. 11–20; 7. 165. 17–26; Syrianus 2. 42. 11–44. 10). For the classes and modes in question see p. 10. It is disingenuous of Hermogenes to focus his polemic on the classification of speeches as judicial, deliberative, and epideictic; these categories are not classes or modes in the relevant sense, and do not feature in Zeno's discussion at all. Also tendentious is the claim that the distinction of class and mode has implications only for style. The classification of a theme as (e.g.) emotional has a direct bearing on how the argument is to be handled. When Sopater analyses the case of the captive concubine accused of poisoning (see Hermogenes 56. 15–17) he observes that it is full of emotion: 'for the city is bereaved of the hero, the man responsible for its liberty is killed by poison; the pathos is enhanced by the fact that the poor captive's being alone and a foreigner adds to her misfortune' (Sopater 28. 7–10); and this diagnosis informs Sopater's treatment of the captive's case throughout. Compare e.g. Sopater 313. 29–314. 1, or (for the class based on character) 309. 19 f., 315. 23 f. Classes and modes may be useless without an understanding of issues, and do not affect division at the relatively abstract level with which Hermogenes is here concerned (see on *28. 7–14); but his opponents could reasonably retort that effective application of issue-theory and the principles of division requires an understanding of classes and modes.

35. 15–17 Correct division: Person and act are partial determinants of a division; we will see in later sections how their different combinations define variant forms of the issues. But first the issues themselves have to be introduced.

35. 17–36. 5 the origin of the term 'issue': The point was disputed; Hermogenes mentions the theory that it derived from στάσις in the sense of 'dispute, political conflict', but does not pursue the question. A common (κοινόν) name is purely conventional; a contingent (συμβεβηκός) name reflects the nature of the object—as, e.g., in the supposed derivation of 'Nile' from the fresh mud (νέα ἰλύς) which it deposits (*RG* 4. 202. 1–4, 7. 173. 25–174. 2, cf. Syrianus 2. 48. 3–10).

36. 7–43. 14 The systematic presentation: A traditional structure for issue-theory (see e.g. Cicero *Or*. 45, *De Or*. 2. 104–13; Quintilian 3. 6. 44, 56) was based on three questions: does it exist? what is it? is it a good one? These questions correspond to the issues of conjecture, definition, and quality. This structure underlies Hermogenes' system (42. 7–10); the number of issues is raised to thirteen by a complex series of subdivisions to the third question, and by the addition of a fourth, procedural question (the status of which had been uncertain since it was first introduced by Hermagoras: Cicero *Inv.* 1. 16; Quintilian 3. 6. 68–85; *RG* 4. 278. 29–279. 9; cf. *42. 5–43. 8). Hermogenes' system is represented diagrammatically in Figure 1. In summary form:

(1) Are the facts of the case in dispute?
    (*a*) yes: the issue is *conjecture.*
    (*b*) no: go to (2).

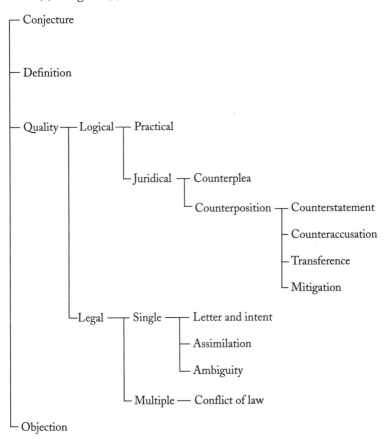

FIGURE 1. Hermogenes' system of issues

(2) Is the correct categorization of those facts in dispute?

    (*a*) yes: the issue is *definition*.

    (*b*) no: the issue is *quality*; go to (3).

(3) Does the dispute focus on the implications of substantive features of the acts in question, or on the implications of the law under which the charge is brought (or of some other relevant legal instrument)?

    (*a*) act: the issue is *logical*; go to (4).

    (*b*) law: the issue is *legal*; go to (9).

(4) Is the dispute concerned with a past or future act?

    (*a*) future: the issue is *practical*.

    (*b*) past: the issue is *juridical*; go to (5).

(5) Does the defence deny that the act in question was *prima facie* illegal?

    (*a*) yes: the issue is *counterplea*.

    (*b*) no: the issue is *counterposition*; go to (6).

(6) Is responsibility for the act accepted or transferred?

    (*a*) accepted: the issue is *counterstatement*.

    (*b*) transferred: go to (7).

(7) Is responsibility transferred to the victim?

    (*a*) yes: the issue is *counteraccusation*.

    (*b*) no: go to (8).

(8) Is responsibility transferred to an accountable third party?

    (*a*) yes: the issue is *transference*.

    (*b*) no: the issue is *mitigation*.

(9) If the dispute focuses on the implications of a law or legal instrument, is there one instrument or more than one (or one divided into more than one part)?

    (*a*) one: go to (10).

    (*b*) more than one: go to (12).

(10) Is the literal interpretation of the law agreed?

    (*a*) yes: go to 11.

    (*b*) no: go to 13.

(11) Is an implied meaning of the instrument substituted for its explicit meaning, or added to it?

    (*a*) substituted: the issue is *letter and intent*.

    (*b*) added: the issue is *assimilation*.

(12) If the dispute is concerned with more than one legal instrument (or one divided into more than one part), then the issue is *conflict of law*.

(13) If the literal meaning of a legal instrument is disputed, then the issue is *ambiguity*.

(14) Is the validity of the charge contested on the basis of an explicit legal instrument? If so, the issue is *objection*; we must now consider whether the challenge is countered:

- (*a*) by questioning the interpretation of the law under which it is made: the objection is *documentary* (corresponding to the legal issues).
- (*b*) by arguing that some feature of the act in question constitutes a relevant difference from the norm: the objection is *non-documentary* (corresponding to the logical issues).

36. 7–9 **The matter to be judged** is the one survival in Hermogenes of the elaborate substructure with which Hermagoras and his successors had tried to furnish issue-theory; for an attempt to reconstruct the history of this substructure see Heath 1994*b*. In its early forms it involved a two- (or, in Hermagoras, three-) phase analysis of the question. In the first phase the issue is determined from the initial propositions of the two parties (e.g. the case is qualitative if an accusation of homicide is met with a claim of justification); in the second phase the grounds of the initial propositions are examined to determine more closely the matter on which the jury has to decide (e.g. whether the stated degree of provocation justifies the homicide). By the second century AD internal tensions had caused the two phases to collapse into one: the charge (αἴτιον) and response (συνέχον, the 'key point') determine both the issue and the matter to be judged (κρινόμενον). Minucianus innovated by making this scheme the basis for his account of valid and invalid themes; themes lacking issue were diagnosed as defective in respect of one of these three elements (an approach which later commentators found less satisfactory than that of Hermogenes: *RG* 4. 139. 24–140. 11, 143. 5–14; cf. 5. 57. 21–58. 3, 69. 30–70. 6). But in Zeno the whole scheme has been abandoned, and likewise in Hermogenes. Zeno, however, follows earlier theorists in thinking of the matter to be judged as a question (e.g. was this homicide justified?); for Hermogenes it is identified simply with the facts of the case (e.g. the homicide committed in these circumstances).

36. 9–12 **If the matter is unclear:** For conjecture as a 'proof of existence' (ἔλεγχος οὐσιώδης) cf. 42. 7 f. and the note to *36. 7–43. 14; compare e.g. Theodorus *ap.* Quintilian 3. 6. 36. Alternatively, conjecture could be characterized as the denial of the charge (e.g. Cicero *De Or.* 2. 105, Quintilian 3. 6. 32); this was the approach favoured by Zeno (325. 19 f.) and Minucianus (Syrianus 2. 61. 8–10; *RG* 4. 202. 20–4, 214. 16 f., 5. 150. 5–16).

The sign is 'clear' only in the sense that the facts which constitute the sign are not in dispute; it is not clear that they are a sign of the crime alleged, this being the point in dispute. After 'from a sign that is clear' the manuscripts add 'or from suspicion concerning the person'; this must be an interpolation, since Hermogenes was criticized for precisely this omission (*RG* 4. 210. 27–212. 1; 5. 85. 10–87. 23, especially 86. 25–8). Generally in conjecture one act is treated as a sign or indication that the accused has committed some other, and criminal, act; however, in some cases judgement is based on suspicion arising from person alone (*31. 12–18), and Hermogenes' formulation therefore seemed to need supplementation. But he probably did not mean to restrict 'sign' here to act.

36. 12–15 **A man is apprehended:** For the example see *49. 16–19. Strictly, the question is not who committed the homicide, but whether the accused did so.

37. 1–13 **If the matter to be judged is clear:** The second question is whether the facts are 'complete', i.e. whether they meet all of the conditions we normally associate with a given description. E.g. a typical instance of temple-robbery would involve the theft of consecrated objects from a temple; if it is private property that is stolen the act is 'incomplete' by comparison with that norm, and there is room for dispute about the description to be applied to it: is the man guilty of ordinary theft rather than temple-robbery? For this example see *62. 3–5.

37. 14–20 **If the matter to be judged is clear and complete:** If the fact and the appropriate categorization of the fact are agreed, the dispute may focus on its evaluation. This qualitative dispute may turn on the implications of some aspect of the act itself (e.g. whether it constitutes a culpable assault given that the victim struck the first blow), or on the correct interpretation of the law under which the act is brought to trial; these are the logical and legal species of quality respectively. The logical species is preferred (cf. *39. 20–40. 6), since reliance on purely legal argument may seem to be (in a pejorative sense) legalistic; this contrast is already found in Gorgias fr. 6: 'preferring mildness and fairness to inflexible justice, correctness of reasoning (λόγων ὀρθότης) to legal exactitude (νόμου ἀκρίβεια)'.

38. 1–8 **The logical issue:** Deliberative oratory evaluates future acts: would the course of action proposed be just, honourable, and prudent? Aristotle too distinguished deliberative and forensic oratory on the basis of their past or future reference (*Rhet.* 1358ᵇ3–5). If Hermogenes' definition of the practical issue is taken strictly, it would cover any debate

about reward or punishment: e.g. whether the tyrannicide's reward should be conferred on a claimant, whether the father's disinheritance of his son should be ratified. Some rhetoricians did accept this view (criticized by Zeno 350. 10–351. 5); Hermogenes was clearly not among them (see e.g. 38. 15 f., 59. 18–60. 1). Where the verdict in such cases turns on the evaluation of specific past acts (whether the claimant has satisfied the conditions of the award, whether the son's behaviour warrants disinheritance), they are juridical rather than practical.

38. 12 f. If he denies altogether that the act was forbidden: At first sight it may not be apparent how counterplea can avoid collapsing into definition: a claim that the act is legitimate cannot be sustained unless the prosecution's description of the act (which of course represents it as criminal) is disputed; but a dispute about the description of an act is definition. An example may help to clarify the distinction:- A husband kills a hero as an adulterer, and is charged with harming the public interest (see p. 115 below). The husband cannot deny that the killing of a hero weakens the city militarily, and is therefore against the public interest; so he cannot argue (as in definition) that the charge incorrectly describes the act in question, which is not a complete or (therefore) genuine instance of the crime alleged. He can, however, argue that it is unreasonable to make the killing of an adulterer the subject of a criminal charge, since such killings are licensed by the law (see *43. 3–8). This is obviously a weaker response than in definition.

38. 15 f. A farmer disinherits his son: Declamation assumes the father's right to disown a son for unsatisfactory behaviour, subject to judicial review (see Russell 1983, 31 f. and, for the legal background, Wurm 1972). The possibility of judicial review entails that the father's right is not unlimited, but the limit is left conveniently unspecified; many declamation themes invite an exploration of the limits to a reasonable exercise of this power. Lucian's *Disinherited Son* (discussed in Berry and Heath, forthcoming) is a good example; see also Russell 1983, 97–105.

38. 16–39. 19 If the defendant concedes that the act . . . was a wrong: In counterplea the defence maintains that its act is legitimate in itself; in counterposition it is conceded that the act is illegitimate in itself, but maintains that it is justifiable (or at least excusable) in the given circumstances. If responsibility for the act is accepted, the defence must put forward a counterstatement, that the act was justified in the circumstances because of some beneficial consequence. Alternatively, responsibility may be shifted to the victim by counteraccusation (e.g. a claim that the assault was justifiable retaliation), or to a third party by transference (e.g. a claim that one committed the crime because terrorists were holding one's family hostage). The weakest of these defences is mitigation, in which some feature of the situation is offered as an explanation of the act, even though it does not allow an alternative placing of the blame; e.g. that one acted in anger, or was a victim of circumstances. (Hermogenes mentions in passing at the end of this paragraph a different way of distinguishing transference and mitigation: see further *75. 11–76. 2.) According to *RG* 4. 238. 15–17, 5. 97. 6–8, Minucianus was the only theorist before Hermogenes to have treated the four counterpositions as separate issues; but since Zeno treats them separately (325. 9 f., 345. 15–349. 22) this is unlikely to be true.

39. 11–14 **An ambassador:** This theme is discussed in Cicero *Inv.* 2. 87–91, 124. In a related theme a man is prevented from fulfilling some obligation (such as military service) by a flood (*Rhet. ad Herennium* 1. 24; Cicero *Inv.* 2. 96 f., 124; Quintilian 7. 4. 14); this would count as mitigation in Hermogenes' scheme, there being no accountable third party to receive the blame (see 39. 17–19).

39. 15 f. **The ten generals:** The case is based on the trial of the generals after the battle of Arginusae, on which see MacDowell 1978, 186–9. For its popularity among declaimers see Stephens 1983; apart from Hermogenes' commentators, the theme is found in Apsines 326. 23 (evidently assumed to be well known), and an adaptation appears in Zeno 347. 20–348. 23, Sopater 223. 13–227. 22; Sopater also refers (225. 20) to a treatment of the theme by Metrophanes. There is a papyrus fragment of an exercise on the theme (PYale II. 105), dating from perhaps the first century.

39. 20–40. 6 **legal issues:** Legal argument originally fell outside the system of issues. Hermagoras defined issue as 'a proposition in accordance with which we grasp the underlying act in which there is a question in reference to which the dispute arises' (fr. 10: φάσις καθ' ἣν ἀντιλαμβανόμεθα τοῦ ὑποκειμένου πράγματος ἐν ᾧ ἐστι τι ζήτημα καθ' ὅ ἐστιν ἡ ἀμφισβήτησις; thus PS 329. 10–12, cf. 318. 10–12; abbreviated in *RG* 7. 173. 10–12, Quintilian 3. 6. 21); only the logical issues are concerned with the act (*37. 14–20), and Hermagoras accordingly made a distinction between logical issues and legal questions (Cicero *Inv.* 1. 17, Quintilian 3. 6. 61 f.). This distinction was rejected by some later rhetoricians (cf. Quintilian 3. 6. 45 f., 54 f.); it is ignored in the thirteen-issue system (cf. Zeno 325. 4–17), although there remains a sense that

legal argument alone is insufficient (cf. *37. 14–20, and pp. 141, 152 f. below).

39. 22 **verbal instrument:** The term ($\dot{\rho}\eta\tau\acute{o}\nu$) is also used in the sense of the literal meaning of a verbal instrument as distinct from its spirit ('letter and intent' = $\dot{\rho}\eta\tau\grave{o}\nu$ $\kappa\alpha\grave{\iota}$ $\delta\iota\acute{\alpha}\nu o\iota\alpha$). See p. 224.

40. 6–19 **a single instrument:** In letter and intent one party tries to show that the implicit intention of the law is narrower than its explicit formulation, and thus that the present case lies outside the intent of the law. This involves drawing a distinction which the law does not explicitly make (e.g. 'it says "an official", but that cannot mean an official even when acting in a private capacity'). In assimilation one party tries to extend the application of the law to cases which it does not explicitly cover. Here a distinction has to be blurred (e.g. 'It says "wife", but that must include unmarried partners as well').

40. 11–13 **an alien:** See *82. 11–13.

40. 18 f. **The son of a (female) prostitute:** The sexes are reversed at Syrianus 2. 198 f.; a variant at Quintilian 7. 6. 3 turns on a woman who becomes a prostitute after the birth of her son, which Hermogenes would class as definition (cf. 64. 6–13).

40. 20–41. 12 **two or more verbal instruments:** Conflict of law arises when each party appeals to the explicit content of a different law, so that the two laws (or two parts of one law) appear to contradict each other in the given circumstances. A legal code should in principle be consistent; but consistent laws may be put into conflict in particular circumstances (cf. Demosthenes 24. 34 f.; Quintilian 7. 7. 2; Syrianus 2. 195. 7–12; *RG* 4. 264. 1–18, 5. 106. 13–17).

41. 5–8 **A disinherited son:** For this example see *85. 1–4.

41. 9–12 **A victim of rape:** See *87. 14–16.

41. 13–42. 4 **Ambiguity** involves a dispute about what the explicit content of a single law really is; the law can be read in two ways, and each party appeals to a different reading.

41. 16–20 **If a prostitute wears gold:** See *91. 2–5.

41. 21–42. 4 **A man has two sons:** Since word-division (like accentuation) was not generally indicated in Greek manuscripts the collocation of *panta* and *Leōn* is ambiguous. This is a traditional example: Quintilian 7. 9. 6. Sopater (*RG* 5. 108. 18–109. 15) claims that the case is invalid unless the brothers are differentiated in some way which would give grounds

for arguing that the father would have preferred one to the other; cf. Metrophanes at *RG* 7. 695. 27–36 for the importance of arguments about the father's preference. An argument in Pantaleon's favour might be that, given the flexibility of Greek word-order, the ambiguous collocation could have been avoided if Leon were the named heir; their father would therefore have phrased the will differently had he meant that.

42. 5–43. 8 objection is different: Both species of objection arise out of a challenge to the validity of the proceedings. To mount that challenge the defence must cite the provisions of some legal instrument; this might take either of two forms:

(i) It might be argued that there is a defect in the proceedings as such, e.g. a violation of the bar on double jeopardy (as at *42. 15–19) or of a time-limit (*80. 3–9). The prosecution will have to show that the law which is cited to this effect has been misinterpreted or misapplied; the substantive argument about the case will therefore be preceded by a procedural argument conducted in accordance with one of the legal issues. This is the documentary species of objection.

(ii) It might be argued that the proceedings are invalid because there is explicit legal warrant for the act charged; e.g. if someone kills an adulterer and is charged with homicide (and provided there is no evident complication, such as the adulterer being a eunuch: *60. 20–61. 1) the defence will claim that the act was explicitly permitted by the law against adultery (as at *43. 3–8). Here the prosecution must show that the circumstances of this killing make it relevantly different from the killing licensed under the law (e.g. the killing was done with excessive cruelty, or after an unreasonably long delay: see *43. 3–8). Thus the debate arises out of the citation of a law, but is about the act in question. This is the non-documentary species.

The division of questions falling under these two species is quite different, and there is little logic in their being classed as a single issue. (Metrophanes separated them to give a fourteen-issue scheme; in this he was followed by Evagoras, Aquila, and Syrianus, who mistakenly attributes the scheme to Hermogenes himself: 2. 55. 5–8.) There is also a terminological anomaly. In Hermogenes most issues are named after their key head; e.g. the argumentative structure of counterplea (the issue) is centred on counterplea (the head), which also has a supporting role in many other issues. Non-documentary objection fits this pattern: the crucial head is the prosecution's objection, conceding the act in principle but objecting to it in given circumstances (e.g. he deserved to be killed, but not then, there, by you, in that way, etc.). But in documentary objection there is no place for objection (the head). In fact, the subdivision of objection conflates a system of nomenclature based on crucial heads with Hermagoras' original use of the term μετάληψις in the sense 'transference' for a defence based on a procedural exception (*36. 7–43. 14). Syrianus' evidence suggests that this awkward duality existed already in Minucianus (2. 55. 3 f.). In Zeno, however, the duality does not arise (338. 31–340. 20). Objection in his system corresponds to Hermogenes' non-documentary species; cases which Hermogenes would class as documentary objection are treated by Zeno under letter and intent (Sulpicius departs from Zeno on this point). It is possible that Zeno preserves the original form of the thirteen-issue system; if so, it may have been Minucianus who introduced the problematic refinement (see further *79. 18 f.).

42. 15–19 The same charge shall not be tried twice: Cf. 44. 16–20. Hermogenes analyses the first question as letter and intent: can the law of double jeopardy be meant to apply to such serious cases, or to thwart the god's will? But some rhetoricians found the law ambiguous: it prohibits two δίκαι for the same offence, but this word may mean 'punishment' rather than 'trial' (Zeno 340. 29–35; *RG* 4. 272. 18–24, 284. 26–285. 4, 286. 6–9, 805. 13–19; 7. 230. 20–9, 239. 2–5, 243. 2–7; Quintilian 7. 6. 4 raises the question whether 'twice' refers to the prosecutor or the prosecution). The second, conjectural question in this case is whether the defendant is a murderer. He does not have to claim that the oracle is false (ruled out by *33. 11); oracles are proverbially riddling, and he can argue that the reply is simply obscure (*RG* 4. 286. 15–29; Hermogenes associates ambiguity and oracles at 90. 13–15).

43. 3–8 Both an adulterer and an adulteress: The legal right to kill an adulterer summarily is a standard assumption in declamation (for the historical background see Lysias 1. 30, Demosthenes 23. 53; MacDowell 1978, 124 f.). In Hermogenes' example the objection turns on place and time, but other elements of circumstance (see p. 13) can have the same function; e.g. if the husband burns the house down with the couple inside, objection might be made to the manner of the killing (Syrianus 2. 154. 13–18).

43. 11–14 the discussion will . . . be comparatively extensive: Cf. *Rhet. ad Herennium* 2. 12.

79

CONJECTURE (43. 16–59. 9)

Division (43. 16–53. 13)

Conjecture has a unique structure. In other issues, some act is given and one party asserts that this act is criminal (or worthy of reward, or whatever the case may require), while the other party denies it. In the standard form of conjecture, the given act is innocent (or at least is not part of the charge) in itself, but is treated as a sign that some other act, which is criminal, has been committed. The point in dispute is whether the inferred crime was in fact committed as alleged. The distinction between the inferred crime and the given act on which the inference is based is the key to Hermogenes' model strategy. The argument has two main phases. The primary phase concentrates on the alleged crime: is it intrinsically likely to have been committed? A secondary phase concentrates on the sign: does it really warrant an inference to the crime? In an optional preliminary phase the defence may call into question the validity of the proceedings; once the charge has been established the way is open for exploitation using common topics for emotive force. Hermogenes' division (43. 17–21) is summarized in Figure 2.

A. Preliminary Argument

44. 1–20 Exception: This head is not to be used in all cases (43. 18). Even when an exception could in principle be devised, it may be tactically prudent to suppress it; e.g. objecting to a serious charge because of the time elapsed since the alleged crime might give a poor impression of the defendant's character or confidence in his own innocence (*RG* 4. 317. 30–318. 2). Similarly, one might vary its position: it may be better to bring the exception in at a later stage, if leading with it could be thought to imply a lack of confidence in one's case. The ancient commentators stress that Hermogenes gives the 'natural' order of the heads, but that the speaker may wish to vary this in particular cases (*RG* 4. 307. 6–11, 28–32, 319. 21–320. 11, 7. 258. 23–8; on natural and artificial order see Ch. 1 n. 63); this agrees with Hermogenes' stress on the need to exercise judgement (see especially *78. 10–21).

44. 1–11 Exception arises in four ways: This classification seems arbitrary. In particular, why is time singled out for special mention? Any element of circumstance could provide the basis for an exception (*RG* 4. 316. 2–23, 5. 123. 6–124. 10); for example, in the cases Hermogenes cites

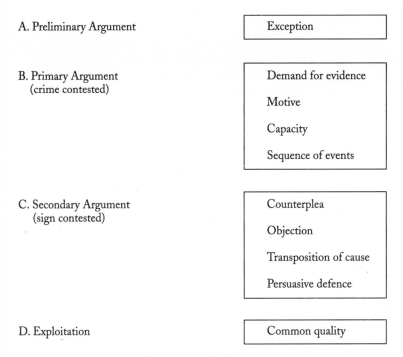

A. Preliminary Argument	Exception
B. Primary Argument (crime contested)	Demand for evidence Motive Capacity Sequence of events
C. Secondary Argument (sign contested)	Counterplea Objection Transposition of cause Persuasive defence
D. Exploitation	Common quality

FIGURE 2. Conjecture

to illustrate his other categories, the ten young men and the triple-hero have exceptions based on person, the dissolute son one based on act.

44. 2 f. **The father of a dissolute son:** See *31. 6–11, *54. 9–55. 8.

44. 4–6 **Ten young men:** For ten defendants cf. the trial of the Arginusae generals (*39. 15 f.); but for present purposes a conjectural case is needed. We must assume that a collective trial is not strictly illegal (the issue would then be objection), but contrary to normal practice and unfair. Sopater argues that, since the person and act are identical for all the co-defendants, there can be no unfairness in returning a single verdict (*RG* 5. 124. 10–16); but to make an exception the defence needs no more than the possibility of relevant differences (e.g. in motive: Syrianus 2. 66. 27–67. 21).

Since this is a case of conjecture, the oath not to marry is not seen as an illegal act in itself, but as evidence of immorality; the prosecution must therefore rest on a common prejudice in favour of marriage rather than on legislation promoting it (contrast Russell 1983, 33). The theme appears also in Apsines 223. 25–224. 2, 276. 14–277. 22, and Zeno 314. 32 f.; in Fortunatianus 87. 12–16 and [Augustine] 144. 25–9 an oath not to marry is suggested as possible grounds for disinheritance. The declaimer would be able to draw material from the thesis on whether one should marry (e.g. Aphthonius 42–6; [Hermogenes] *Prog.* 24–6), one of the subjects most commonly prescribed to students according to [Dionysius] 261. 13–22.

44. 6–9 The triple-hero: Hermogenes' example of a charge based on another's act at 30. 21–31. 1; see also 50. 5–10. For the hero in declamation see Russell 1983, 24 f.

44. 11–20 If the exception is based on a verbal instrument: The exception (παραγραφικόν rather than παραγραφή: cf. *RG* 4. 317. 2–6, 323. 14–19) is a spoiling device, designed only to make the prosecution's case seem weaker. If a strong exception, based on an explicit provision of the law, can be made, it must be argued out at length; the issue is then objection.

44. 16–20 A man tried for homicide: See *42. 15–19.

B. Primary Argument

The main part of the case begins by focusing on the alleged crime. The two parties argue over the plausibility of the allegation:

(i) is there evidence?
(ii) would and could the defendant have done it?
(iii) does the alleged sequence of events hang together?

45. 1–46. 7 Demand for evidence: The body of the argument begins by looking at the non-technical proofs in the case (*RG* 4. 328. 11–24, 336. 13–16: on technical and non-technical proofs see e.g. Aristotle *Rhet.* 1355^{b}35–40; Quintilian 5. 1; Anon. Seguerianus 188–91; Apsines 260. 18–261. 15; Cicero *Pro Caelio* 54 with Austin ad loc.). If there are witnesses, the defence will have to undermine their credit; but if the prosecution lacks 'hard' evidence of this kind the defence will try to exploit that weakness, while the prosecution stresses the unreliability of witnesses and emphasizes the importance of the technical proofs (46. 3–7: cf. Aristotle *Rhet.* 1376^{a}17–32, 1376^{b}31–1377^{a}7; Anon. Seguerianus 189). A prosecutor in this position who is unwilling to lead off with the weakest part of his case could delay his reply to the demand for evidence until after the presentation of his technical proofs, i.e. after the sequence of events (*RG* 4. 336. 9–13, Syrianus 2. 72. 9–12).

45. 2–20 **A girl's mother:** The case is co-confirmatory conjecture (*57. 11–58. 2: *RG* 5. 125. 19–126. 17 misses this point). The adultery gives the mother a motive (jealousy) for the alleged poisoning, and if this motive is granted then the circumstances of the girl's death count strongly against her; but the adultery will be denied, and the demand for evidence refers to this second conjectural question. The case appears with minor variants at Seneca *Contr.* 6. 6, Calpurnius Flaccus *Decl.* 40, Zeno 331. 14–332. 26; without the adultery at [Quintilian] *Decl. Min.* 354, Julius Victor 376. 33–7.

45. 15 f. **as Demosthenes does:** Demosthenes 54. 31–6.

45. 20–46. 3 **If there are no witnesses:** The defendant emphasizes the absence of witnesses by considering every aspect of the alleged act to which testimony might be required and is not available. The use of the six elements of circumstance (p. 13; cf. 42. 22–43. 3) for elaborating or amplifying an argument is standard; cf. 47. 9–11.

46. 8–47. 7 **Motive and capacity:** The technical proofs begin with an analysis of the person (or persons: 46. 24–47. 7) involved in the case, to determine whether or not the alleged crime was something which the defendant would and could have undertaken. An interesting early example of argument from motive and capacity is found in Gorgias' *Palamedes*: Palamedes could not have betrayed the Greeks (6–12), nor had he any motive to do so (13–21). Gorgias places the demand for evidence after this (22–4), perhaps a less effective order than Hermogenes' (21 would lead neatly into 25 f., in effect a persuasive defence: if I was clever enough to commit the crime I could not have been stupid enough to want to commit it).

46. 9–18 **the topics of encomium:** see *30. 10–12.

47. 2–5 **the rich youth who maintains disinherited sons:** See *48. 6–9; other indications of a rich young man's desire to be tyrant are shouting encouragement to prisoners (*49. 10–14) and weeping when he looks at the acropolis (*49. 21–3, 51. 1–3). The case is discussed by Julius Victor 387. 15–35; in [Quintilian] *Decl. Min.* 260 the charge is harming the public interest, and accordingly the issue is counterposition.

For rich young men and their characteristics see *29. 19–22. Disinherited sons (see *38. 15 f.) are likely to be of disreputable character (this is the reason for their disinheritance), and resemble disfranchised citizens in being marginalized members of society who stand to gain from revolution (see Russell 1983, 31 f.).

47. 8–48. 2 **Sequence of events:** The term means literally 'the things from beginning to end'; cf. *Lucian *Tyrannicide* 14. This head gives a step-by-step analysis of the sequence of events alleged by one or other party (cf. Zeno 326. 24 f. *in quo persequimur ordine criminum signa non simul omnia sed carptim singula*), in order to establish its coherence and plausibility and to highlight its implications. It is distinguished from the main narrative (which precedes the argumentative heads) by its systematic use of argument and amplification (e.g. *RG* 7. 284. 1–6). The necessary techniques of argument have been practised in the preliminary exercises of confirmation and refutation (p. 15).

Rhetorical terminology for the narrative and quasi-narrative elements in a speech is complex. 'Narrative' (διήγησις) may be used as a generic term covering any form of exposition of facts, or as a technical term for the main narrative section of a speech, as distinct from the argumentative section. 'Statement' (κατάστασις) is applied to a species of narrative in which the exposition is slanted for the speaker's advantage (e.g. Apsines 251. 3–9); all rhetorical narrative takes this form, and some theorists therefore prefer to call the main narrative section of the speech statement rather than narrative (e.g. Sopater in the *Division of Questions* invariably speaks of the statement). Theorists who have this preference sometimes express the distinctiveness of statement by describing narrative in general as a plain (ψίλη) exposition of the facts (Syrianus 2. 64. 20–65. 3, 127. 6–12); statement itself may also be described as plain (Troilus in *PS* 52. 12 f.), but then the contrast is with the handling of facts in the argumentative section of the speech. So too *RG* 4. 356. 15–19 recognizes the slanted nature of rhetorical narrative—retaining that term—but still describes it as plain by contrast with the argumentative handling of the facts.

There are two ways in which the exposition of facts may be elaborated in the argumentative section: demonstration (i.e. showing that the facts are as stated), and amplification (i.e. enhancing the perceived significance of those facts). The sequence of events in conjecture is demonstrative (cf. Syrianus 2. 78. 6–10). Some theorists regarded sequence of events as invariably demonstrative, by contrast with presentation (see *59. 16 etc.), which is always amplificatory (*RG* 7. 408. 3–10, 556. 11–19 contrast 24–7); but this is not Hermogenes' usage. In Hermogenes, sequence of events (i.e. what happened) normally refers to the material used in certain heads. In other issues it designates material handled by way of amplification in the presentation and in certain subsequent heads (see *59. 16, *66. 13–67. 1); but in conjecture it designates material handled demonstratively (but also by amplification: *47. 9–11) in a head which is also called sequence of events.

47. 9–11 can be amplified: For the amplificatory use of the elements of circumstance cf. *45. 20–46. 3.

47. 11–13 If this belongs to the prosecutor: A head 'belongs' to one party if it is used positively in the construction of that party's case. The prosecution in a conjectural case must establish that its reconstruction of events is probable; the defence need only show that this reconstruction is improbable, or at least that it is not necessary. So the sequence of events in most cases will be used constructively by the prosecution. But in some cases the defence can argue constructively that an alternative reconstruction of the events is probable (47. 14–48. 1), and the head will then belong to both parties in common.

47. 17–48. 2 A charge of conspiring to establish a tyranny: In this example, two opposed accounts of events can be given. One is based on a hostile interpretation of the quashing of the charge (if he was confident of his brother's innocence he could have let justice take its natural course; if not, then he gave protection to a possible conspirator); the other is based on a friendly interpretation of the tyrannicide (loyally putting right the damage he had done by mistake). Each party will have, under subsequent heads, to reinterpret the event on which the other's reconstruction is based (he had quarrelled with the tyrant and feared for his life, or believed that the tyranny was about to fall and wished to disguise his guilt; brotherly affection clouded his judgement when he made the request). Hence, where both sides make positive use of the sequence of events, subsequent heads are also used on both sides.

48. 1 f. It is not possible: Commentators (Syrianus 2. 77. 27–78. 6, *RG* 4. 363. 12–23, 5. 131. 12–23, 7. 288. 18–291. 2) show that it is possible for the sequence of events to belong to the defence alone, citing a case in which a man who has suffered a series of calamitous misfortunes denounces himself for some crime; his son speaks against him, arguing that he has accused himself falsely in despair. Since there is no evidence of the man's guilt other than his confession, the sequence of events favours the defence.

C. Secondary Argument

In response to the analysis of the sequence of events, attention shifts from the alleged crime to the events which are cited as evidence of it:

(i) are they innocent in themselves?

(ii) are they open to an explanation which does not imply the alleged crime?

(iii) do they support the prosecutor's allegation, or undermine it?

48. 3–9 **Counterplea:** The defence asserts the legitimacy of its acts; the reference is (of course) to the sign and not to the alleged crime. Since the sign is not the subject of a charge this head may seem superfluous, but the defence will use it to cast a shadow over the prosecution (is it reasonable to bring someone to court on account of an innocent act?) and to dispel the sinister interpretation placed on its acts by the prosecution. This move is not possible if the charge is based on another's act (*30. 21–31. 1); in such cases the defence is compensated by a stronger exception (*44. 6–9). Nor is it possible if a criminal or disreputable act is being cited as sign of some more serious crime (Syrianus 2. 79. 24–80. 9).

Minucianus placed the counterplea after the transposition of cause; some other rhetoricians agreed that this was the best order for the defence to follow, since it might seem provocative to claim the freedom to perform contested acts before their innocence has been exhibited (*RG* 4. 313. 20–314. 13, 373. 29–374. 10; 5. 121. 24–122. 12; 7. 257. 16–22, 299. 20–301. 5, 315. 10–19; Zeno 325. 27, 326. 30–2, places counterplea first, but says that it is not always used). In some cases this might be wise (see *51. 8–11), but in general Hermogenes' order gives the defence an effective progression: the acts in question are not illegal (counterplea); they have an innocent explanation (transposition of cause); indeed they refute the allegation based on them (persuasive defence).

48. 6–9 **A rich youth maintains all disinherited sons:** See *47. 2–5. Hermogenes gives the structure of the argument, not its tone; in practice a less blunt and arrogant formulation would be advisable. For example, the youth might give a philanthropic and democratic colouring to his counterplea by pointing out that wealthy men often provide support for less fortunate citizens.

48. 10–49. 6 **Objection** seeks to refute the counterplea by identifying a circumstance which makes the particular case an exception from whatever general rule the defence has appealed to (cf. 42. 21–43. 8, 81. 8–12). In the example just mentioned, the objection is based on person: disinherited sons, having brought misfortune on themselves by their bad behaviour, do not deserve support.

48. 11–14 **If one of the opposed parties:** Counterplea is always used by the defence, objection by the prosecutor; but the order is variable, the

counterplea coming after the objection in the division of some issues (61. 3–6, 74. 9–14, etc.). The doctrine that objection is always opposed by counterplea was questioned by Menander (Georgius *ap.* Schilling 1903, 745; cf. sch. Demosthenes 21. 26 (93b), 22. 22 (65)), who argued that an objection may be opposed by a further objection; if one party objects to the way in which something was done, the other party can retort that doing it in any other way would have been equally or more objectionable.

48. 14–49. 6 **by refutation or by counter-representation:** Refutation rebuts an opponent's claim outright; counter-representation concedes it up to a point (perhaps hypothetically) and shows that it is does not warrant the desired conclusion. For example, after questioning the defence's claim that the maintenance of disinherited sons is legitimate in principle, the prosecution may go on to argue that in any event to maintain so many of them is sinister (cf. Syrianus 2. 81. 23–82. 5). These techniques can be generalized beyond counterplea and objection (*76. 17–77. 2; cf. *RG* 4. 380. 12–18, [Hermogenes] *Inv.* 136. 20–138. 13, 163. 15–164. 9, Quintilian 4. 5. 13–17, 7. 1. 16).

48. 18–21 **An adolescent who uses cosmetics:** See 30. 1–2, 51. 13–16, 52. 1–5; the case is based on one of Aristotle's illustrations of the fallacy of affirming the consequent: *SE* 167^{b}8–11, *Rhet.* 1401^{b}23 f. The defence's counterplea is that there is no law against the use of cosmetics. The prosecutor's refutation does not mean that the use of cosmetics is strictly illegal, but simply that it is disgraceful (for males: in this case person is the aspect of circumstance on which the objection turns). The counter-representation will remind the jury that there cannot at any rate be a defence for the use of cosmetics for immoral purposes, thus bringing back into focus the connection between the sign and the alleged crime which the counterplea seeks to sever (*RG* 4. 380. 3–12, 7. 296. 9–15).

49. 7–50. 19 **Transposition of cause:** The defendant gives an innocent, or indeed praiseworthy, gloss to his acts; 'gloss' ($\chi\rho\tilde{\omega}\mu\alpha$) is in fact a common term for this head (Hermogenes uses it at 31. 10 f., 50. 10; see Matthes 1958, 140 f., Calboli Montefusco 1986, 17 f., and Fairweather 1981, 166 f. on the Latin equivalent *color*). The prosecutor must respond by showing that this explanation is less plausible than his own. One approach is to identify internal inconsistencies in the defence's story; another is to show that the defendant's behaviour in other contexts is inconsistent with the motive claimed ('if this were true, he would behave like this; but he does not': Porphyry *ap. RG* 4. 398. 17–399. 26; *RG* 7. 313.

25–314. 18; Menander *ap.* sch. Demosthenes 19. 101 (228); Demosthenes 19. 109 f. is the model).

49. 10–14 **A rich young man comes in a nocturnal revel:** An adaptation of the case in *47. 2–5, 48. 6–9. In Syrianus (2. 83. 27–84. 3, 87. 13–18) the rich young man is identified as Alcibiades.

49. 16–19 **A man is apprehended:** See 30. 19–21, 36. 12–15, 54. 5 f., 55. 2. In a variant the man is found standing by the corpse with a bloody sword in his hand (Zeno 327. 11–13, *RG* 7. 231. 20–6 etc., *PS* 251. 12–16; bloody sword but no corpse at Syrianus 2. 83. 15–18); this is an incomplete conjecture (lacking person: cf. 54. 5 f.), which can be made complete by identifying the man as Odysseus and the corpse as Ajax (*Rhet. ad Herennium* 1. 18, 1. 27, 2. 28–30; Cicero *Inv.* 1. 11, 1. 92; Quintilian 4. 2. 13 f.; cf. *29. 7–11).

The defendant shows that his act was praiseworthy by enlarging in general terms on the obligation to bury corpses; this is the thesis, a technique practised in the preliminary exercises (p. 16 f.; cf. *67. 13–18). Since the defendant is being tried for meeting (as he claims) a basic human obligation there is scope here for indignation (Apsines 235. 11 f., cf. *51. 8–11; for βαρύτης see Hermogenes *Id.* 364. 1–368. 21).

49. 21–3 **A rich young man constantly looks at the acropolis:** Another adaptation of *47. 2–5, 48. 6–9; see 51. 1–3. There is an extensive treatment in Zeno 325. 19–327. 7; in *RG* 8. 413. 15–17 and [Quintilian] *Decl. Min.* 267 it is an abdicated tyrant who sheds the incriminating tears, and the case is complicated by an amnesty.

49. 23–50. 2 **One should realize:** This qualification does not cure the inadequacies of Hermogenes' assignment of different kinds of gloss to different kinds of sequence of events (49. 7–23). There are two problems. First, the categories of sequence of event cannot be kept distinct; for example, an utterance is also an act (e.g. of encouragement) and may be prompted by emotion. So it is a mistake to single out mitigation and its application to one category of event: mitigation may apply to utterances and other acts (perhaps the youth who called out to the prisoners was drunk, or was moved by pity); and the other counterpositions may be relevant alongside mitigation (by burying the body the man saved the city from pollution, a counterstatement). Secondly, a thesis is not a defence but the amplification of a defence (as we shall see in the division of several other issues). So to say that acts can be glossed in the manner of a thesis leaves out a step; an innocent or meritorious intention has to be exhibited before a thesis can usefully be developed. In some cases, such

as the burial of the body, the possible meritorious intention is so obvious that thesis-style amplification can be introduced very quickly; but these cases need not be based on acts. Conversely, cases in which the sequence of events is *prima facie* so prejudicial to the defence that the innocent intention needs to be stated with great care need not be based on words; Apsines cites the young man who weeps when he looks at the acropolis as a paradigm of this kind of case (243. 12–15, 273. 10–14). Hermogenes' presentation tries to harness to an unhelpful classification of sequence of events a clumsy conflation of two schemes, one giving the logical structure of the transposition of cause (a counterposition), the other suggesting two ways of developing it (emphasizing argument about intention, or thesis-style amplification) depending on how heavily the facts of the case seem to weigh against the defence. For ancient discussion of these points see especially *RG* 4. 364. 5–30, 392. 16–395. 8, 397. 15–30, 5. 135. 1–11; sch. Demosthenes 19. 101 (228), where the source is Menander (cf. Georgius *ap.* Schilling 1903, 745 f.). For an example of multiple counterpositions in the transposition of cause see *Libanius *Decl.* 44. 59–64.

50. 2–19 **If the trial arises out of what others have done:** Hermogenes makes the simple point that a consistent gloss must be put on the speaker's own acts; but if the charge is based on the acts of others (*30. 21–31. 1) the defence can offer a number of incompatible explanations speculatively (indeed, this show of ignorance may help to dissociate him from the acts).

50. 5–10 **The enemy erect a statue of a triple-hero:** See 30. 23–31. 1, *44. 6–9.

50. 20–52. 5: **The persuasive defence:** Having shown through transposition of cause that the prosecution's interpretation of events is not necessary, the defence now tries to show that it is impossible: if the alleged crime had been committed, these events would not have occurred.

In some cases the sign is something that would necessarily attend the alleged crime (e.g. a would-be tyrant stockpiling weapons for his coup); the persuasive defence is then not available (51. 3–11; cf. Sopater 17. 6–14). In such cases the defence must fall back on the weaker argument that the entailment cannot be reversed: the crime would entail the sign, but the sign does not entail the crime (51. 16–52. 5). This is similar to the transposition of cause (52. 4 f.), but the defence needs to dwell on the point since in these cases the prosecution will try to collapse the distinction between sign and crime by what is in effect a forcible definition: doing this is tantamount to committing the crime (51. 12–16); it is forcible because the sign is not strictly part of the crime, although it may be a concomitant (cf. *RG* 4. 404. 17–30). For forcible arguments in general see *73. 16–74. 4.

There was a range of standard counters to the persuasive defence (Syrianus 2. 88. 19–28; *RG* 4. 405. 27–407. 3, 5. 138. 20–139. 2). The prosecution might argue that the act in question could not have been avoided in the circumstances (e.g. the vigilance of the jailers compelled the youth to deliver his message to the prisoners in this risky way), or appeal to the defendant's carelessness (e.g. misjudging his own self-control, the youth did not realize that he would give away his ambitions when he looked at the acropolis), or to the city's good fortune and the favour of the gods.

51. 1–3 Where you look and cry: See *49. 21–3.

51. 8–11 Pericles' house is struck by lightning: For themes involving Pericles under suspicion of seeking tyranny (see Plutarch *Per.* 16 for the roots of this idea in contemporary comedy) see *RG* 7. 263. 18, Syrianus 2. 68. 1–3; cf. Kohl 1915, 29 f. Syrianus 2. 80. 9–14 suggests that the necessary connection between the sign and crime rules out counterplea as well as persuasive defence in this case. There are indeed obvious dangers if the counterplea is not handled cautiously, and it might be wise to delay the counterplea until after the stockpiling of arms has been given a favourable gloss (cf. *48. 3–9). The defendant might claim that he intended to equip men who could not afford their own armour (Syrianus 2. 68. 3–5 etc.); this patriotic motive provides the defence with good material for the exception (discussed at length by Syrianus 2. 68. 1–69. 10) and for indignation (cf. *42. 16–19).

51. 13–16 the adolescent using cosmetics: See *48. 18–21.

51. 19–52. 1 Those who intend to be tyrants: See *51. 8–11.

D. Exploitation

The speakers have presented their arguments, and can now take their position as proven; the final phase is devoted to reinforcement and amplification.

52. 6–53. 13 Common quality: In the epilogue both parties recapitulate (52. 11, 14 f.). The prosecutor, taking the defendant's guilt as proven, uses the techniques of common topic (*RG* 4. 415. 8–15, 7. 329. 1–16; cf. p. 15) to bring home to the jury the gravity of the offence and so provoke them to anger; the defendant, taking his innocence as proven, strives to enlist the jury's sympathy (he may use the common topic against malicious accusers to this end; cf. *Libanius *Decl.* 44. 68–71). The generalizing nature of these techniques distinguishes common quality from considerations focused on the individual quality of the prosecutor or defendant (see *61. 6–15). In addition to recapitulation and common topics, both sides employ the heads of purpose (52. 19–53. 1; cf. p. 15) to show the jury that returning one or other verdict is their proper course of action. For extensive discussion of these techniques in epilogues see Apsines 296. 13–329. 23, Anon. Seguerianus 198–253, Quintilian 6. 1 f.

52. 6 f. epilogues and second speeches: Aphthonius comments on the similarity between common topic and 'second speech and epilogue' (17. 3; cf. Nicolaus *Prog.* 36. 13 f., 39. 18–20). 'Second speech' in this context implies the division of a case between two speakers, the first laying the argumentative foundation and the second using extended amplification (cf. *RG* 4. 418. 4–8, 422. 18–22; [Hermogenes] *Meth.* 444. 13–26 refers to Demosthenes 25 and 26 as examples).

52. 12 f. as Demosthenes does: Demosthenes 19. 177.

52. 16 f. the presentation of children, wives, relatives, and so forth: For these external devices for moving pity see e.g. Quintilian 6. 1. 30–3.

53. 1–13 In general, epilogues: For the connections between prologue and epilogue see e.g. Quintilian 6. 1. 12, Anon. Seguerianus 3, 19 f., 237 f. The stylistic and rhythmical differences are analysed in *RG* 7. 344. 21–345. 2, 345. 24–347. 12.

53. 12 f. in my treatment of the prologue: The reference is probably to the treatise on invention which Hermogenes mentions elsewhere (*Id.* 378. 18 f.), and which was presumably organized (like Apsines and Anon. Seguerianus) according to the parts of a speech. But in the fifth century Syrianus (2. 3. 3–7) could only infer its existence, and had no direct knowledge of it. The treatise *On Invention* transmitted among Hermogenes' works is incorrectly attributed; its first book is devoted to the prologue, but contains nothing that corresponds to the reference here.

Variant Forms (53. 14–59. 9)

In addition to the standard kind of conjecture, Hermogenes identifies a number of variant forms in which the model strategy needs to be adapted. The variants arise:

(i) when no resources for argument can be drawn from one or other of the basic pair, person and act (e.g. if the theme says only 'someone', one cannot base arguments on the attributes of the person);

(ii) when more than one person and/or act is involved in the charge;

(iii) when a second conjectural question arises which is not itself part of the charge but stands in some logical relation to it.

A. Simple Incomplete Conjecture

If person gives no basis for argument (e.g. the defendant is 'someone') heads relating to person (motive, capacity) are omitted. Likewise, act-related heads (sequence of events etc.) are omitted if act gives no basis for argument (e.g. there is evidence that a crime has been committed, but the only grounds for suspecting the defendant arise out of character); Hermogenes argues that this cannot occur in a simple case.

54. 3–8 An incomplete case based only on acts: There is a person as well as an act in all cases; the criterion of completeness is the capacity of person (or act) to sustain argument (*29. 12 f.).

Confusingly, the terminology for incomplete questions was reversed by later rhetoricians; in Hermogenes a question that is incomplete ἐκ πραγμάτων is based on act only, but in Syrianus it is incomplete in respect of act, i.e. based on person only; cf. Gloeckner 1901, 35 f.

54. 5–8 A man is apprehended: See *49. 16–19.

54. 9–55. 8 An incomplete, simple conjecture based only on person: Hermogenes returns to the controversy raised in *31. 6–11. His target in denying the possibility of this class of conjecture is Minucianus, who had proposed the disappearance of the dissolute's father as an example. For discussion see RG 4. 128. 18–29, 131. 4–136. 5, 432. 8–439. 7; 5. 142. 24–145. 3; 7. 133. 13–136. 11, 349. 3–353. 16. Although Hermogenes' view had some advocates (mentioned by Sopater, RG 4. 434. 26 f.), including Metrophanes (RG 7. 350. 5–351. 1) and Georgius (ap. Schilling 1903, 761–3), the overwhelming majority of rhetoricians sided with Minucianus (RG 7. 349. 6–10); the opponents include Harpocration (RG 7. 349. 25, 350. 29), Tyrannus (Georgius ap. Schilling 1903, 761–3), Menander (sch. Demosthenes 19. 101 (228), citing Isocrates Against Euthynus as a real instance of conjecture based only on person), and Evagoras and Aquila, followed by Syrianus (2. 35. 1–6). Sopater and Marcellinus found Hermogenes' position so misguided as to be inexplicable except as the product of misplaced rivalry (see e.g. RG 4. 128. 14–29, 131. 11–132. 1, 133. 25, 134. 20; 5. 55. 16–18, 57. 6–9).

Zeno 327. 8–328. 29 appears at first sight to agree with Hermogenes; he illustrates conjecture based only on person with a double case (the same example as Hermogenes *56. 14–20), and gives no example of a simple conjecture based only on person. However, he does this unselfconsciously, without any hint that the matter is controversial. It may therefore be significant that Zeno does not formally introduce the distinction between simple and double questions until after his discussion of incomplete questions, and that he makes no attempt to correlate these two ways of classifying questions. If Zeno antedates Minucianus (Heath 1994*a*), it may be that Minucianus was the first to superimpose the two classifications on each other, and that the dissolute son was devised to fill the vacant slot which this innovation brought to light.

In Minucianus' interpretation of the case the sign must be the son's dissolute character, which is an aspect of his person; the act (the father's disappearance) gives no grounds for suspecting the son specifically. Hermogenes argues that the act does give grounds for suspecting the son when taken in conjunction with his bad character; there is therefore an intermediate act (*31. 1–6), which has no direct reference to the defendant but can be referred to him indirectly in the light of some other factor. In the paradigm of this category the other factor is Archidamus' acts (his mismanagement of the invasion of Attica), while here it is the son's bad character; nevertheless the fact of the father's disappearance means that here too, according to Hermogenes, there is an act on which argument is based. Hermogenes supports his contention by pointing to the act-related arguments which the son will use. He will argue that there are possible explanations for the disappearance which do not incriminate him (a transposition of cause of the speculative kind discussed at *50. 2–19), and that the inference 'if you had murdered him he would have disappeared' cannot be reversed to give 'he has disappeared, therefore you murdered him' (a persuasive defence of the weaker kind discussed at 51. 16–52. 5; cf. *RG* 4. 434. 24–435. 19).

Hermogenes' analysis of the case is plausible, in part because the defence can play on the uncertainty whether the father has been murdered at all. Minucianus perhaps formulated the case in this way on the grounds that the father's disappearance, since it leaves his death open to doubt, *a fortiori* cannot be a sign that the son killed him (cf. *RG* 4. 132. 2–16). If we modify the case to remove this feature, Hermogenes' general thesis may seem more doubtful:- The father of a dissolute son is found murdered; the son is accused. Since it is now clear that someone murdered the father the scope for arguments based on act is radically restricted. The son will of course point out that someone else might have murdered him; but this must always be true in a valid conjectural theme, and does not weaken the presumption that the son is the most likely culprit. If so minimal an argument is enough to exclude incomplete cases based on person alone, then incomplete cases based on act alone must also be impossible, since the prosecution will always have a minimal argument based on person, that the 'someone' charged *could* have committed the crime (capacity).

In this modified example the act gives grounds for concluding that someone murdered the father, but does not point to the son; the charge against the son is based solely on person (i.e. his character and the motive suggested by his status as the dead man's heir). In this respect the case resembles the incomplete double conjectures which Hermogenes accepts at *56. 14–20, in which objective circumstances suggest that one of two parties committed the crime, but only arguments from person will help to decide which of the two it was.

55. 6–8 Archidamus being tried for receiving bribes: See *31. 1–6.

B. Double Conjecture

Typically, two parties bring charges against each other; thus both speeches combine elements of prosecution and defence, and each head will be treated from both perspectives.

55. 13–17 Aeschines and Demosthenes: A close variant (with gold stolen from the acropolis; Demosthenes is found composing a defence on a charge of sacrilege and Aeschines burying gold: note that the orators have exchanged roles) is found at Sopater 19. 17–28. 2; cf. Syrianus 2. 79. 19–21 (also in *RG* 7. 204. 7–9 with 'two orators', as in 56. 5–8 below). In another variant the compromising acts result in Demosthenes and Aeschines both being prosecuted by Hyperides (*RG* 5. 124. 17–20, 141. 6–10; 7. 354. 1–4).

55. 17–56. 3 Here the demand for evidence is omitted: Hermogenes' assumption is that each party will undercut its own demand for evidence in replying to the opponent's demand, so that the head is fruitless for both sides; cf. Zeno 328. 9–14. But it is arguable that in some cases the difference of person will give point to the demand for evidence. Minucianus (see Sopater 18. 7–20) gave as an example a case in which doctor and layman accuse each other of poisoning: the layman can ask for witnesses to his acquiring the poison, but the doctor cannot reasonably do this since he has access to poisons professionally (cf. *RG* 4. 442.

19–443. 4, 444. 8–32; Tyrannus *ap. RG* 7. 357. 26–358. 14). Sopater (unlike his namesake the commentator) rejects this example, arguing that the demand for evidence should relate to the crime itself; but in certain cases one party has less opportunity to commit the crime undetected (e.g. in 56. 15–17 the stepmother might argue that her unobserved access to the young man's food was less), and it will then be reasonable to develop the demand for evidence in this way.

55. 18–22 opposing one thing to another: The technique has been practised in the preliminary exercise of comparison (*RG* 7. 366. 7 f.; cf. Aphthonius 31. 18–20: 'Those engaged in comparison should not compare whole with whole, since that is tedious and lacks competitive energy, but head with head; that does have competitive energy').

C. Incomplete Double Conjecture

In some cases, person will give no grounds for argument (e.g. the parties are 'two politicians': without further information there is no argument based on person which will not apply equally to both); in others, act will give no grounds for argument (e.g. there is evidence that a crime has been committed by one of the two, but the only grounds for suspecting one party or the other arise out of their respective characters).

56. 4–13 A double, incomplete case based on acts: The example is derived from *55. 13–17 by replacing the determinate proper names with identical indeterminate appellatives; since the two parties are identical, neither can derive any advantage from arguments about motive and capacity.

56. 14–20 A double conjecture based only on persons: Objective circumstances pick out two suspects but give no grounds for deciding which of them committed the crime; the verdict therefore turns solely on the characteristics of the two persons. For the example of the stepmother see Zeno 319. 31 f., 327. 31–328. 14, Sopater 28–32 (see *34. 16–35. 14 above); further arguments in *RG* 4. 448. 8–449. 8, 450. 5–18. The wicked stepmother is a common motif in declamation (e.g. *58. 19–21; Quintilian 2. 10. 5 refers disparagingly to 'stepmothers more cruel than any in tragedy' as a declamatory cliché), and in terms of motive she has the weaker position; but she can argue that the concubine had more intimate access to the hero, and therefore greater capacity—indeed, her own motive made her suspect and so decreased her capacity to commit the crime.

D. Conjunct Conjecture

In double conjectures there are two charges, and the case could in principle be decomposed into two underlying simple questions; in conjunct conjecture there is a single charge that is logically interlinked with some other disputed claim, so that a second conjectural question has to be examined in order to reach a conclusion about the primary one. Hermogenes identifies three possible forms, each needing a different modification of the model strategy.

56. 24–57. 11 **Incident conjecture:** The defence's explanation of its acts (transposition of cause) presupposes some disputed statement of fact ('I did *that* because *this* happened': but did *this* really happen?). The second or 'incident' conjecture is treated as a digression after the transposition of cause from which it arises.

56. 26–57. 11 **A man convicted of treason:** For this case see *RG* 4. 454. 14–456. 23, 7. 372. 28–374. 7, Apsines 267. 3–268. 15, Sopater 51. 1–54. 11; Russell 1983, 51. Suspicion of the general's complicity is raised by his killing the prisoner before he had disclosed details of the conspiracy; the alleged adultery gives the defender a plausible alternative motive. The prosecution will question, not just whether the general was in reality motivated by the adultery, but whether the adultery took place at all; so when the transposition of cause is reached a subsidiary conjectural question (did the prisoner commit adultery?) is raised. The prosecution may cast doubt on the likelihood of a man in the prisoner's situation having an affair with his captor's wife, or her accepting the advances of one so placed; the defence could point out that if he had simply wished to silence the prisoner he could have killed him more discreetly, and without the disgrace of publicizing his wife's infidelity.

The defence's counterplea is of course that killing an adulterer is legal (see *43. 3–8); the objection will be based on person—can this law be applied where a matter of overriding public interest is at stake? In the persuasive defence (57. 10 f.) the general cannot argue that he would not have killed the prisoner if he had been party to the conspiracy; so this head is of the kind discussed at 51. 16–52. 5: complicity would have entailed, but is not itself entailed by, the killing.

57. 11–58. 2 **Pre-confirmatory conjecture:** The charge presupposes some disputed statement of fact ('Given that *this* happened, the defendant's act is highly incriminating': but did *this* really happen?). The 'pre-

confirmatory' conjecture must be treated before the main question is tackled.

57. 14–58. 2 **A rich general:** The prosecution must show that the poor man's sons were traitors; if not, the father cannot have been party to their treason and the case collapses. The defendant is not under the same logical necessity to establish the sons' innocence, but his case will be strengthened by whatever doubts can be raised about the prosecution's basic premise. In favour of the prosecution's premise are the rumour of the sons' guilt (which the general claims prompted him to act, a detail made explicit in the extended treatment of the theme in Sopater 32. 27–42. 9) and the third son's confession; but the prospect of torture offers an obvious gloss on the confession, and rumour is untrustworthy (given the enmity between the two men one might even suggest that the rumour was concocted by the general himself). Having established the sons' guilt the prosecution must still implicate the father. The crucial point here is the father's failure to proceed against the general; is this a guilty party lying low, or an inability to take action only to be expected in a man overwhelmed by misery? A failure to take legal proceedings is crucial also to the different illustration of pre-confirmatory conjecture in Zeno 331. 1–9.

One point which emerges from Sopater (35. 20–36. 2) is Porphyry's suggested exception, not accepted by all rhetoricians: the father can cast doubt on the validity of a prosecution in view of the irregularity of the treatment of the sons. The sceptics' position seems sounder. A general in the field may be assumed to have wide summary powers, subject to subsequent judicial review if those powers are abused; to raise the procedural point at this stage simply draws attention to the father's failure to proceed against the general.

In the related theme at Calpurnius Flaccus *Decl.* 7 a different sign of the sons' guilt is substituted for the third son's confession: the poor man has two sons, neither of whom confesses under torture; their bodies are thrown out of the camp and are buried by the enemy, who then withdraw; the father prosecutes the rich general for homicide. If the sons were in fact traitors there is no case against the general; the execution of traitors is clearly not a crime. So the sole point in dispute is about the sons' guilt, and the case is a simple conjecture.

For the enmity of rich and poor in declamation see *80. 3–9.

58. 2–16 **Co-confirmatory conjecture:** This is the most difficult conjunct category, and ancient sources give conflicting accounts of it. In

pre-confirmatory conjecture the second question arises out of a presupposition of the charge itself (e.g. a charge of complicity presupposes the original crime). In incident conjecture it arises out of one of the arguments for the defence (the gloss it places on the signs of guilt adduced by the prosecution). The remaining possibility would seem to be a question arising out of one of the arguments for the prosecution. This is indeed the account which Zeno gives of co-confirmatory conjectures; he identifies two species, with the second question arising either out of the alleged motive or out of the sign (the text at 331. 12–14 is corrupt, but 332. 27 f. shows the subdivision intended). Zeno's example of the first kind (331. 14–332. 26) is the case which Hermogenes mentions at *45. 2–20; adultery is cited under the head of motive, and this allegation is argued out before the speaker returns to the main charge. His second kind is illustrated by the following theme (332. 27–333. 29):- A young man swears that he will make himself tyrant; another swears that he will kill him if he becomes tyrant, and the next day is found murdered; the first young man is charged with conspiracy. In this case the oath is taken as a sign of the conspiracy; in the transposition of cause the defence will argue that it is insignificant (e.g. that it was drunken horseplay). To establish that the sign is significant the prosecution will point to the murder; since the defendant denies that he was the murderer a second conjecture arises at this point, in which the defendant's oath raises suspicion against him.

In this example the charge of conspiracy rests on one sign, the oath. The murder confirms the significance of the oath, but there is no dispute of fact about the oath itself; conversely, the oath confirms the murder, but in the sense of confirming the factually disputed claim that the murder was committed by the accused. Thus the oath and the murder are mutually supporting, but the relation is asymmetrical. Hermogenes' definition of co-confirmatory conjecture in terms of signs which establish each other (58. 2 f.) could carry that sense; but the logical structure of his example (58. 3–14) is in fact somewhat different. Here the charge of complicity rests on two signs, the adultery and the murder; the (factually disputed) claim that the woman committed adultery with the servant confirms the (factually disputed) claim that the servant was the murderer, and *vice versa*. Thus in this case there are three factually disputed claims (complicity, adultery, and the identity of the murderer), where Zeno's exposition would lead us to expect only two.

Hermogenes recommends (58. 14–16) that the questions proceed in parallel; in Zeno they are treated separately, as are incident and pre-confirmatory conjectures in Hermogenes (57. 4–11, 57. 19–58. 2). Sopater agrees with Hermogenes in recommending parallel treatment of the questions in co-confirmatory conjecture (54. 17–55. 4), and discusses Hermogenes' example (67. 2–75. 6). But his first co-confirmatory case (54. 13–67. 2) has a logical structure more like Zeno's:- A man and his wife fall ill with the same disease, and send for a doctor who is the man's friend; the husband dies, the wife recovers; the doctor marries the wife, and is accused of poisoning the husband. The marriage suggests a motive, and this taken with the circumstances of the husband's death raises a suspicion against the doctor; but the doctor will deny the alleged liaison with the wife. Likewise in the case of the mother accused of poisoning her daughter (Zeno 331. 14–332. 26, Hermogenes *45. 2–20) the servants' allegations suggest a motive which, taken with the circumstances of the girl's death, raises a suspicion against the mother.

There is, therefore, considerable obscurity in the category of co-confirmatory conjecture. This obscurity gets worse the more one reads. Some later theorists took the distinguishing feature of co-confirmatory conjecture to be the interlinking of two charges (*RG* 4. 460. 19–461. 22, 465. 2–15; Syrianus 2. 94. 5–13); one charge constitutes the matter to be judged, the other is adduced to support it. This leads to a different interpretation of the case of the young man who swears that he will make himself tyrant (and its more common variant in which it is a rich man who swears and a poor man who is his political enemy who reacts and is murdered); now it is the murder (not the oath) which is treated as the sign of the conspiracy (cf. *RG* 7. 382. 12–23, 383. 18–384. 17).

Sopater 42. 26–43. 2, 51. 9–15 treats the case of the rich man who swears to make himself tyrant as incident, rather than co-confirmatory, conjecture. A dispute about the interpretation of Demosthenes *On the False Embassy* likewise reflects disagreement about the relationship between these two categories. Some interpreted the speech as co-confirmatory conjecture, with events in Phocis and in Thrace forming the basis of the two charges. Menander criticized this view, and interpreted the case as incident conjecture (sch. Demosthenes 19. 1 (1a), 19. 101 (228), 19. 179 (368a–b)); Aeschines' gloss on the main charge (i.e. his claim that his role in the loss of Phocis has an innocent explanation) is countered by the accusation that he had accepted bribes; since Aeschines denies the claim of bribery a second conjectural question arises. But this departs (as Menander recognized) from the normal view of incident conjecture, since the second question focuses not on the defence's gloss but on the prosecution's reply to the gloss. So Menander was in turn criticized by those who saw the same two charges (responsibility for the destruction of Phocis and receiving bribes) as the two components of a co-confirmatory conjecture (*RG* 7. 374. 9–29).

In a variant of the case of the rich man who swears to make himself tyrant at *RG* 5. 79. 26–9 and sch. Demosthenes 19. 101 (228) the rich man is charged with murder, not conspiracy; in *RG* 5. 141. 16–19 he is charged with both. At *RG* 4. 451. 13–24 cases of this latter kind, in which there are two charges, both of which are to be judged, are termed complex (συμπεπλεγμένος), as distinct from conjunct (συνεζευγμένος); but *RG* 5. 141. 13–23 reverses the terminology.

58. 4–14 **Prisoners are to be released:** The charge of complicity against the woman presupposes (*a*) that it was the slave who killed the husband (otherwise there is no crime which she can be suspected of having been party to), and (*b*) that the slave and the woman were lovers (otherwise she has no motive). But (*a*) is uncertain, and (*b*) will be denied by the woman. If the slave killed the husband, then he was probably the woman's lover—for this provides him with a motive; conversely, if they were lovers, it probably was the slave who killed the husband. Thus stated the argument is circular; but as Hermogenes points out (58. 12–14) there are other circumstances (the husband's prior suspicion, the fact that the woman freed the slave, the coincidence of the man's death with the freeing of the slave) which give us an entry into the circle.

The case is seriously distorted in *RG* 4. 461. 9–20: the freeing of the servant establishes complicity; complicity establishes adultery; adultery establishes that the servant was the murderer. But the charge to be judged is complicity; this should depend on, not establish, the other allegations.

E. Conjecture based on Intention

In some cases there is no dispute that the act in question was committed by the defendant, but it is maintained that the defendant's state of mind when the act was committed negates criminal responsibility; e.g. it is claimed that the defendant was insane. If the prosecution denies this claim, we have a conjecture based on intention. If the prosecution concedes the claim but questions its adequacy as a defence, the issue will be mitigation.

58. 19–21 **A stepmother:** For the stepmother cf. *56. 14–20. A similar example in Zeno 334. 29–335. 16 omits the wounding of her own son.

59. 4–9 **other classes of conjecture:** For Hermogenes' reluctance to multiply classes unnecessarily cf. 71. 3–17. Other classes of conjecture included the paradoxical, recognized by Minucianus (*RG* 4. 472. 6–473. 10; cf. 7. 394. 13–395. 2; rejected by Sopater 78. 6–20; cf. Gloeckner 1901, 36–8). His example is a magician who promises to kill a tyrant within a stated period; the tyrant is killed by lightning; the magician claims the tyrannicide's reward. One would assume that this is paradoxical in the sense that the disputed claim to agency cannot be resolved by standard criteria of likelihood; this is the implication of sources which observe that this category resembles conjecture based on intention in having no sign (*RG* 4. 210. 29–211. 14, 5. 85. 23–86. 7). Another view is that the paradox lies in a reversal of the normal pattern for conjecture: instead of an accusation denied by the alleged agent, it is the agent who asserts the act and an opponent who denies it. Our source (*RG* 4. 472. 11–23) suggests as a better example a man who accuses himself of murder when his lover is found dead; compare the unfortunate man who denounces himself in the note to *48. 1 f.

DEFINITION (59. 10–65. 8)

Division (59. 10–61. 20)

Definition was defined at *37. 1–13 in terms of the incompleteness of the matter to be judged. There is no disagreement about what was in fact done; but what was done deviates in some respect from a paradigmatic instance of an act of that kind, and there is therefore disagreement about how to characterize the act; e.g. the accused concedes that he stole property from a temple, but he did not steal the temple's property; does his act constitute temple-robbery?

Since the act is conceded in definition, one cannot make the distinction between a primary phase of the argument concerned with the crime and a secondary phase concerned with the sign which we observed in conjecture. It is nevertheless possible to identify two phases of argument in this issue as well. The first argues out the definition proper; an optional secondary phase provides a qualitative defence of the act charged. There is also a preparatory phase in which the act in question is presented in terms which support the speaker's preferred way of characterizing it; this phase was absent from conjecture, since a speaker cannot begin by presenting an act when the point at issue is precisely whether it was performed (*RG* 4. 309. 8–310. 4, 481. 12–24, 589. 12–28; 5. 119. 23–120. 9). Hermogenes' division (59. 11–15) is summarized in Figure 3.

A. Presentation	Presentation

B. Primary Argument (definition proper)	Definition
	Counterdefinition
	Assimilation
	Legislator's intention
	Importance
	Relative importance

C. Secondary Argument	Counterposition
	Objection
	Counterplea

D. Exploitation	Quality
	Intention
	Common quality

FIGURE 3. Definition

A. Presentation

59. 16 **The presentation is actually the sequence of events:** The first speaker begins with a presentation of what has occurred, not as part of a demonstration that the act in question was really performed (like sequence of events in conjecture: *47. 8–48. 2), but in order to amplify an act the performance of which is acknowledged. A basic technique of

amplification is to analyse the circumstances of an act, showing how each increases the gravity of the crime (or, where the first speaker is not prosecuting but presenting a petition, the act's merit); when Hermogenes says below that the presentation is amplified using 'the concomitants of the sequence of events' (60. 3 f.) he means the elements of circumstance. See *45. 20–46. 3, 47. 9–11 for amplification based on circumstance; the technique is illustrated in *Syrianus' commentary on this passage.

B. Primary Argument

The first main phase of the argument is concerned with how the act thus presented is most aptly characterized; the prescribed sequence of heads constitutes a standard package which will recur in other issues (65. 11 f. with *66. 4–67. 1, 72. 3–5). Both parties define the terms in which the act has been described by the charge. The defendant offers a strict definition, and insists on a distinction between that description and the act performed; the prosecutor's looser definition tries to blur the distinction, and offers a supplementary argument to show that the two things are effectively equivalent. Each side will back up its position by trying to show (i) that it conforms to the law's intention, and (ii) that the concern it expresses is both important, and more important than that of the opposition.

59. 17–60. 6 **definition:** The first speaker has presented the act with moderate amplification; he naturally does not dwell on the act's incompleteness with respect to the standard description (e.g. the philosopher who claims the reward for tyrannicide will amplify the ending of the tyranny without stressing the fact that the tyrant was not killed). The opponent's first head seizes on this omission; it argues that because of what was not done the act fails to satisfy the strict definition of the description proposed (e.g. that the tyrant's survival rules out by definition the proposed description of the philosopher's act as tyrannicide).

59. 18–60. 4 **A philosopher persuades a tyrant to abdicate:** The case of the philosophical tyrannicide, which Hermogenes uses to supply brief running illustrations throughout his summary of the primary argument, is found also in Anon. Seguerianus 217; a variant in *Sopater 95. 22–98. 11 substitutes an orator for the philosopher. There were many other definitional themes based on the tyrant's reward: is it tyrannicide if the tyrant is forced or induced to commit suicide (*Lucian Tyrannicide; cf. Quintilian 7. 3. 7, RG 8. 607. 21–4)? Or if the claimant brings it about that someone else strikes the blow (variously in Zeno 319. 32–4, 338. 7–14;

Sopater 98. 12–100. 17; *RG* 4. 561. 18–563. 19, 7. 464. 26–465. 2; [Quintilian] *Decl. Min.* 345, 382)? Or kills him in mistake for someone else (*RG* 4. 579. 16–580. 14, 5. 160. 16–161. 4, 8. 396. 7–16)? Or is insane when he strikes the blow ([Hermogenes] *Inv.* 165. 10–166. 11)? Or kills him for some reason other than his being a tyrant (*RG* 5. 160. 21–161. 13; Seneca *Contr.* 4. 7; Quintilian 5. 10. 36)?

60. 6–8 **counterdefinition:** In response the first speaker must propose a looser alternative definition under which the act does qualify. Of course, despite Hermogenes' use of quasi-dialogue form to show the argument's logical structure, the first speaker is in reality pre-empting the strict definition rather than responding to it; so the strict definition makes its first appearance as a counterposition cited by the first speaker, to which he offers the looser counterdefinition as a solution. The speaker will naturally ensure that it is presented in an unfavourable light; *RG* 7. 416. 29–418. 17 mentions Demosthenes *Against Meidias* 25–8 as a model for the prejudicial citation of the opposing side's definition (see *63. 6–13 for the importance of this speech in accounts of definition).

60. 8–14 **assimilation:** This head (in Greek συλλογισμός, whence 'syllogism') develops the first speaker's response to the strict definition further: in all important respects what is covered by the looser counterdefinition amounts to the same thing as what is required by the strict definition (e.g. the tyrant's abdication is in effect as good as his death). Counterdefinition and assimilation are two parts of a complex response to the definition (at *66. 7–12 the reference to assimilation seems implicitly to include counterdefinition; conversely Zeno 337. 15 f. absorbs assimilation into his counterdefinition; cf. *RG* 5. 154. 9–20). *RG* 7. 420. 12–421. 14 observes that the sequence of counterdefinition and assimilation is an instance of the more general pattern of refutation and counter-representation (for the terminology see *48. 14–49. 6); the opponent's definition is first rejected, and then accepted as valid in a limited sense which makes the counterdefinition its equivalent. This claim of equivalence sets the opponent the task of showing that some important concern is embodied in the strict definition which the looser counterdefinition fails to capture; the next three heads focus on this point.

60. 10–14 **in just the same way that . . . counterplea opposes objection:** For the opposition of objection and counterplea see *48. 11–14.

60. 14 f. **Legislator's intention:** First, each party argues that its position reflects the underlying intention of the law; e.g. it might be argued that the law establishing a reward for tyrannicide was meant to encourage

people to put an end to tyranny—an intention which the philosopher's act has met; or else that it was meant to make tyranny a capital crime—an intention thwarted by the crucial omission in the philosopher's act. The preliminary exercise of proposal of law has provided practice in the kinds of argument required here (see p. 17 above).

60. 15–18 **Importance . . . Relative importance:** The first speaker argues that what was done (e.g. ending a tyranny) is inherently important, and more important than what was not done (e.g. exacting the extreme penalty for tyranny); the second speaker argues that what was not done is inherently important, and more important than what was done.

In these two heads each party is trying to establish the significance of the concern expressed in its interpretation of the law; they return, therefore, to the sequence of events treated with moderate amplification in the presentation (*59. 16; cf. *RG* 4. 489. 13–18), and engage in more elaborate amplification to show the overriding importance of the act (or the omission). Hermogenes does not refer explicitly to the sequence of events here, but its inevitable involvement in importance and relative importance emerges clearly in the treatment of parallel heads in other issues (cf. *66. 13–67. 1).

Other rhetoricians analysed the primary argument in definition in slightly different ways:
(i) Some, including Minucianus (Nilus *ap*. Gloeckner 1901, 39, cf. 80 f.; cf. *RG* 7. 402. 2–403.6) and Zeno (337. 12), did not recognize presentation as a distinct head: the statement is followed directly by the definitional heads. The conventional view is that presentation briefly recapitulates facts expounded in the narrative, with moderate amplification (*RG* 4. 480. 22–481. 12, 5. 150. 28–151. 15, 7. 407. 12–408. 12; cf. 5. 166. 4–10). It differs from the narrative because it is not a plain exposition (*RG* 4. 488. 6–489. 18, 491. 27–31, 589. 4–6; 7. 403. 9–14, 550. 32–551. 3); conversely it differs from counterdefinition, which goes over the same facts, in not being argumentative (*RG* 4. 495. 27–496. 3). However, this lack of argumentative function raised for some the question whether presentation was a head at all (*RG* 4. 481. 28–482. 6). In one sense no rhetorical narrative is a plain exposition (see *47. 8–48. 2); if, therefore, the narrative proper is tendentious and amplificatory, what need is there of a separate head to do the same work? Alternatively, the presentation can be seen as definition's substitute for narrative (Syrianus 2. 101. 18–22; I do not see how to reconcile this with the inclusion of statement at 2. 101. 9, where Rabe's supplement is secured by the parallel with 2. 64.

9–12). Thus one scholion to Demosthenes 21. 13 identifies the passage as the beginning of the statement (50a), another as the first part of the presentation (50b); the latter note reports the view that definition has no narrative, but concludes that in it statement and presentation are identical. *RG* 4. 655. 8–656. 5 notes that not all cases require a narrative (cf. Nilus *ap*. Rychlewska 1940–7, 180 f.) and suggests that where there is a narrative, presentation is merely a preface to following heads; where there is not, presentation expands as a partial substitute for it.

(ii) The terms definition and counterdefinition were variously applied. In Minucianus' scheme (cf. Syrianus 2. 99. 7–9, 103. 24–6; *RG* 4. 491. 25–7, 7. 402. 2–403.6), since there was no separate head of presentation, definition was the first speaker's statement of his position and counterdefinition was the opponent's reply. Zeno (337. 12–16) also omits presentation, but has the same assignment of definition and counterdefinition as Hermogenes. Thus:

	Hermogenes	Minucianus	Zeno
1st speaker	Presentation	Definition	—
2nd speaker	Definition	Counterdefinition	Definition
1st speaker	Counterdefinition	—	Counterdefinition

The commentator Sopater argues firmly for Hermogenes' arrangement (*RG* 5. 152. 6–153. 4). By contrast, the terms have a variable application in Sopater's *Division of Questions*: definition is applied to the head used by the other party (whichever that may be), and counterdefinition to one's own response (contrast e.g. 82. 6–83. 11 with 91. 16–25, respectively defence and prosecution in the same case; 93. 23–94. 7 has a confusing comment on this practice). These schemes share the obvious premise that definition precedes counterdefinition, but apply it differently. Minucianus attributes definition to the party which speaks first in the debate; Sopater reasons that in any one speech the other party's definition will first be counterposited and then solved by the counterdefinition; Hermogenes' usage rests on precedence in the underlying logical structure of the debate (the prosecutor or petitioner rests his initial claim simply on the act performed; it is the second speaker who first invokes a point of definition to contest that claim).

(iii) There were various alternative arrangements of the last four heads (see *RG* 4. 483. 17–485. 16, 510. 3–15, 518. 17–520. 21; 5. 153. 13–156. 20; 7. 425. 20–427. 3, 432. 3–433. 9; Nilus *ap*. Rychlewska 1940–7, 197 f., 202; sch. Demosthenes 21. 70 (214a)):

(*a*) Some (including Minucianus: *RG* 4. 485. 7–16, 5. 155. 10–156. 20) placed relative importance before importance. This difference was in part a matter of alternative ways of constructing a climax; Hermogenes' ordering of heads places a positive (important) before a comparative (more important), while the alternative scheme has a comparative followed by a superlative (*RG* 4. 484. 2–485. 6, 518. 17–519. 27). Harpocration saw the order as variable according to the needs of the case (*RG* 4. 519. 27–520. 6; cf. 7. 432. 7–21). Zeno has only relative importance (337. 21–3).

(*b*) Some rhetoricians placed assimilation after importance and relative importance; others likewise postponed legislator's intention. In Hermogenes' arrangement a block of demonstrative arguments is followed by graduated amplification; in the alternative schemes the postponed head functions as a summary or conclusion for the whole primary argument (e.g. the philosopher might say: 'Since I have shown that the more—indeed the most—important thing is ending the tyranny, it follows that what I did is as good as killing him and/or that this is what the legislator had in view; so my act satisfies the proposed description').

(iv) After relative importance Syrianus has two further heads (2. 113. 1–114. 19). In the request for intention (cf. the *coniectura voluntatis* in Zeno 337. 23–8), the first speaker interprets the act as having been performed with an intention which brings it within the definition he has proposed (e.g. why did I approach the tyrant, if not with a view to ending the tyranny? or—in a case based on prosecution—why did you do this, if not with criminal intent?); the second speaker responds with a gloss (cf. *49. 7–50. 19), or by appealing a second time to the legislator's intention. The addition of these heads seems unnecessary; motive, as one of the elements of circumstance, would naturally be raised in the sequence of events (as in *Lucian *Tyrannicide* 14), and it will reappear in the final phase.

C. Secondary Argument

Importance and relative importance are amplificatory heads, and so bring us back to the sequence of events. A defendant may now wish to supplement the primary argument by mounting a qualitative defence of his act in response to the sequence of events. In Hermogenes' scheme the heads are similar to those used in the secondary phase of conjecture—there is an obvious likeness between transposition of cause and counterposition (cf. *RG* 4. 617. 26–618. 2, 7. 504. 28–31); but the order is different. In conjecture the act cited as a sign of the crime is not in itself criminal, so the defence can assert the intrinsic legitimacy of that act by counter-plea before providing the innocent gloss which disarms it as an indication of the alleged crime. In definition, however, the act allegedly is criminal; so the defence must first give the act an innocent gloss (by means of a counterposition) in order to prepare for a climactic assertion of legitimacy in the counterplea.

60. 19 **The counterposition is not relevant in this example:** The secondary argument does not arise in cases based on a petition rather than a prosecution, since there is no crime to defend (*RG* 4. 532. 20–533. 14); Hermogenes therefore changes his example at this point.

60. 20–61. 1 **A man finds a eunuch with his wife:** The case of the adulterous eunuch is found also in Seneca *Contr.* 1. 2. 23; in a simpler variant the eunuch is prosecuted for adultery (*RG* 4. 541. 24 f., 5. 158. 13–15, 7. 217. 12–24; Syrianus 2. 114. 1). The simpler variant is evidently definition; there were those who denied that the more complex version used here by Hermogenes is definition, arguing that the case must be counterplea, since it turns on the claim that killing an adulterer is permitted (*RG* 5. 158. 8–159. 6). But Hermogenes' (and Minucianus': Nilus *ap.* Gloeckner 1901, 49; see also Schilling 1903, 747 f.) analysis recognizes that the fundamental point in dispute is the eunuch's status; this has to be argued out before the defendant can produce his counterplea to fullest effect— hence its relegation to the secondary phase (cf. *RG* 7. 438. 15–442. 10). Analogously, if the prosecutor denied that the victim had in point of fact been caught in adultery we would clearly have a conjectural case; Quintilian uses this example at 3. 6. 17 to illustrate his insistence that issue arises from the first point of dispute between the two parties (3. 6. 4 f.). The definitional nature of the present theme can be seen if one compares it with the case in which a husband is prosecuted for killing as an adulterer a man who has won the prize for heroism three times (see p. 115 below); that case is straightforwardly a counterplea, there being no doubt that an adulterer has been killed. (For the comparison of these two cases see *RG* 5. 158. 8–159. 6; Lollianus in *PS* 330. 14–331. 3; and see Heath 1994*b*, 114, 122–8 for the theoretical problems underlying the disputed classification of the adulterous eunuch.)

Some rhetoricians found in the case of the eunuch a class of definitions which are 'indirect' (*RG* 4. 532. 27–533. 5; Syrianus 2. 100. 6–20, 115. 17–116. 24), in the sense that the matter for judgement (e.g. is this man guilty of murder?) is distinct from, but depends on, the disputed question (e.g. can a eunuch be an adulterer?); Zeno calls this class of definition ἐγκρινόμενον (338. 19–24: in his example a man raids a cenotaph and is prosecuted for robbing a grave): see *64. 15–19.

61. 3 f. **objection:** A counter-representation: the prosecutor concedes that the eunuch deserved to die, but objects to one of the killing's circumstances, i.e. its summary manner.

61. 5 f. **counterplea:** If the defence has conducted the primary argument successfully, the objection can be dismissed; it has been shown that the eunuch does fall within the definition of adulterer, and summary killing is therefore legitimate (see *43. 3–8).

Syrianus has a less restrictive view of the possible forms of secondary argument in definition; as well as counterpositions, he envisages arguments based on objection, definition, or conjecture (Syrianus 2. 114. 20–115. 15). *RG* 4. 486. 13–22 also recognizes conjectural arguments; e.g. in the case of the philosophical tyrannicide there is the question whether the ex-tyrant will try to regain power—a possibility which would weaken the philosopher's claim that voluntary abdication is effectively equivalent to tyrannicide. The handling of the case in *Sopater 95. 22–98. 11 shows how the philosopher can respond to this attack using the conjectural heads of motive and capacity.

D. Exploitation

In conjecture the conclusion to the question of fact leads directly into the epilogue; having made out one's case that the defendant is a murderer, the common topic against murder follows at once. In other issues, where the dispute turns not on the fact but on the description or evaluation of the fact, the exploitation is more complex. When, for example, a homicide has been admitted and defended, the common topic against murder will need some preparation if it is to excite indignation against the defendant; an examination of the individual's character and intention will add the finishing touch to the argument and open the way to the use of common quality in the epilogue.

61. 6–15 **Quality:** First, the speaker's interpretation of the act is set in the context of the agent's character and life in general. E.g. the prosecutor has argued that the husband cannot appeal to the right to kill adulterers (since the eunuch was not an adulterer), and that the counterpositional defence is inadequate; it follows that the defendant has committed an unjustified homicide; but this claim will be more effective if it can be shown that such an act is congruous with the defendant's previous behaviour. If the defendant's previous behaviour has been blameless,

there is of course an even more urgent need to pre-empt his appeal to it
(*RG* 4. 538. 21–539. 21); the prosecutor will therefore seek to cast doubt on
or minimize the defendant's good qualities and acts, and will argue that
they do not constitute good reason for ignoring his present misdeeds—
or indeed that his previous good conduct makes his present descent into
lawlessness even more shocking. The defence on its part will draw attention to the discrepancy between its previous record and the present allegation against it, or will play down past misdeeds.

The status of this head was a matter of discussion among rhetoricians
(see *RG* 4. 536. 23–537. 10, 542. 19–21; 7. 442. 11–443. 14, 446. 20–448. 4;
Gloeckner 1901, 34; Schilling 1903, 760). The view favoured in the scholia to Hermogenes is that it and intention are transitional heads, paving
the way for the epilogue. Its focus on individual rather than common
quality was held to count against Minucianus' view that it was part of the
epilogue. Metrophanes regarded it as the last and most important of the
heads of argument; but invoking the individual's previous life goes
beyond the case in hand, and this digressive aspect might be held to put
it outside the argumentative section of the speech. Some rhetoricians sit-
uated a digression on the defendant's previous life as a regular part of the
speech between argument and epilogue (Hermagoras fr. 22; *PS* 52. 14–18,
270. 28–271. 3, 271. 15–19; Heath 1989, 90–4); sch. Demosthenes 19. 237
(455b) and 21. 77 (242a–b) reproduce the discussion of the status of quality in terms of digression.

61. 6–14 on the concomitants of person: For the topics of encomium cf.
*30. 10–12, 46. 9–18. For the richness of content associated with determi-
nate individuals see *29. 13–16, *30. 3–9. If the defendant is not a determinate individual he will have no prior history on which the argument
about quality can be based; partially determinate persons create expectations on which an argument can be based (e.g. what one expects of a
father or a rich young man; cf. *29. 16 f., *29. 19–22), but where the person is wholly indeterminate (30. 12 f.) the argument must be based on
extrapolation from the present act (strictly speaking, of course, this
involves a circularity of argument).

61. 15–18 Intention: Having shown (if possible) the consistency of his
interpretation of the particular act with the defendant's life and character, the prosecution has a firm platform from which to expatiate on his
criminal intention.

61. 18–20 common quality: The digression on the defendant's previous
life and the elaboration of his criminal intention have given the prosecu-

tor a way of attaching the common quality (in the case of the eunuch, the common topic against murder) securely to the individual defendant. At this point all the epilogue techniques discussed under conjecture (*52. 6–53. 13) become available; Hermogenes does not repeat the discussion. In subsequent issues he makes no explicit mention of common quality; its implication with individual quality and intention is simply taken for granted.

Variant Forms (61. 21–65. 8)

In addition to the standard kind of definition, Hermogenes identifies a number of variant forms, all of them double.

62. 1–10 **counterdescription:** In simple cases the second speaker denies that the act satisfies the definition of the description proposed; in counterdescriptive cases he denies this and also proposes an alternative description (carrying, naturally, a lesser penalty), arguing that the strict definition of this alternative description is satisfied by the act. The two parties therefore offer rival descriptions of the act as if mutually exclusive ('You are *this*': 'No, I am *that*': 'You are not *that*, but *this*').

62. 3–5 **A man steals private property from a temple:** For the theft of private property from a temple see 37. 8–13. If my property is stolen from a friend's house, I have been robbed and not my friend; but if the theft of my property takes place in a temple the violation of the sanctuary makes the more serious description 'temple-robbery' seem plausible. The example goes back to Aristotle (*Rhet.* 1374ª3 f.) and is often referred to by Quintilian (3. 6. 38, 41, 4. 2. 69 f., 4. 4. 3, 5. 10. 39, 7. 3. 9 f., 21–4); it appears also in Zeno 336. 19–26, 338. 3–7; Sopater 102. 10–105. 21. In Cicero *Inv.* I. 11, 2. 55 there is a curious inversion: sacred property is stolen from a private house—is this sacrilege?

62. 5–9 **Just as with double conjectures:** See *55. 18–22. Some rhetoricians thought assimilation impossible in counterdescriptive definitions, since the dispute collapses if both sides claim that the two descriptions are effectively equivalent (*RG* 4. 552. 13–554. 18). This is incorrect: the prosecutor will argue that the degree of impiety displayed in committing a robbery in a temple makes it equivalent to being a temple-robber in the strict sense; the defendant will argue that stealing private property is plain theft wherever it happens. More plausible is the view (*RG* 4. 554. 18–555. 3) that importance and relative importance are not doubled; the prosecutor will simply amplify, the defendant simply diminish the one act.

62. 11–64. 3 **by inclusion:** In counterdescription the prosecutor rejects the defence's description of the act; here it is accepted, and a more serious description added to it. The two parties offer definitions that may intersect ('You are *this*': 'No, I am *that*': 'You are indeed *that*, but you are *this* as well').

62. 15–63. 13 **A man serving as ambassador:** The rape of the ambassador's daughter is found with a slight variation (the ambassador replaced by a general going on campaign) in Zeno 338. 10–18, Syrianus 2. 107. 7–19, Sopater 105. 23–110. 17. The case sets in opposition the father's private and public roles; the model is Demosthenes *Against Meidias* (*63. 6–13).

63. 6–13 **Demosthenes did this:** In *Against Meidias* Demosthenes maintains that the defendant's aggressive behaviour towards him was not just an assault, but also an offence against the festival, since it occurred during the Dionysia and while he was serving as *khorēgos* in the dithyrambic competition (Demosthenes 21. 31–5; cf. MacDowell 1990, 13–23); most later commentators assimilate this charge to the standard declamatory offence of harming the public interest (cf. *65. 22–66. 4), although a minority treat it as a charge of impiety (see Libanius' hypothesis, with MacDowell 1990, 424–30; sch. Demosthenes 21. 31 (103), 127 (447); *RG* 4. 524. 3 f., 556. 19–24; sch. Demosthenes 21. 51 (159) points out that this misunderstands the amplificatory force of the references to impiety in 51–5).

Demosthenes' speech is analysed in the scholia as follows: prologue (1–7), preliminary confirmation (8–12), statement (12–23), arguments (24–76), digression (77–125, cf. *61. 6–15), epilogue (126–227). The division of the argumentative section adopts some of the variants discussed above (p. 105–7). The core consists of a counterposed definition (Meidias' claim that the offence was against Demosthenes: 29 f.) and Demosthenes' response, the response comprising counterdefinition (it was both an offence against Demosthenes and a public offence: 31–3), assimilation (an offence against Demosthenes during the festival and while he was *khorēgos* is equivalent to an offence against the festival: 33 f.), legislator's intention (there would have been no need for a law concerning the festival if it added nothing to the law of assault: 34 f.), relative importance (51–69), and importance (70–6). Prefaced to that core is the solution to a counterposed exception, also based on definition, in which Meidias argues that he is being prosecuted under the wrong law (25–8). In 36–40 Demosthenes has detached part of Meidias' definition, in which parallel cases in which a private settlement was reached are cited as evidence that the offence was not public; Demosthenes deliberately obscures the force of this argument by misrepresenting it as a plea of mitigation (cf. 36: 'thinking that, if he shows that many others have suffered . . . you will be less angry at what I have suffered') alongside the mitigation counterposed and solved in 41–50.

63. 13–20 **But in counterdescription:** Hermogenes claims that the prosecutor will use counterdescription when the more serious charge entails the less serious charge; in other words the prosecutor will reject the defendant's characterization of the act when it is entailed by his own (as robbery is entailed by temple-robbery). At first sight this is paradoxical. But where the lesser charge is entailed by the greater there is no need to dwell on it; the prosecutor can afford to lay exclusive stress on the more damaging description—a more forceful rhetorical strategy. Where the connection between two descriptions is contingent (as between rape and harming the public interest), the prosecutor needs to keep the less damaging description before the jury's attention as the material basis for the graver charge. Cf. *RG* 7. 461. 1–463. 12.

64. 1–3 **has this head in its division:** Hermogenes speaks very loosely here; inclusive definition differs from counterdescription by its overall logical structure rather than by the use of an additional head (cf. *RG* 4. 560. 14–26, 5. 162. 29–163. 13).

64. 3–14 **double according to person:** This category is also known as that 'by dispute' (Syrianus 2. 120. 11–15); two persons make rival claims for a single description ('I am *this*': 'No, I am *this*').

64. 5 **performed as a whole by two persons:** The two persons do not act in concert throughout (like the tyrannicides Harmodius and Aristogeiton), but each performs part of the act; e.g.:- A man ascended the acropolis to kill the tyrant; the tyrant fled; a second man encounters the tyrant by chance and kills him; they dispute the reward (Zeno 319. 32–4, 338. 7 f.; *RG* 4. 561. 18–563. 19; Sopater 98. 12–100. 17).

64. 13 f. **opposing head to head:** In this class of definitions, as in the two preceding, the two questions are argued out in parallel: each party asserts his own and attacks his opponent's version of each head before proceeding to the next head. In the remaining classes each question is handled in a distinct sequence of heads.

64. 15–23 **incident:** The formal structure of incident definition is the same as incident conjecture (*56. 24–57. 11); the similarity in the

underlying logical structure is not so immediately apparent. The defence in incident definition in responding to the charge (e.g. 'you revealed the mysteries') proposes a strict definition ('nodding is not revealing') and adds a further point ('and he was an initiate anyway') to which the prosecutor in turn opposes a strict definition ('a dream is not initiation'). This is parallel to incident conjecture, where the defence in denying the prosecution's claim as to fact ('you are implicated in the conspiracy') makes another claim in the transposition of cause ('the prisoner committed adultery with my wife') which the prosecution in turn denies. See *RG* 4. 572. 1–573. 4.

64. 15–19 **An uninitiated man:** Hermogenes' formulation of this example obscures part of its point: the initiate nods assent (Syrianus 2. 119. 7–10; *RG* 4. 572. 13 f.; also Sopater 110. 19–124. 16, discussed by Russell 1983, 53–5). So the first question is whether nodding reveals (literally 'speaks out') the mysteries; the second, whether a man to whom the mysteries have been revealed in a dream is uninitiate.

Zeno's classification of double definitions (338. 1–29) like Hermogenes' has five categories; four coincide with those of Hermogenes, and indeed have substantially identical illustrations (read *retineat* at 338. 13; in 338. 16 f. delete Halm's supplement *non* and read *addit alterum crimen*). But he has no category corresponding to incident definition; his fourth category (ἐγκρινόμενα, cf. note to *60. 20–61. 1 above) cannot be equivalent (as suggested by Jaeneke 1904, 145 f.; Calboli Montefusco 1986, 88 f.), since the logical structure is different. Incident definition involves two questions (was the nod revealing the mysteries? was the man still uninitiate after his dream?), but in ἐγκρινόμενα a single question (can a eunuch be an adulterer?) settles the case; Syrianus (2. 100. 6–20, 115. 17–116. 24) accordingly treats this 'indirect' category as a species of simple definition. Hermogenes could not have accepted Zeno's view of the category, which makes the issue depend on the disputed question and not (contrary to the basic principle stated at *36. 7–9) on the matter for judgement; see Heath 1994*b*, 127 f.

65. 1–8 **dual definition:** Two descriptions are both asserted by one party and both denied by the other.

65. 3–5 **A priest must be pure and of pure parentage:** The opposition argues that the claimant is (i) impure, since he killed his father, and (ii) of impure parentage, since his father was an adulterer; the claimant replies (i) that killing an adulterer does not bring impurity and (ii) that an impurity contracted by his father after his own birth is irrelevant.

There is a brief division of this theme in *RG* 4. 577. 2–578. 29. In Zeno 338. 25–8 the claimant has successfully prosecuted his father for treason; the son's unfilial act and the father's crime are alleged to disqualify him.

COUNTERPLEA (65. 9–71. 17)

Division (65. 9–67. 21)

In counterplea the defence asserts that its acts were legitimate. Theorists recognized various possible bases for this assertion (*RG* 4. 233. 17–235. 3, 587. 15–588. 11; 5. 164. 5–9, 7. 197. 5–24, 542. 31–543. 13; Syrianus 2. 129. 17–130. 12; cf. Calboli Montefusco 1986, 110–12). The standard categories are compliance with the norms of law, nature, custom, or, according to some, art (*65. 18–20); Minucianus added the purely negative claim that there is nothing to forbid the act. Hermogenes' definition (38. 12 f., cf. 48. 5 f., 67. 1–3) if taken strictly would limit the issue to cases in which no law forbids the act; but *60. 20–61. 6, where the counterplea rests on the law permitting the summary killing of adulterers (see *43. 3–8), suggests that Hermogenes did recognize counterpleas based on positive legal warrant as well.

There is however a problem when the defence appeals to the explicit provisions of a legal instrument licensing the act: how in this case does counterplea differ from objection? Consider an example:- A husband kills as an adulterer a man who has won the prize for heroism three times. The husband might be charged with murder (Syrianus 2. 129. 19–22, *RG* 4. 595. 27 f.) or with harming the public interest (*RG* 4. 587. 23 f., 588. 16 f., 615. 8–20; 7. 487. 29–31, 490. 27–491. 21). In either case he will appeal to the law about adulterers, and the prosecution will reply that this law cannot be used to justify the destruction of one of the city's most valuable military assets. The case is consistently classed in ancient sources as a counterplea; but since the defence questions the validity of the prosecution on the basis of an explicit legal warrant for its act, it is not immediately obvious why the case should not be classed as objection. The distinction between counterplea and objection was discussed inconclusively by ancient commentators (*RG* 4. 289. 24–290. 18, 5. 116. 18–117. 2). One theory held that the description under which the act is charged is crucial; but the killing of the triple-hero is treated as counterplea irrespective of whether the charge against the husband is murder or harming the public interest. More promising is the suggestion that in counterplea the licence for the act is contested in principle, but in objection it is conceded in principle but contested on the basis of a specific circumstance. In the case of the triple-hero the prosecution will deny outright that it is legitimate to kill a triple-hero as an adulterer; contrast e.g. the case of the woman who kills her husband as an adulterer (treated as objection by *Sopater 247. 8–252. 2), where the prosecution concedes that the killing of the husband as an adulterer is permitted, but denies that it is permitted to his wife.

As in other issues, a primary and a secondary phase of the argument can be distinguished. The primary phase is the counterplea proper; the nature of this primary argument ('the act is legitimate') makes it possible to preface an elaborate spoiling action. The secondary phase has the same general form as the secondary argument in definition. Hermogenes' division (65. 10–13) is summarized in Figure 4.

A. Presentation

65. 14 **Presentation:** The initial formulation of the charge is treated as in definition; see *59. 16.

B. Preliminary Argument

There follows an elaborate series of spoiling moves. Arguments against the charge are adduced from:

(i) the act charged: is it open to prosecution at all?
(ii) the person: is he or she liable to a charge of this kind? and:
(iii) the charge itself: does it describe the act correctly?

As one might expect, this last point is argued out using the sequence of heads found in the primary argument of definition.

65. 14–22 **Part of right:** The legitimacy of the act in question is briefly affirmed so as to put in question the validity of the prosecution (cf. *44. 1–20 on exception in conjecture); the argument will be repeated more elaborately later as the substance of the defence. The term (*RG* 4. 596. 7–9, 5. 164. 5–10; cf. *partes iuris* in *Rhet. ad Herennium* 2. 19, Cicero *Inv.* 2. 68, *Or.* 45) refers to the different subdivisions of right according to which the assertion of legitimacy may be made (e.g. it was in accordance with law, custom, or nature).

65. 18–20 **A painter paints a shipwreck:** Hermogenes illustrates the standard division of counterplea using an example which, being based on an act and its contingent consequences (68. 11–13), in fact has some

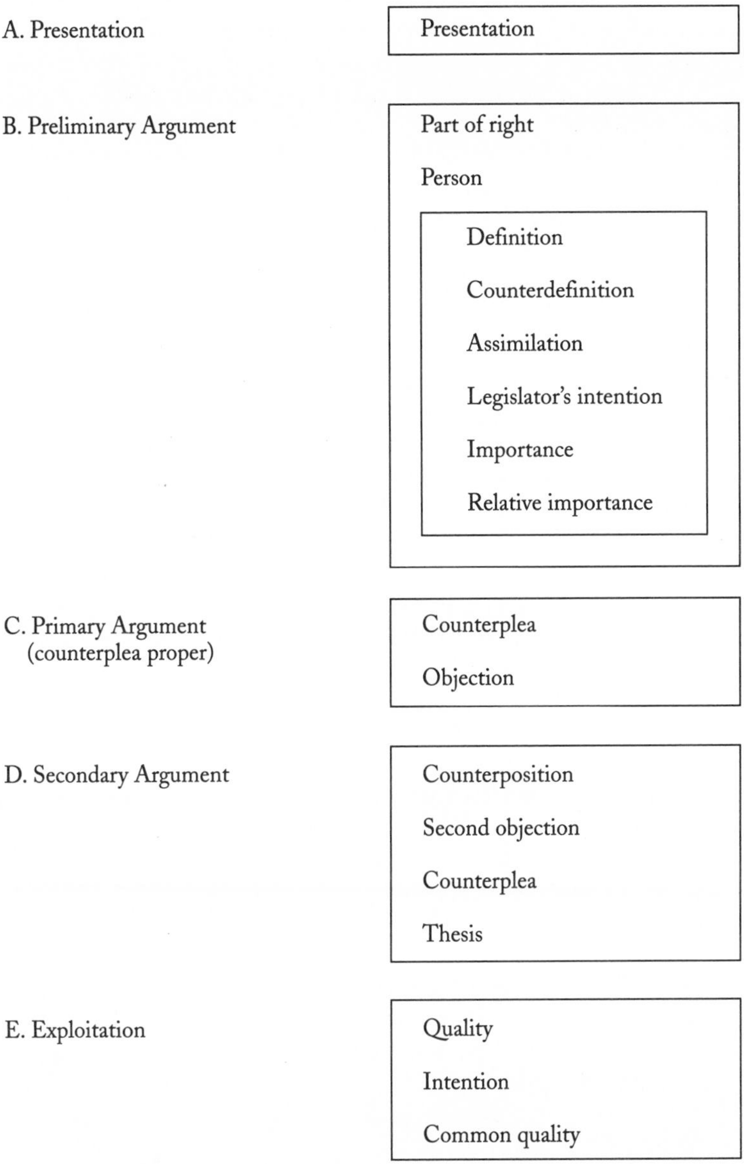

A. Presentation

> Presentation

B. Preliminary Argument

> Part of right
>
> Person
>
> > Definition
> >
> > Counterdefinition
> >
> > Assimilation
> >
> > Legislator's intention
> >
> > Importance
> >
> > Relative importance

C. Primary Argument
(counterplea proper)

> Counterplea
>
> Objection

D. Secondary Argument

> Counterposition
>
> Second objection
>
> Counterplea
>
> Thesis

E. Exploitation

> Quality
>
> Intention
>
> Common quality

FIGURE 4.   Counterplea

additional heads (*68. 10–69. 21). The case of the adulterous triple-hero mentioned above is more straightforward, being based on the act alone.

The painter's case is one of a cluster of related themes illustrating counterplea based on the practice of an art or profession. The orator whose encomium of death or tyranny prompts a rash of suicides (*RG* 8. 407. 14–16) or conspiracies (*RG* 5. 80. 29–32) is similar, as is Aeschylus prosecuted for *Eumenides* (Apsines 230. 5 f., alluding to the anecdote that the appearance of the fearsome chorus caused miscarriages). These too are based on act and contingency. Based on act alone are the painter Micon, prosecuted for a picture of the battle of Marathon in which the Persians are shown bigger than the Greeks (Sopater 126. 26–145. 8, cf. Russell 1983, 56–8), the artist who portrayed the Sicilian expedition (see on *68. 6–8), Euripides prosecuted for his *Heracles* (POxy. 2400), Epicurus prosecuted for his denial of divine providence (Himerius *Or.* 3: cf. Ch. 1 n. 67), Plato prosecuted for the *Republic* (Syrianus 2. 135. 17–19), or Thucydides prosecuted for his *Histories* (Syrianus 2. 135. 20–5, alluding to the idea that Thucydides presented the Athenians in a hostile light, resenting his own exile: cf. *Vita* 4; Dionysius of Halicarnassus *Thuc.* 41, *ad Pomp.* 3. 15). There is also the painter prosecuted after torturing an Olynthian slave to death to provide a model for the sufferings of Prometheus (Seneca *Contr.* 10. 5).

In the present case, the painter's choice of venue for the display of his work is not as perverse as it may seem; he would be hoping to sell his pictures to sailors who had promised a votive offering in return for escape from storm and shipwreck (see e.g. Cicero *De Natura Deorum* 3. 89; Horace *Odes* 1. 5. 13–16).

65. 22–66. 4 **Person:** Having pointed out that he is being prosecuted for a legal act (e.g. there is no law against painting and displaying pictures) the defendant raises a further doubt: can a private person be guilty of 'public crimes' (a more literal translation of δημόσια ἀδικήματα, a vague charge and therefore convenient for declamation; see Winterbottom on [Quintilian] *Decl. Min.* 260, especially 260. 5; for the tenuous historical background see Xenophon *Hell.* 1. 7. 20, MacDowell 1978, 180 f.)? Naturally this restriction is not explicit in the law (if it were, the issue would certainly be objection: cf. *44. 11–20), so the argument is weak in itself and may readily be countered (see Sopater 132. 2–135. 14 for a model reply); but it may be useful as one step in a concerted effort to convey the impression that the prosecution is on questionable ground. The head

(called by some a 'definitional exception based on person': *RG* 7. 484. 14–23) is obviously omitted if the accused is a public person.

66. 4–6 **Definition:** Refutation is followed by counter-representation (see *48. 14–49. 6): even if a private person could be guilty of a public crime, what he has done does not fall under the definition of public crime. This head (a 'definitional exception based on act') again may be omitted; e.g. a general who destroys a rebellious allied city which he was sent to bring into line can hardly deny that his act, if found to be criminal, would be a public crime (*RG* 4. 601. 6–11, 7. 486. 31–487. 6). He must therefore proceed directly to the counterplea ('my treatment of the rebellious city was legitimate') and its counterpositional supplements ('they deserved it').

If the head is used it sets in train the series of heads characteristic of definition (see *59. 17–60. 18).

66. 7–12 **assimilation:** Counterdefinition is tacitly included with assimilation; see *60. 8–14 (cf. *RG* 4. 604. 1–11, 5. 168. 27–169. 2).

66. 12 f. **legislator's intention:** It is not clear why Hermogenes thinks that this head may sometimes not be relevant. The charge must invoke some law, and if the defence is using a definitional exception to place its act outside the scope of that law (e.g. 'this is not what is meant by public crime'), then the question of the law's intent must arise.

66. 13–67. 1 **Importance . . . Relative importance:** As we observed in definition (*60. 15–18) and as Hermogenes here makes explicit for the first time, the amplificatory heads are based on the sequence of events (see *47. 8–48. 2, *59. 16); the speaker recurs, therefore, at this point to the contents of the presentation, but with greater elaboration.

C. Primary Argument

Since in this issue the legitimacy of the act charged is the main claim of the defence, counterplea can be introduced as a direct response to the sequence of events; it does not have to be approached through a counterposition, as it is in definition.

67. 1–3 **counterplea:** This is the core of the defence, and will be argued out in some detail. The commentators stress that the claim to legitimacy should not be made outright (which may seem arrogant or provocative: cf. *48. 6–9), but be carefully prepared (Syrianus 2. 134. 6–13, *RG* 7. 500. 3–21).

Where the counterplea is based on a law Zeno 345. 9–14 alters the division along the lines of letter and intent (see 82. 10–18 below); the counterplea takes the form of a presentation of the written instrument, and in place of objection there is an appeal to its intent.

67. 3–5 **objection:** On objection see *48. 10–49. 6; for refutation and counter-representation see *48. 16–49. 6. Minucianus placed the sequence of events here (*RG* 7. 498. 17–23, Nilus *ap.* Gloeckner 1901, 40), as does Zeno 344. 30 f.; the effect is to make this head the main focus of the prosecutor's amplification of the act charged.

After this head Syrianus 2. 134. 24–135. 5 has a request for intention. The prosecutor, having entered his objection to the defendant's act, asks why the defendant performed the act despite the circumstance on which the objection rests; e.g. if an otherwise legitimate killing was performed in an unusually cruel way, an objection to the manner would be followed by the argument that the manner of the killing shows that the defendant's intention was not that envisaged and licensed by the law. The defence's response must be to place a favourable gloss on its act by establishing another and innocent intention. Thus the request for intention functions here (as in Syrianus' division of definition, p. 107) as a transition to the secondary argument, the counterposition with which it opens being equivalent to a gloss (cf. *49. 7–50. 19). According to Sopater 127. 19–128. 4 the underlying point at issue in counterplea is precisely the defendant's intentions (cf. Zeno 345. 3 f.: the 'conjecture about intention' is dispersed through the whole speech).

D. Secondary Argument

The secondary argument is identical with that in definition, except that a thesis (setting the particular case in the context of a general principle) is added. It is not clear why thesis should not be equally relevant in definition.

67. 5–8 **counterposition:** In Hermogenes' example the gloss takes the form of a counterstatement; in the case of the adulterous triple-hero, it would be counteraccusation. Some ancient theorists thought that these were the only counterpositions relevant in counterplea, except for the additional head of mitigation in cases based on act and contingency (*69. 13–16); but mitigation is also useful when the act prosecuted is a natural reflex (such as the tears in *Libanius *Decl.* 36), and transference when (e.g.) the people agreed to or acquiesced in the act (cf. *RG* 4. 617. 17–23, 626. 20–5; 7. 504. 18–33). Minucianus denied that counterposition always arises in counterplea (*RG* 4. 617. 11–13, 7. 503. 30–504. 1), but we do not know on what grounds.

67. 9–13 **Second objection ... counterplea:** The secondary argument continues as in definition (*61. 3–6).

67. 13–18 **thesis:** The thesis is used to set the particular case in the context of a more general principle. Thesis has been practised in the preliminary exercises (p. 16 f.); cf. 49. 17 f., 74. 5–9, 82. 1 f., 90. 9.

E. Exploitation

The concluding stages are handled as in definition.

67. 18–21 **quality and intention:** Cf. *61. 6–18, and *61. 18–20 for common quality, here taken for granted.

67. 19–21 **not as a division:** On the sense in which Hermogenes is not dividing see *28. 7–14.

Variant Forms (67. 22–71. 17)

In addition to the standard kind of counterplea, Hermogenes identifies a number of variant forms.

67. 23–68. 5 **more can be found:** See *71. 3–17.

68. 6–8 **Alcibiades, having been recalled from exile:** For this and other themes based on Alcibiades' return from exile see Russell 1983, 123–8 (cf. for Alcibiades in declamation Kohl 1915, 34–8, and note to *49. 10–14 above). Polemo treated the theme (Sopater 142. 5–12). It appears without identification of Alcibiades at *RG* 5. 96. 23 f.

68. 10–69. 21 **the act itself and some other contingency:** The charge is based not simply on the defendant's act, but on the act and some consequence of it. In cases of this kind the defence has two additional resources for argument (*68. 18–69. 13, *69. 13–21).

68. 13–18 **After the battle of Chaeroneia:** The case mentioned here is one of a group of declamation themes concerned with imaginary consequences of the Athenian defeat at Chaeroneia (see Kohl 1915, 73–7); e.g. Philip may offer to exchange the prisoners for Demosthenes (Libanius *Decl.* 21), or to buy him ([Hermogenes] *Inv.* 157. 1–6), or may simply demand his surrender (Apsines 221. 26 f., 226. 9–14, Libanius *Decl.* 19–20, *RG* 4. 102. 2–15). In some of these examples Demosthenes argues in favour of his surrender; these are 'figured' problems (in which the speaker argues one thing in order to achieve the opposite result: cf. note on *81. 4–6). So too are themes in which, for a variety of reasons, Demosthenes proposes his own death (Philostratus 522, 542; Libanius 7.

528. 4–11; *RG* 5. 44. 2–11; Syrianus 2. 165. 2 f.). For figured themes see [Hermogenes] *Inv.* 204. 16–210. 8, [Dionysius] 2. 295–385; Quintilian 9. 2. 67–98; Russell 1983, 36; Schöpsdau 1975.

68. 18–69. 13 **exception:** The contingency is not the defendant's own act: so can he be prosecuted for it? This is no more than a further spoiling device; the response, that one is responsible for foreseeable consequences of one's own acts as well as for the acts themselves, leads into the second additional topic.

68. 22–69. 13 **On what grounds are you bringing me to trial . . .:** Cf. Demosthenes 18. 239–43.

69. 13–21 **mitigation:** The defendant argues that the consequence of his act, on which the charge depends, was not foreseeable given the natural limitations on human foresight.

69. 16–20 **knowledge of division . . . is not enough:** See note to *28. 7–14.

70. 2–14 **by combination:** Two charges are inseparable: each act becomes chargeable in the light of the other; in this kind the prosecution has to bring the two together (or he has no case), and the defence has to separate them (to show that the defence indeed has no case).

70. 14–71. 2 **by distinction:** Here the two charges could in principle be brought separately; the two parties will adopt the same strategy as in double by combination, but for effect rather than out of necessity.

70. 16–18 **adopted many children:** Adoption has the legitimate function of furnishing a childless man with an heir, and so preventing the extinction of his household (MacDowell 1978, 98–108). But it could also be seen as open to abuse: 'most people who adopt children are seduced by flattery, and often motivated by animosity due to family quarrels' (Demosthenes 44. 63). The defendant's frequent changes of adopted son, like his frequent changes of wife, are therefore evidence of a frivolous and self-indulgent approach to life.

71. 3–17 **further classes of counterplea:** For Hermogenes' reluctance to multiply classes unnecessarily cf. 59. 4–9.

COUNTERPOSITION (72. 1–76. 2)

Division (72. 1–74. 15)

In definition and counterplea the defence maintains in the primary phase of the argument that the case against the act charged fails in principle (since the act does not satisfy the description under which it is charged, or is legitimate *per se*); in the secondary phase it is argued that the act was in any case justifiable, or at least excusable, in the circumstances. In counterposition, this distinction cannot be made since it is conceded that the act was in principle liable to the charge; what is secondary in the previous issues therefore becomes the primary and only phase of the argument here. Because this argument now has to bear much more weight (and may be inherently more difficult to sustain, since there is an admitted case in principle against the act) it is given in a more elaborate form, but the underlying structure is familiar: the counterposition itself prepares the way for an eventual counterplea; i.e. the claim that the act was justified or excusable leads in the end into the claim that it was not wrong. Hermogenes' division (72. 3–9) is summarized in Figure 5.

A. Presentation

72. 10 **presentation:** The initial formulation of the charge is treated as in definition; see *59. 16.

B. Preliminary Argument

As in counterplea, we may begin (as a spoiling tactic) with the sequence of heads characteristic of definition.

72. 10–12 **definition:** For this use of definition and the heads which accompany it see 66. 4–67. 1. Rhetoricians disagreed about this section (*RG* 4. 658. 14–662. 13, 5. 175. 12–176. 12, 7. 547. 30–549. 16, 554. 1–555. 12). Harpocration thought it was always relevant. Others argued that it could never be relevant since in counterposition the *prima facie* wrongdoing is conceded by the defence; but it is easy to see how a 'definitional exception based on act' (see note to *66. 4–6) could be invoked when the charge is not specific (e.g. harming the public interest: cf. Sopater *220. 18 f.), and given its spoiling function the argument does not need to be very cogent (cf. Hermogenes' remarks on exception in conjecture, 44. 11–14); see further on *74. 16–75. 10. Minucianus curtailed the sequence at assimilation, thinking the amplificatory heads superfluous (*RG* 5. 175. 26–30, 176. 6–9).

72. 12–18 **after the amplification:** Sequence of events is used 'after' the amplification (i.e. importance and relative importance) if there is a definition; if not it comes 'after' the presentation. The treatment of sequence of events as a separate head implied by 'after' presumably explains Metrophanes' view that in counterposition alone of the issues

A. Presentation

Presentation

B. Preliminary Argument

Definition
Counterdefinition
Assimilation
Legislator's intention
Importance
Relative importance

C. Primary Argument
(counterposition)

Intent
Counterposition
Alternative intent
Objection
Relative importance
Forced definition
Thesis
Second objection
Counterplea

D. Exploitation

Quality
Intention
Common quality

FIGURE 5.   Counterposition

amplification is excluded from the presentation (*RG* 7. 551. 25–32, 555. 20–557. 11); contrast the expression used at *59. 16 (the presentation 'is' the sequence of events) and *66. 13–67. 1 (the sequence of events arises 'in' importance and relative importance). But the underlying point is the same in all these passages. The presentation of the case is amplified using the kind of close analysis of the acts charged that is characteristic of sequence of events; but if the defence uses definition to attack the charge, that point will need to be argued out before the amplificatory elaboration of the charge—which will in that case be subsumed under or annexed to the amplificatory heads with which the definition-sequence culminates. Cf. *60. 15–18; *RG* 4. 662. 15–663. 18.

72. 14–16 **A hero killed his son:** This example turns out at *73. 9–13 not to be very useful for illustrating the full division, although it reappears at 74. 12 f. Hermogenes treats the theme as a counteraccusation, as does Apsines (235. 17 f.); but Syrianus 2. 155. 1–8 seems to treat it as counterplea, and at 2. 41. 15 f. reports the view that it is invalid because self-evident.

C. Primary Argument

As explained above (*72. 12–18), amplification (whether in the presentation or in the definition-sequence) involves an analysis of the sequence of events. The defence has to reply to this analysis, but cannot respond with an immediate counterplea, since it is acknowledged that the act is a *prima facie* wrong; so the defence argues that the intention was innocent as a preliminary to claiming that the act itself was either advantageous or else not the defendant's fault—the counterposition proper. This introduces a sequence similar to that seen in the secondary phase of definition and counterplea. But the sequence is handled more elaborately, since this is where the weight of the defence lies in counterpositions; further amplification, and a tendentious recharacterization of the act backed up by appeal to general considerations, are used to prepare the way for the counterplea. (Not all rhetoricians used this degree of elaboration: in Zeno 345. 15–351. 15 all the heads after objection and relative importance are missing.)

72. 18–73. 2 **intent:** Compare the use of request for intention to effect a transition to the counterposition in Syrianus' division of counterplea (cf. note to *67. 3–5). The defence's statement of its intention is introduced by a common topic on the necessity in general of considering intention as well as outcome; in Zeno (345. 32–346. 1) the head is called *locus communis ex causis*.

73. 2–9 **counterposition:** This is the crux of the case. As Hermogenes observes, in counteraccusation this head is worked out in the manner of the preliminary exercise common topic (p. 15). But the different counterpositions are often interlinked with each other (see note to *49. 23–50. 2), and the counteraccusation against the son can be supported with a counterstatement (i.e. that death is preferable to dishonour, so that the son's death was to his own true advantage).

In Zeno 346. 1–5 the counterposition is worked out using the sequence of events (compare his division of counterplea: see note to *67. 5–8); by contrast in Syrianus (2. 141. 21–5) sequence of events is used by the prosecution to demolish the defence's claim to an innocent intention, i.e. in place of Hermogenes' alternative intent.

73. 8 f. **also with the other issues:** The usefulness of counterposition as a secondary argument in other issues is obvious; for the converse, other issues arising in the course of a counterpositional case, see *RG* 4. 686. 9–29, 5. 179. 2–26.

73. 9–13 **alternative intent:** The prosecutor offers an alternative account of the defendant's intentions. In the case of the hero's son it is difficult to think of an alternative explanation for a father killing his son which will readily carry conviction; so the prosecutor in this case will proceed directly to the objection (cf. 74. 13 f. on using only the relevant heads).

73. 13 f. **Objection:** See *48. 10–49. 6.

73. 14 f. **Relative importance:** Hermogenes indicates the form which relative importance takes in counterstatement ('whether the benefit or the crime is more important'), anticipating the new example introduced at *73. 18–74. 1. Some ancient commentators take the view that this head appears only if there is a counterstatement (*RG* 4. 680. 23–681. 3, 7. 573. 4–8). But the head is obviously relevant in counteraccusation: did the act exceed the victim's deserts (e.g. did the hero's son deserve to be killed for what he did, prostitution normally incurring disfranchisement)? Also in transference and mitigation one may ask whether the outcome is disproportionate to the constraint under which the defendant acted (e.g. there is no excuse for giving way to emotion when such important matters were at stake). So relative importance may be relevant in any of the counterpositions (cf. *RG* 5. 177. 20–178. 1, 7. 574. 9–575. 1).

73. 16–74. 4 **Forcible definition:** Hermogenes applies the term 'forcible' loosely to tendentious or strongly assertive arguments; thus at 48. 15–21, of refutation. In a stricter sense forcible arguments were recognized as a

third class of solution alongside refutation and counter-representation (*48. 16–49. 6). Refutation simply rejects an opponent's claim; but in a forcible argument the opponent's claim is made to work against him, with the paradoxical result that what appears to be a strong point on the opposing side is turned into part of one's own case (see [Hermogenes] *Inv.* 138. 14–140. 8; sch. Demosthenes 19. 134 (291a)). Thus in forcible definition the facts which one party uses to characterize an action in one way are shown in the circumstances to entail exactly the opposite characterization (e.g. the damage done to the city's defences is, in the circumstances, a strengthening of the city's defences; or, conversely, by lifting the siege in this way the general has in effect left the city defenceless).

The doctrine that forcible definition occurs only in counterstatement (*RG* 4. 681. 21–4; attributed to Minucianus at 5. 178. 1–7) again seems too narrow.

73. 18–74. 1 **During a famine:** A counterstatement. The theme is also found at Apsines 232. 17 f. A number of similar themes are found: a general burns his fleet to prevent his troops fleeing (*RG* 4. 657. 2–21 etc., [Hermogenes] *Inv.* 105. 5–7, Apsines 271. 5–10, Zeno 345. 22–346. 19); or he is charged with impiety for cutting down a sacred grove to build ships (*RG* 7. 567. 6–24) or repairing the walls with tombstones (Sopater 198. 18–200. 2); likewise a hero is charged with impiety for taking weapons from a temple (Quintilian 5. 10. 36) or tomb (Seneca *Contr.* 4. 4, [Quintilian] *Decl. Min.* 369).

74. 5–9 **thesis:** An appeal to more general considerations supports the forcible definition; for thesis see *67. 13–18.

74. 9–11 **second objection:** In the counterposition the defence characterized its intentions in such a way as to make an act which is *prima facie* wrong seem praiseworthy (e.g. 'I acted to save the city') or at least excusable (e.g. 'I acted under constraint'); the first objection was a response to that. In the forcible definition and thesis the defence has tried to recharacterize its act more radically so as to abolish the *prima facie* guilt (e.g. 'I acted to save the city and what I did is not even, properly considered, damaging the walls but strengthening them': 74. 3 f.); the second objection responds to this step in the defence's argument (e.g. 'But the way in which you did this was wrong: you should not have acted without the people's consent'). The prosecution also uses forcible definition, giving an equally tendentious characterization of the act so as to obscure the merit or excuse (74. 1 f.); the prosecution's argument in this section

therefore has the overall structure of refutation (forcible definition) and counter-representation (second objection).

74. 11–13 **counterplea:** This claim to have acted legitimately has been the ultimate goal of the defence throughout.

74. 13 f. **use the relevant heads:** For the omission of heads that are not relevant to a particular case cf. 73. 9–13, 78. 15.

Hermogenes divides all four counterpositions in the same way (compare Sopater 205. 14–17), following earlier theorists such as Lollianus (*RG* 4. 648. 9–12, 5. 174. 26–8) who treated counterposition as a single issue; Minucianus and other rhetoricians who treated the counterpositions as four distinct issues more logically used a different division for each (*RG* 4. 647. 17 f., 5. 174. 30 f.; cf. *38. 16–39. 19). The effect can be observed in Zeno 345–54; the most important point is the inclusion of a different range of responses by the prosecution to each counterposition (e.g. in counteraccusation there is an incident issue, in which the charge against the victim is contested; in transference the response may be conjectural or qualitative—was the alleged external constraint real, and was it sufficient to compel this act?).

D. Exploitation

The concluding stages are handled as in definition.

74. 14 f. **quality and intention:** See *61. 6–18, and *61. 18–20 for common quality, here taken for granted.

Variant Forms (74. 16–76. 2)

74. 16–75. 10 **Some of those:** This polemic is directed against Minucianus (*RG* 4. 684. 5–686. 29, 7. 579. 9–582. 17); compare the related section at *34. 16–35. 14 (to which Hermogenes cross-refers at 75. 4 f.). Here too Hermogenes conducts the argument tendentiously; traces of the position of Minucianus' supporters preserved in the commentaries show that they did allege a difference in division. Definition was thought to be irrelevant in private cases (*RG* 4. 659. 29–660. 5, 685. 28–686. 6, 7. 552. 21 f.; cf. the 'definitional exceptions' in counterplea, which question the status of an alleged crime against the public interest: *65. 22–66. 6); there is some suggestion that the second objection arises only in public cases (*RG* 7. 550. 21–3, 578. 11–13); and the distinction between public and private was also thought to bear on the linking of different counterpositions with each other (*RG* 4. 674. 26–675. 9, 686. 1–6).

74. 20–75. 1 **as we have done:** Cf. *67. 22–71. 14.

75. 11–76. 2 **Some have not differentiated:** Hermogenes here takes up
the promise at 39. 17–19. For the distinction between transference as
external and mitigation as internal cf. Apsines 276. 3–7 (and *RG* 4. 245.
15–250. 22, 5. 98. 7–101. 28, 7. 202. 26–204. 4, 205. 20–207. 16; Gloeckner
1901, 42 f.). This too gave rise to problems (cf. *RG* 4. 687. 12–689. 12): if
a defendant has been tortured, did he give way to an external constraint
(Minucianus' view) or to pain and fear (the more common interpretation)? Other distinctions were current. Some thought that transference
referred the act to a person (*RG* 4. 247. 20 f., 5. 101. 20–2); some that
transference defended a fault of omission, mitigation a fault of commis-
sion (*RG* 4. 246. 1–5, 5. 101. 26–8; Menander, reported by Christophorus
ap. Rabe 1895, 247, cf. sch. Demosthenes 22. 17 (53f)); Sopater *ap.* Innes
and Winterbottom 1988, 283, on 360. 27).

Transference may be to a verbal instrument (explicitly so in
Minucianus' definition: Syrianus 2. 144. 2–4); how would this differ from
counterplea based on law? The problem is discussed in Syrianus 2. 146.
24–147. 4, *RG* 4. 246. 10–247. 1, 5. 99. 8–23. One suggestion is that in
counterplea the defence claims a legal right to have acted as it did, while
in transference it claims to have acted under legal constraint; but (e.g.)
in *Libanius *Decl.* 44. 57 the head of counterplea insists precisely on the
point that the act was required by law. In this case the defendant never
has to concede that his act was in fact detrimental to the public interest;
where the detriment is undeniable, as in the related case in *Sopater 220.
11–223. 11, the more cautious strategy of transference has advantages over
an outright and possibly provocative assertion of the act's legitimacy.

75. 21–76. 2 **not . . . a matter of division:** Cf. 69. 16–20, and note to *28.
7–14.

THE PRACTICAL ISSUE (76. 3–79. 16)

The practical issue seeks to make a qualitative assessment of a proposed
future act in order to determine whether the proposal should be adopted.
Some decisions about a future course of action (e.g. the granting of a
reward for tyrannicide or heroism) turn on the qualitative assessment of
past acts; these do not fall within the practical issue for Hermogenes,
although some rhetoricians took a different view (see on *38. 1–8).
Hermogenes' category equates roughly to deliberative oratory, but he

classifies some deliberative questions as legal rather than practical; again, some rhetoricians took a different view (see on *76. 6–11).

The division follows the heads of purpose (see p. 15), and is summarized in Figure 6. This division differs from that of other issues, since it provides a checklist of topics to consider rather than a structured sequence of steps in an argument. The order in which the heads are given here is sometimes seen as natural (see the discussions in *RG* 4. 713. 12–717. 9, 742. 1–18, 5. 182. 18–186. 20; cf. e.g. sch. Demosthenes 23. 18 (20, 22, 24)), but in practice the sequence is varied to suit the case in hand and the outlook of the audience (Syrianus 2. 180. 9–11, cf. e.g. sch. Demosthenes 15. 11 (5b), 16. 6 (2)). A degree of fluidity in the order of the heads is indeed inevitable, since any head may be opposed by any of the others; e.g. the claim that a course of action would be advantageous may be more effectively countered by a claim that it is unjust or not feasible than by meeting the proposer on his own ground.

Legality (Custom)
Justice
Advantage
Feasibility
Honour
Consequence

FIGURE 6.   The Practical Issue

76. 6–11 **It may be documentary or non-documentary:** The practical issue is part of the logical subdivision of quality, and is therefore concerned with an evaluation of the act (see *37. 14–20). In the documentary species reference is made to some verbal instrument, and so the kinds of argumentation associated with the legal issues are relevant (76. 12–14); but the dispute is nevertheless about the act as such, not about the verbal instrument. Where a deliberative question turns primarily on the interpretation of a verbal instrument the issue would (for Hermogenes) be legal rather than practical; e.g. a speaker advising the Athenians to take to their ships after receiving the 'wooden wall' oracle would be using

a legal issue (ambiguity), provided that the decision is made to turn on the interpretation of the oracle rather than on an assessment of the strategic options *per se* (cf. Sopater 377. 2–379. 5, Syrianus 2. 203. 5–209. 8).

Hermogenes' definition of the practical issue at *38. 1–8 implies a broader category, covering any debate 'whether this should or should not happen, whether or not to grant this', irrespective of whether the argument is logical or legal. This view of the practical issue was in fact very widely adopted. One consequence of the broader view is that deliberative themes which Hermogenes would classify as legal are reclassified as practical (Syrianus 2. 195. 19–196. 17, opposing Hermogenes and Metrophanes; cf. *RG* 7. 691. 27–692. 7 on the 'wooden wall', 7. 223. 25–224. 9, 646. 12–14). On this view, themes in which the dispute is about the verbal instrument constitute the documentary species of the practical issue, while themes which are about the act are non-documentary, even if they make reference to a verbal instrument; consequently all themes which Hermogenes would classify as practical are held to fall under the non-documentary class. (Views on the distinction between documentary and non-documentary cases are surveyed in *RG* 7. 592. 19–594. 17, cf. 4. 705. 15–26, 724. 4–22; Syrianus 2. 162. 10–17; for an attempt to establish an intermediate class see *RG* 5. 181. 2–182. 15, 187. 13–29.) Hermogenes' position seems more satisfactory, since it recognizes a fundamental difference in argumentative strategy between decisions which turn on legal and logical considerations respectively, and (within the latter) a less fundamental difference between those which do and those which do not involve reference to a particular text (see *76. 12–77. 2).

A second unsatisfactory consequence of the broader view of the practical issue is that it came to embrace various categories of theme (e.g. requests for a reward, self-denunciations) irrespective of the underlying logical structure of the dispute (see e.g. Syrianus 2. 162. 18–167. 9). As Russell observes (1983, 63) 'there is . . . not much rationale in this classification'.

76. 6–10 when Philip occupies Elateia: This theme is also found in Apsines 245. 3–7. For an account of the crisis following Philip's seizure of Elateia in 339 BC see Demosthenes 18. 169–79. Hermogenes' classification of this case as documentary shows that he thought that it raises a legal question, presumably of letter and intent (cf. Syrianus 2. 163. 25–164. 4): does the law apply when Athens is confronted with open aggression? A contrary view (*RG* 5. 187. 21–9) is that there is no question about the law, the question being whether the course of action proposed should be adopted despite an acknowledged violation of the law.

76. 10 f. Cleon requests the title 'Pythian': See 76. 18–22. Pericles was mockingly compared to Zeus in contemporary comedy (Cratinus fr. 258 Kassel–Austin), and Aristophanes calls him 'the Olympian' in *Acharnians* 530 (cf. Telecleides fr. 18 Kassel–Austin). The epithet entered into the biographical tradition (see Plutarch *Per.* 8. 2, 39. 2, with Stadter ad loc.), and was then taken up by later rhetoricians; Aristides alludes to this 'honour' conferred on Pericles in his speech *On the Four* (3. 124), and composed a declamation in which an unnamed speaker proposes the withdrawal of the honour during the plague (fr. 118 Behr = Syrianus 2. 173. 3–11; a similar theme in [Hermogenes] *Inv.* 96. 23–97. 5). The theme cited here develops this idea. Cleon, being a lesser figure than Pericles, has a lesser title attached to him; but his requesting the honour for himself reflects the traditional image of his extravagant self-promotion (see especially Aristophanes *Knights*, Thucydides 4. 28). It should not be assumed that the declaimers took such inventions too seriously; the splendid theme in which Cleon does away with himself after a performance of *Knights* and Aristophanes is charged with causing his death (*RG* 4. 234. 1–3, 235. 4–6, 588. 5–7) can only have been a deliberate and witty invention.

76. 12–77. 2 Legality: If (e.g.) the Elateia example (see *76. 6–10) is thought to involve a question of letter and intent, the heading of legality will be handled using the pattern of argument set out under that issue. In non-documentary cases, where there is no law to be invoked, established custom (which can be treated as an unwritten law) is available as a substitute (cf. Apsines 293. 12–294. 14). For Hermogenes, documentary and non-documentary cases differ only in respect of the appeal to law or custom. Russell comments that the distinction between the two species is 'not a fundamental one' (1983, 63), but they do require different techniques of argument; the speaker in a documentary case must take account of the wording of a particular text and the assumed intention of its author, and it is helpful therefore to be referred to the handling of legal issues as a model.

The possibility of argument from custom made alleged innovation (as in the case of Cleon's title) a popular basis for practical themes (cf. [Hermogenes] *Inv.* 137. 11–14, 144. 17–146. 13, 149. 15–22).

76. 17–77. 2 **by refutation and counter-representation:** See *48. 14–49. 6.

76. 18–22 **Cleon requests the title 'Pythian':** See *76. 10 f.

77. 3–5 **Justice:** A deliberative assembly will wish to be reassured that the course of action proposed is just (see Heath 1990, 391–6); since this may depend on the previous behaviour of another party (e.g. people are readier to declare war on a proven aggressor or to conclude an alliance with the victims of injustice) the juridical issues are relevant here. Thus in Thucydides the Corcyrean ambassadors seeking an alliance with Athens try to pre-empt by a counteraccusation the Corinthian argument that this would be unjust (1. 34).

77. 6–19 **Advantage:** Aristotle saw advantage as the distinctive concern of deliberative oratory (*Rhet.* 1358ᵇ20–9); this analysis is too simple (Quintilian 3. 4. 16), but the topic remains centrally important. Hermogenes' fourfold treatment of the topic allows the speaker to show that adopting the proposal will lead to the retention and acquisition of good things and the removal and avoidance of bad things, while rejecting the proposal will lead to the opposite results.

77. 7–9 **Accepting Olynthus as an ally:** Cf. Demosthenes 1. 25.

77. 20–78. 21 **Feasibility:** One commentator (*RG* 7. 605. 12–606. 8) compares the pairing of advantage and feasibility to that of motive and capacity in conjecture (*46. 8–47. 7).

78. 6–9 **as Demosthenes does:** There is an extensive analysis of Philip's resources in Demosthenes 2. 5–10, 14–21; but Hermogenes is in fact conflating 1. 21–4 (Philip's despondency, Thessalians, Illyrians, finance) with 2. 17 (mercenaries and guards).

78. 10–21 **Corresponding to this:** This is Hermogenes' clearest statement of the distinction between the theoretical division of an issue and its application, which must always adapt itself to the needs of the particular case; rhetorical practice, which involves an element of judgement, cannot be reduced to a theoretical system (p. 4). For the contrast made here between nature and art cf. *44. 1–20 and Ch. 1 n. 63.

78. 22–79. 6 **Honour:** Hermogenes achieves an unusually contorted form of expression in his illustration by casting it all in questions; the use of conditional statements in 77. 12–19 is much clearer. One is reminded of the exercise recommended by some handbooks on preliminary exercises (see [Hermogenes] *Prog.* 5. 6–9; Theon *Prog.* 62. 10–21, 74. 3, 101. 8–24), in which the student is required to treat a theme using one grammatical construction throughout; cf. Bonner 1977, 257 f.

79. 7–16 **Consequence:** The distinction between advantage and consequence is obviously not a sharp one, and is discussed inconclusively by ancient commentators (*RG* 4. 761. 9–762. 14, 763. 17–25, 7. 613. 25–616. 10). One difference does emerge from Hermogenes' discussion. Under advantage the speaker will stress the advantages to be gained from the successful implementation of his proposal, but here the consequences of an unsuccessful (or even partial) implementation are reviewed as well.

79. 10–14 **As in the *Philippics*:** Cf. Demosthenes 4. 18.

79. 14–16 **as in *On behalf of Megalopolis*:** Cf. Demosthenes 16. 30 f.

OBJECTION (79. 17–82. 3)

79. 18 f. **Objection can . . . be documentary or non-documentary:** We have seen how in other issues an attack on the validity of the prosecution can be introduced as a spoiling action before the main body of the argument (*44. 1–20, *65. 14–66. 6, *72. 10–12). In objection the defence promotes this preliminary move into a primary component of the argument by citing an explicit provision of the law which (it is claimed) invalidates the prosecution. This may happen in two ways (see *42. 5–43. 8): the law cited may invalidate the prosecution on procedural grounds, or it may explicitly license the act charged. In the first instance the prosecution must contest the defence's interpretation of the law, and legal argument about the procedural validity of the case precedes the substantive argument about the act in question. In the second instance the prosecution does not contest the defence's interpretation of the law (if it did, the case would fall straightforwardly under one of the legal issues); instead there is an attempt to show that the particular circumstances of the act remove it from the scope of the law.

A distinction between documentary and non-documentary species is found also in the practical issue (*76. 6–11). The documentary species of both issues have in common a first phase divided according to one of the legal issues (76. 12–14, 79. 19–21). The subsequent phase of the argument in the practical issue is logical, involving a qualitative assessment of the proposed action; likewise Hermogenes claims that the second phase of documentary objection is divided according to one of the logical issues, although this is not wholly convincing (see on *80. 1–3). But the parallel between objection and the practical issue breaks down with the non-documentary species. Non-documentary practical cases do not refer at

all to a legal instrument; by contrast, non-documentary objection necessarily arises out of an appeal to a legal instrument, even though the argument that ensues is logical.

Since the two species of objection have completely different divisions,
it may be thought incongruous that they are subsumed under a single
issue. In Zeno 338. 31–340. 13 objection covers only the latter (non-
documentary) class; procedural argument based on the interpretation of
a law is more logically assigned to the legal issues. See the note to *42.
5–43. 8 for the possibility that Minucianus created this awkwardness by
trying to combine a scheme like that found in Zeno with Hermagoras'
original and rather different system.

As noted earlier (*42. 5–43. 8), Metrophanes and later Neoplatonist
rhetoricians, including Syrianus (2. 55. 5–8, 152. 11–153. 6, 157. 3–17), recognized two distinct issues; but the scheme which results has its own
problems. The non-documentary species retains the name objection;
the documentary species is called exception (παραγραφή), and is subdi-
vided in turn into complete and incomplete exception (158. 3–12).
Complete exceptions reject the procedural validity of the primary case
in principle; this occurs in cases of double jeopardy (159. 18–26).
Incomplete exceptions reject the primary case on circumstantial
grounds, e.g. because it is brought by someone without right of access
to the courts, or before the wrong court, or after a time-limit (159.
26–160. 25); such exceptions are incomplete, because the prosecution
would have been valid if it had been brought in other circumstances,
e.g. by someone else, or before a different court, or sooner. Syrianus'
paradigm of incomplete exception is Aeschines' attempt to thwart
Timarchus' prosecution by bringing a counter-prosecution for prostitution; if successful this would deprive Timarchus of access to the courts,
but it would not prevent someone else (e.g. Demosthenes) from continuing the case against Aeschines. But this kind of legal process is of
little interest from the point of view of issue-theory; it consists in reality of two distinct cases, each with its own issue. Thus in Syrianus'
paradigm there is a conjectural case concerning Timarchus' alleged
prostitution, and a distinct conjectural case concerning Aeschines'
alleged malpractice as ambassador; the purely procedural fact that one
of the cases has been brought to forestall the other has no bearing on
the way either case is divided. Sopater accordingly argues that a case may
be an exception in a procedural sense (i.e. brought to forestall some other
legal action) without being an exception in a sense relevant to issue-
theory (268. 2–269. 1). He limits exception to cases involving double

jeopardy (i.e. Syrianus' complete exception), but fails to make it clear why these should not be handled under some other issue.

Documentary Objection (79. 19–80. 20)

79. 19 **a complete procedural exception:** Documentary objection is a 'complete' exception in the sense that its success would wholly invalidate the prosecution; contrast the use of exceptions as a spoiling move designed to weaken, rather than destroy, the opponent's case in other issues (cf. *44. 11–20). Other explanations of the term (*RG* 4. 292. 18–29) invoke the distinction between complete and incomplete exceptions found in Syrianus (above), or identify complete objection with the documentary species and incomplete with the non-documentary.

80. 1–3 **The question following the exception:** According to Hermogenes the division of the first question may follow either a legal issue or definition; the second question is logical. The term 'logical' was formally introduced as a species of quality (37. 20), but in a broader sense it includes conjecture and definition (see e.g. Zeno 325. 6 f.); thus the second question in documentary objection may be conjectural (as in the example at 42. 19). There remain two problems.

First, if the initial question is definition then it is a logical dispute about the categorization of certain facts, not a legal dispute about the written instrument on which the exception is based; the distinction between documentary and non-documentary objection therefore collapses. See *RG* 4. 777. 23–779. 29, 5. 192. 1–19, 7. 619. 23–621. 27, which argue that the first question will always be legal, although the head of definition will sometimes have especial prominence. The same problem besets the suggestion of some commentators that the first question may even be conjectural: *RG* 4. 778. 16–18, 7. 242. 8–11, 619. 23–30, 622. 30–623. 4. The inclusion of conjecture was presumably required to accommodate the paradigm case in which the exception presupposes a disputed statement of fact about the circumstances of the prosecution: Aeschines' contention that Timarchus has no right of access to the courts rests on the contested claim that Timarchus has prostituted himself. But there is no reason why this kind of case should have a special place in issue-theory (*79. 18 f.).

Secondly, it is not clear why Hermogenes specifies that the issue of the second question must be logical. There seems to be no reason why an exception should not be entered and argued out on legal grounds in a case that will itself turn on a legal question. The problem is recognized at *RG* 7. 624. 17–625. 3; Sopater 268. 1 f. allows the substantive case to be either logical or legal.

80. 3–9 **Anyone opposing a law:** Apart from the commentators, the case appears only in a catalogue of rhetorical problems at *RG* 8. 409. 19–26. The idea of a time-limit within which judicial review of legislation must be sought is derived from Demosthenes' *Against Leptines*; there, however, the expiry of the time-limit does not prevent the quashing of the law, but means only that the law's proposer will not be subject to personal penalty (Demosthenes 20. 144, cf. MacDowell 1978, 50 f.). In the formulation of the present case at *RG* 4. 283. 13–23 the time-limit is one year, as in Demosthenes.

Conflict between rich and poor is a popular motif in declamation (see Russell 1983, 21 f., 27–30; [Dionysius] 381. 13–382. 7); cf. 57. 14–58. 2 and the note to *81. 4–6, and for a fully worked example e.g. *Libanius *Decl.* 36. An attack on the poor man during his absence on an embassy is also found in the following ingenious theme (*RG* 7. 237. 8–17; Marcommanus *ap.* Sulpicius Victor 340. 14–341. 28):- A poor man returns from an embassy to find that his son has been murdered, and that his two rich enemies have unsuccessfully prosecuted each other for the murder; he wishes to charge them both, but they enter an exception under the principle of double jeopardy.

Non-Documentary Objection (81. 1–82. 3)

Hermogenes' model strategy for non-documentary objection is an adaptation of counterplea (for the relation between objection and counterplea based on law see p. 115 f. above). The preliminary spoiling action is omitted; since the defence will maintain outright that the charge is explicitly invalidated by a law there is no need for a preparatory undermining of its validity. Hermogenes' division (81. 1–4) is summarized in Figure 7.

A. Presentation

81. 4–6 **A man who has fought heroically:** A variant of this case appears at *RG* 8. 404. 1–8:- A man commits a murder, and then kills the tyrant and requests the victim's death as his reward; but the victim's family find his servants disposing of the body and realize that he was killed before the reward was granted; they prosecute him for murder.

The hero's reward has been met before (see the case in *47. 17–21). A hero (or other public benefactor) allowed to name his own reward has

A. Presentation

B. Primary Argument

C. Secondary Argument

D. Exploitation

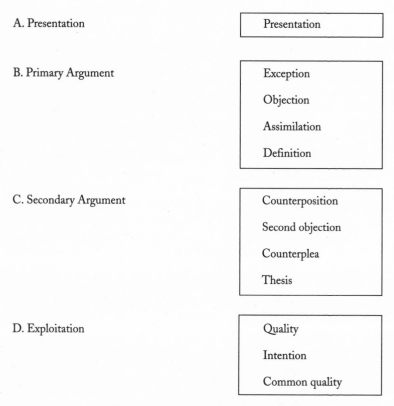

Presentation

Exception
Objection
Assimilation
Definition

Counterposition
Second objection
Counterplea
Thesis

Quality
Intention
Common quality

FIGURE 7.   Non-Documentary Objection

apparently been granted the legal right to act in ways that would otherwise be illegal, and that are certainly unjust; such rewards are therefore a fruitful source of interesting rhetorical problems, and the request for the death of a personal or political enemy, although open to mockery (see Synesius *De Insomniis* 20, quoted by Russell 1983, 21), was a popular basis for declamation themes. In the simplest form, someone opposes the request (Syrianus 2. 164. 12–14). If the killing is delayed, the person claimed may ask to be put to death at once (Apsines 319. 3–12, cf. Sopater 316. 12–317. 10); this is a 'figured' case (see note on *68. 13–18), for the petitioner's real aim is to win so much pity that the grant is revoked. In [Quintilian] *Decl. Min.* 294, by contrast, the victim wants his death to be deferred; he has a prosecution for treason outstanding against the claimant and wants the case to be heard before he is killed (if the prosecution is successful, then the claimant will of course no longer be in a position to take the deferred reward).

In accordance with the conventional hostility between rich and poor in declamation (*80. 3–9), the claimant is usually a rich man and his victim poor. If the granting of the poor man's death leads other poor men to withdraw from politics, the claimant may be charged with harming the public interest (Syrianus 2. 49. 16–26). The request need not be for the enemy's death. In Sopater 145. 9–161. 25, the request is apparently for his living person (the rich man requests that his poor enemy be 'handed over' to him; when the poor man learns of the award he kills himself, and the rich man is charged with causing his death); likewise in Sopater 286. 4–306. 20. The rich man in *Libanius *Decl.* 36 was less ambitious, asking only for part of his poor enemy.

81. 6 **Presentation:** The initial formulation of the charge is treated as in definition; see *59. 16. In most issues the presentation is used for moderate amplification (see on *59. 16, *72. 12–18); commentators suggest that the amplification should be fuller in objection since the amplificatory heads of the definition-sequence (importance and relative importance) will be omitted (*RG* 4. 785. 2–8, 786. 23–787. 24, 795. 4–8, 7. 627. 18–28, 628. 24–629. 16).

B. Primary Argument

In the primary argument the defence enters its procedural exception, citing the legal instrument which allegedly invalidates the prosecution. This head is a counterpart to the counterplea in the primary argument of the issue counterplea (*67. 1–3), and the prosecution responds accordingly with an objection (cf. *67. 3–5) showing how the circumstances of the act in question remove it from the scope of that instrument. Since the prosecution's strategy depends on the validity of this distinction, the rest of the primary argument exploits elements of the definition-sequence concerned with establishing or blurring distinctions.

81. 6–8 **Exception:** Note that Hermogenes specifies (81. 1 f.) that the exception is based on a verbal instrument, just as in the documentary species; contrast the variety of exceptions suggested in conjecture (*44. 1–11). As Hermogenes points out there, the fact that the exception is based on explicit legal provisions is what gives the issue of objection its strength (*44. 11–20).

81. 8–12 **Objection:** The objection is to the time of the killing; before the request was granted the killing was illegal. The supplementary point that the request might not have been granted had the victim been able to speak against it shows why the circumstance invoked is important.

81. 12–16 **Assimilation:** In previous issues assimilation has come after definition. But the objection has drawn a distinction based on circumstance between this case and that covered by the legal instrument; assimilation regularly has the function of blurring a distinction (cf. *60. 8–14), and is therefore an appropriate response to the objection.

81. 13–16 **not by way of a division:** Compare 67. 19–21, and see on *28. 7–14.

81. 16–18 **Definition:** The definition follows as a formal restatement of the distinction introduced in the objection; cf. *60. 10–14 for the habitual opposition between definition and assimilation.

Syrianus 2. 156. 2–5 suggests that other heads of the definition-sequence (legislator's intention, importance, and relative importance) may be used here; Sopater 246. 16–18 includes importance (see p. 224). The majority view among the commentators is that in objection amplification is concentrated in the presentation, and the other amplificatory heads are omitted (see on *81. 6).

C. Secondary Argument

The rest of the argument follows the same pattern as the secondary argument in counterplea.

81. 16–18 **Counterposition:** In this case, the counterposition is counter-accusation. Note the appeal to the people's judgement; the defendant tries to manœuvre the prosecution into criticizing the people's decision, and thus appearing to be undemocratic in outlook.

81. 18–20 **Second objection:** The second objection is to the manner of the hero's request to the people. A fuller working-out of the argument might suggest that the hero deceived the people and distorted their decision by concealing the fact that his victim was already dead. The assembly which granted the proposal that someone be put to death might not have been willing to grant a request that a previous illegal killing be condoned; so its decision cannot be used to justify the murder.

81. 20–82. 1 **counterplea:** See *61. 5 f., 67. 9–13.

82. 1 f. **Thesis:** See *67. 13–18.

D. *Exploitation*

The concluding stages are handled as in definition.

82. 2 f. Quality and intention: See *61. 6–18, and *61. 18–20 for common quality.

LETTER AND INTENT (82. 4–83. 18)

In this issue, before the debate turns to the inherent qualities of the act charged, one of the parties has to argue away an apparent conflict between its position and the explicit provisions of a legal instrument. Some argued that it is invariably the prosecutor who is in possession of the letter of the law (*RG* 7. 212. 13–16, Syrianus 2. 193. 5–11); Hermogenes (40. 10) agrees with Minucianus (*RG* 7. 212. 3–13, cf. 4. 256. 11–257. 4, 5. 103. 13–28) that this is not invariably so. But the apparent disagreement is illusory. According to the commentators the defence is held to possess the letter where the case arises out of a request or claim (as distinct from prosecutions); e.g.:- A man disables himself and claims a disability allowance. The more common view of such cases is that the petitioner takes the place of the prosecutor, on the grounds that he speaks first (*RG* 4. 212. 25 f., 258. 4–15, 490. 17–23, 501. 6–9, Syrianus 2. 110. 6–8, 113. 12–14). But others see the petitioner as the defendant in such a case, despite speaking first, since he is defending his claim; his opponent is then seen as the prosecutor (*RG* 4. 218. 17–26, 258. 15–17). On either view, it is the first speaker (prosecutor or claimant) who appeals to the letter of the law, and the second (defendant or opponent) who appeals to the intent. The point has no effect on Hermogenes' exposition, since he formulates his division as if for a straightforward case of prosecution and defence.

Cases are rarely based on legal argument alone (cf. *37. 14–20, *39. 20–40. 6); arguments over the interpretation of the law (or some other document with legal force, such as a will) are typically part of a larger structure involving considerations of equity. Sometimes the legal issues will be combined with one of the logical issues (see 90. 9–15, and cf. p. 225 on Sopater), but Hermogenes also builds the more general considerations of equity into the recommended division of each of the four legal issues. In the primary phase the legal arguments are set out; then in the secondary phase the focus of the dispute turns to the act charged itself, and considers whether it is justifiable or excusable. Hermogenes' division (82. 5–9) is summarized in Figure 8.

A. Presentation

82. 10–13 **presentation:** Since the prosecutor is to insist on the letter of the law, it is important to begin by setting the conflict between act and

A. Presentation	Presentation
B. Primary Argument	Intent Exclusion of further distinctions Second intent Assimilation Definition
C. Secondary Argument	Counterposition Objection Relative importance Forced definition Thesis Second objection Counterplea
D. Exploitation	Quality Intention Common quality

FIGURE 8.   Letter and Intent

law clearly before the jury. In 82. 5 f. this head is described as a presentation of the verbal instrument; according to the more precise formula used here it is a presentation of the act as a violation of the law (or other legal document) on which the case rests. In other issues the act is presented with a degree of amplification; e.g. in counterstatement the prosecutor is likely to dwell on the danger to which the city was exposed when the general secretly breached the wall (cf. *73. 18–74. 1). In letter and intent the act in question may be innocuous *per se*; the presentation will therefore focus on the act simply as a contravention of the law, and amplification will be achieved by arguments about the importance of the law (cf. *RG* 4. 800. 23–801. 9, 802. 19–803. 17).

82. 11–13 **It is a capital offence:** See 40. 11–13; this is a standard example of letter and intent (Quintilian 4. 4. 4, 7. 6. 6 f., Zeno 351. 23–352. 6, Sopater 348. 28 f., Apsines 273. 2–5), which Cicero uses to contrast the easily comprehended problems set to young students with the complexities of detail and documentation that must be mastered in real advocacy (*De Or.* 2. 100).

B. *Primary Argument*

In the primary argument an appeal is made from the explicit content of the law to its implicit intention; typically this appeal makes a distinction that is not explicitly drawn in the law, and the ensuing debate is concerned with the legitimacy and relevance of that distinction. The heads used are broadly those of the standard definition-sequence, although the order is different.

82. 13–18 **Intent:** The claim that one must consider the intention with which an act was performed as well as the act itself has been met in counterposition (*72. 18–73. 2). Here the head is more complex (cf. *RG* 4. 806. 2–11); because the act outwardly considered conflicts with the terms of the law, the defendant has at the same time to consider the legislator's intention (cf. *60. 14 f., 66. 12 f.) in order to establish that what he intended to do is not what the law was intended to prevent. Cf. Aristotle *Rhet.* 1374^{b}11–14.

In counterposition intent is opposed by alternative intent (*73. 9–13), in which the prosecution argues for a less favourable construal of the defendant's behaviour. Here, since the case for the prosecution rests on the letter of the law, there is no need to question the defendant's claims about his own intention; the argument therefore continues on other lines.

82. 18–83. 2 **exclusion of further distinctions:** The defence rests on a distinction between what the law explicitly forbids (e.g. foreigners going onto the city walls) and what it is intended to prevent (e.g. foreigners going onto the city walls without good cause); the first and crucial step for the prosecutor is to question the legitimacy of any appeal to distinctions not made explicit in the law.

83. 2–8 **second intent:** Each side must now show why its interpretation of the law—accepting or excluding the implicit distinction—best fits the intention of the legislator. Note that the prosecutor cannot dismiss the legislator's intention as irrelevant, and insist solely on the letter of the law; it is common ground that the legislator's intention is authoritative. The prosecutor has instead to show that the interpretation which excludes implicit distinctions is the one which the legislator intended; his appeal to the letter of the law is one piece of evidence in his favour (why did the legislator not make the distinction explicit if that was what he meant?), but he must also show that the intention he attributes to the legislator is a sensible and just one.

83. 8–10 **Assimilation:** Since the prosecutor has placed at the centre of the dispute the question whether it is legitimate to draw a certain distinction not expressed in the law, the defence (precisely because its case rests on that distinction) will want to remove the question of its legitimacy from the centre of the dispute. This is done by suggesting that it makes no difference whether the distinction is made or not, since the desired conclusion (e.g. that it is not a criminal act for a foreigner to go on the wall in those circumstances) is self-evidently valid whether or not the legislator made the distinction explicit (this, indeed, is why the legislator did not bother to make it: 83. 4–6). Assimilation thus has its usual function of blurring a distinction (cf. *60. 8–14).

83. 10 f. **Definition:** The prosecutor responds by insisting on the difference that the distinction makes. Definition and assimilation are habitually opposed (*60. 10–14); here, as in objection (*81. 12–16), it is definition which comes second.

C. Secondary Argument

The secondary argument reproduces the primary argument of counterposition (73. 2–74. 14), except that intent and alternative intent are omitted. The defence has already touched on the question of intention in the primary argument (*82. 13–18); since the prosecution's case rests on the terms of the law rather than the inherent harmfulness of the act, we do not in this issue have the amplificatory presentation of the act which in counterposition compels the defence to exhibit the innocence of its intentions (*72. 12–73. 2).

83. 11 f. **counterposition:** See *73. 2–9. The defence is stronger here precisely because the prosecution does not attempt to show that the act charged was inherently harmful.

83. 12–14 **Objection:** See *48. 10–49. 6, 73. 13 f.

83. 15 f. **Relative importance:** See *73. 14 f.

83. 17 f. **The rest of the heads:** These are forcible definition, thesis, second objection, and counterplea; see *73. 16–74. 13.

D. Exploitation

The concluding stages (82. 9) are also handled as in definition; see *61. 6–18 for quality and intention, and *61. 18–20 for common quality.

CONFLICT OF LAW (83. 19–88. 2)

As Hermogenes says (41. 4 f., 83. 20 f.), conflict of law is like letter and intent doubled: each party will have to argue away the explicit content of the law which the other party cites and substitute an implicit intention, while maintaining the explicit intention of its own law. (Hermogenes notes that the two parties may appeal to different parts of the same law: other rhetoricians found far more complex variants; cf. Calboli Montefusco 1986, 167–78.) The structure is the same as letter and intent, except that each party will also try to argue that its own position is the more inclusive, i.e. that it preserves the underlying concerns of the other side's law. Hermogenes' division (84. 4–15) is summarized in Figure 9.

A. Presentation

85. 1–4 **A disinherited son:** See 41. 5–8. A simpler theme based on the title to a ship abandoned in a storm appears at *Rhet. ad Herennium* 1. 19 (an invalid is left on board: the case is treated as letter and intent); another variant with ingenious complications is found in Cicero *Inv.* 2. 153 f. Some (Syrianus 2. 197. 2–17, *RG* 7. 646. 12–14) denied that this is a conflict of law, analysing it as practical; see on *76. 6–11 for the theoretical point at issue here.

85. 4 f. **Presentation:** As in letter and intent; see *82. 10–13.

A. Presentation

Presentation

B. Primary Argument

Intent
Alternative presentation
Alternative intent
(Exclusion of further distinctions)
Second intent
(Assimilation)
(Definition)

C. Secondary Argument

Counterposition
Objection
Relative importance
Inclusive and included
Forced definition
Thesis
Second objection
Counterplea

D. Exploitation

Quality
Intention
Common quality

FIGURE 9.   Conflict of Law

B. *Primary Argument*

A modified version of the primary argument in letter and intent; the involvement of two laws entails additions (alternative presentation and intent) and omissions (exclusion of further distinctions).

85. 5–9 **Intent:** See *82. 13–18.

85. 9–12 **alternative presentation:** Thus far the pattern has followed letter and intent; now it diverges. As well as its interpretation of the intent of the first party's instrument, the second party has its own legal instrument to set against the first.

85. 12–15 **alternative intent:** The second party's legal instrument, in turn, is treated symmetrically by the first party.

85. 16–86. 3 **exclusion of further distinctions:** This head will in most cases not be useful. Both parties are following the same strategy, advancing the explicit content of one law and proposing an interpretation of the other which rests on distinctions which are not explicitly made in it; there cannot therefore be any argument about the legitimacy in principle of appealing to distinctions which are not made explicit. If the making of implicit distinctions is not brought into question, assimilation and definition (which are prompted by the questioning of distinctions: *83. 8–10) are also irrelevant.

Hermogenes repeats his insistence that he is not engaged in a full division: see on *28. 7–14, and 67. 19–21, 81. 13–16, and 86. 15–17. Here the point is that heads which are irrelevant in theory may in practice sometimes prove useful. The exclusion of further distinctions is, as a matter of general principle, irrelevant; but a speaker who can find a way to use it in a particular case (perhaps making his opponent's distinctions seem more remote from the law than his own) should not be deterred by the general principle.

86. 3–17 **second intent:** At 84. 9 Hermogenes includes the second intent (that of the legislator: see *83. 2–8) among the heads which are omitted as equally balanced, but he is right to reinstate it here. Its function is to show that the proposed interpretation of the law (or, here, both laws) is reasonable. Since this is just as necessary in conflict of laws as in letter and intent there seems to be no good reason why this head should go the same way as the exclusion of further distinctions (cf. *RG* 7. 648. 14–24).

C. Secondary Argument

86. 18–21 **counterposition:** See *73. 2–9, 83. 11 f. The counterpositions in the example are a counteraccusation against the disinherited son (whose status is evidence of his bad character, which can be elaborated by means of a common topic) and a counterstatement in his favour (since his heroism preserved the ship and its cargo, to the general good).

86. 21–87. 2 **objection:** See *48. 10–49. 6, 83. 12–14. Since two opposed counterpositions have now been introduced, the heads which follow are naturally doubled; each party takes the role of (so to speak) defendant in his own and prosecutor in the opponent's counterposition.

87. 2–9 **relative importance:** See *73. 14 f., 83. 15 f. The conflict of law gives this heading a distinctive colouring: it is not only the material implications of the two positions that are compared (e.g. which has the more important consequences for the city?) but also the authority of the two laws (e.g. which has the greater sanction of antiquity?). For the superiority of old and unrevised laws see e.g. Antiphon 5. 14, Demosthenes 23. 70, 80; for the special prestige of Solon e.g. Aeschines 1. 6, Demosthenes 22. 25–32, 24. 142.

87. 9–19 **which is inclusive and which is included:** Relative importance compares the intrinsic authority of the two laws; the test of inclusiveness compares their respective claims to be upheld in the given circumstances. Upholding the more inclusive law will subsume and preserve the legitimate concerns of the other; insistence on the less inclusive law will annul the other.

As before (see *60. 19, *72. 14–16) Hermogenes finds that his chosen example is not ideal for illustrative purposes (a striking sign of carelessness here, since the head which it fails to illustrate is the one which is distinctive to conflict of law: 84. 15–20). The son's position is in fact fairly clear: he will argue that his opponent's position simply contradicts the law governing title to a ship abandoned in a storm; his own position preserves the law excluding a disinherited son from his father's property, since he is not claiming title to the ship as son—the law's underlying concern is with inheritance, and his claim does not impinge on this. The opponent will find this head more difficult to handle, and Hermogenes' change of example is presumably intended to provide a more balanced illustration.

87. 14–16 **A man raped two young women:** See 41. 9–12. The rape-victim's choice (see Russell 1983, 34, who oddly calls it the rapist's choice)

was a fruitful source of declamation themes. This case is found in Seneca *Contr.* 1. 5, Quintilian 7. 7. 3. It was controversial. Some argued that the simultaneous rape invalidates the theme on grounds of impossibility. Others argued that it was invalid on the grounds of equivalence, there being no distinction between the offence and the person of the victim and the order of the two crimes being undefined (*RG* 5. 106. 25–107. 9, 202. 25–9; 4. 819. 6–12); Minucianus replied that the equivalence is broken by the different requests (*RG* 4. 270. 9–25, cf. 4. 137. 19–25, 266. 19–267. 24, 7. 225. 1–20; Nilus *ap.* Gloeckner 1901, 46), and Hermogenes' illustrative use of the theme supports this view (the question of which is more inclusive can only arise if the requests are different). Syrianus 2. 196. 9–17 treats the case as practical; cf. Julius Victor 384. 3–6, and see note on *85. 1–4.

87. 19–88. 1 **Forcible definition:** See *73. 16–74. 4.

88. 1 f. **The thesis and what follows:** i.e. thesis, second objection, and counterplea; see *74. 5–13, 83. 17 f.

D. *Exploitation*

The concluding stages (84. 15) are handled as in definition; see *61. 6–18 for quality and intention, and *61. 18–20 for common quality.

ASSIMILATION (88. 3–90. 4)

This issue reverses letter and intent. Where letter and intent makes a distinction in order to set aside the explicit content of the law in favour of an implied meaning, assimilation blurs a distinction so that the explicit content of the law can be extended to cover something not explicitly stated (Quintilian 7. 8. 1 formulates the relation to letter and intent clearly, cf. 7. 10. 3).

The structure is essentially that of definition (88. 8–10), but there are some differences in the primary phase. Hermogenes' division (88. 4–8) is summarized in Figure 10.

A. *Presentation*

88. 11–14 **It is illegal to ridicule anyone by name in comedy:** The case combines traditions about fifth-century laws restricting comedy by name (see Halliwell 1991 for a survey and assessment of the evidence) with the reference to portrait-masks in comedy at Aristophanes *Knights* 230–2.

A. Presentation

> Presentation

B. Primary Argument

> Letter
>
> Assimilation
>
> Definition
>
> Legislator's intention
>
> Importance
>
> Forced definition
>
> Relative importance

C. Secondary Argument

> Counterposition
>
> Objection
>
> Counterplea

D. Exploitation

> Quality
>
> Intention
>
> Common quality

FIGURE 10.   Assimilation

The case is briefly discussed in Sopater 383. 27–384. 15; in *RG* 8. 388. 17–21 the charge brought is evasion (κατασοφισμός = Latin *circumscriptio*, for which see Seneca *Contr*. 6. 3, Zeno 335. 29–336. 26), rather than a breach of the law as such. The variant at *RG* 8. 388. 26–389. 2 is probably a corruption of the theme which Zeno (337. 1–14) treats as definition:- A dramatist is charged under the law when a performance of his comedy evokes calls of 'That's so-and-so!' from the audience.

88. 14 f. **Presentation:** Hermogenes has designated the presentation in other legal issues as presentation of the verbal instrument, i.e. a presen-

tation of the act as a contravention of the letter of the instrument (see *82. 10–13); here, since the letter is possessed by the other party, the presentation is 'of the fact'.

B. Primary Argument

The primary argument differs in a number of details from that of definition. As one would expect, the assimilation precedes the definition (cf. *81. 12–18, 83. 8–11, 84. 9 f.). There is no counterdefinition; this may be (as *RG* 4. 837. 1–7 suggests) because it is tacitly included with assimilation (see on *60. 8–14, *66. 7–12), but I suspect that here the omission is deliberate, and is compensated by the inclusion of forcible definition among the amplificatory heads. In the issue of definition there is a dispute over what constitutes (e.g.) tyrannicide or adultery; so assimilation, the head which actually blurs the distinction, is prepared by a counterdefinition. There is no such dispute here, since neither party asserts that the act in question is an instance of what is explicitly mentioned in the law; the claim is that the two are nevertheless sufficiently similar for the provisions of the law to be extended to cover the act. So here the assimilation does not need to be prepared by counterdefinition, but instead is justified by a tendentious recharacterization of the act (forcible definition) in the course of the following amplification. This illustrates how one party's possession of the letter of the law forces a weaker argumentative strategy on the other (cf. Quintilian 7. 8. 2, *RG* 4. 834. 13–29).

88. 15–17 **Letter:** The explicit provisions of the law are set out in opposition to the charge.

88. 17 f. **Assimilation:** See *60. 8–14; as always, assimilation blurs a distinction, here that between what is explicitly mentioned in the law and what has been done.

88. 18 **Definition:** See *59. 17–60. 6.

88. 18–89. 10 **Legislator's intention:** See *60. 14 f.

89. 10 f. **Importance:** See *60. 15–18.

89. 11 f. **Forcible definition:** See *73. 16–74. 4.

89. 12 f. **Relative importance:** See *60. 15–18.

C. Secondary Argument

The secondary argument (88. 6–8) consists of counterposition, objection, and counterplea; this follows the pattern set in definition (60. 19–61. 6).

A more elaborate structure is found in letter and intent (83. 11–18) and conflict of law (86. 18–88. 2), modelled on the primary argument of counterposition (73. 2–74. 14); the greater elaboration in these issues may have been meant to compensate for the absence of amplificatory heads in the primary argument.

Syrianus 2. 200 has request for intention and gloss before the counterposition, as in definition (cf. p. 107), and sees conjecture, definition, and counterplea as alternative possibilities for the secondary argument.

D. Exploitation

The concluding stages (88. 8) are handled as in definition; see *61. 6–18 for quality and intention, and *61. 18–20 for common quality.

89. 14–90. 4 **There are many classes of assimilation:** These kinds of assimilation are variants not of the issue (as with the kinds distinguished in conjecture, definition, or counterplea), so much as of the head; i.e. they are ways in which the effective equivalence of the letter and the act may be argued. Hence they have no effect on the division (89. 14 f.). In Hermogenes' scheme 'greater' and 'lesser' apply to what is specified in the law (e.g. the law licenses killing, which is greater than and therefore implicitly includes the beating administered), as in Quintilian 5. 10. 88; in Syrianus 2. 198. 24–199. 16 and *RG* 5. 105. 13–27, 206. 14–207. 2 the terminology is reversed.

Minucianus recognized an additional category, distinguishing similarity from equality (*RG* 7. 1023. 28–30, Nilus *ap.* Gloeckner 1901, 43 f.; cf. Calboli Montefusco 1986, 192 f.).

89. 21 f. **A hero shall receive a reward:** The reasoning behind this example is that if there is a reward for heroism there should be a penalty for desertion; the law rewarding heroism therefore implies that the general's action against the deserter is legitimate (cf. *RG* 5. 206. 22–5; in *RG* 5. 105. 24–7 the theme is reversed: a legal penalty for desertion grounds a hero's claim to a reward).

AMBIGUITY (90. 5–92. 11)

The difficulty faced in ambiguity is that both sides appeal to the explicit contents of the same law, but the explicit content to which each side appeals is different because the law is read in different ways. Obviously, where the law is so uncertain the party which can produce stronger 'logical' arguments in its own support will have a great advantage; this is why Hermogenes says that ambiguity tends not to occur as a self-sufficient issue (90. 9–15). It is perhaps because he does not believe that it will in general be used on its own that Hermogenes gives this issue rather cursory treatment. Some denied that the issue had any validity on its own (see Syrianus 2. 201. 15–22, *RG* 4. 845. 8–14, 7. 226. 13–24, 682. 16–683. 18). Hermogenes' division (90. 6–9) is summarized in Figure 11.

A. Presentation	Presentation
B. Primary Argument	Alternative presentation Legislator's intention Inclusive and included
C. Secondary Argument	Counterposition Objection Thesis
D. Exploitation	Quality Intention Common quality

FIGURE 11. Ambiguity

A. Presentation

91. 2–5 **If a prostitute wears gold ornaments:** See 41. 16–20. The case is found at Cicero *Inv.* 2. 118, Theon *Prog.* 129. 19 f.

91. 5 f. **Presentation:** See *82. 10–13.

B. Primary Argument

The response to the presentation is an alternative construal of the law's explicit content; both parties then attempt to show that their position corresponds to the implicit intention of the law and is the more inclusive. Since the dispute is about the explicit content of the law, there is no need for headings such as exclusion of distinctions, definition, and assimilation.

91. 6 f. **Alternative presentation:** In conflict of law, the alternative presentation is of a different law (*85. 9–12); here, it is of the same law differently construed.

91. 7–12 **Legislator's intention:** See *60. 14 f.

91. 12–15 **Inclusive and included:** See *87. 9–19.

C. Secondary Argument

91. 15–92. 2 **counterposition:** See *73. 2–9. Note that here it is the prosecutor rather than the defendant who uses counterposition (in the form of a counteraccusation). It is a reasonable assumption that this will be the pattern wherever counterposition arises in ambiguity; a defendant with a plausible counterpositional argument to offer would not have based the defence on an ambiguity in the law. But in some cases of ambiguity, such as the dispute between Leon and Pantaleon (*41. 21–42. 4), there will be no counterposition; the argument is purely about the correct reading of the will, and in the absence of circumstantial detail no logical question is raised at all.

92. 2–7 **objection:** See 73. 13 f. The objection here is based on person; because the behaviour of a professional prostitute cannot be judged by the same criteria as that of free women, the moral attack on the defendant in the prosecutor's counteraccusation is misconceived.

Hermogenes states elsewhere (*48. 10–49. 6) that objection is always opposed by counterplea, but that head is missing here. Where the defence uses a counteraccusation to justify the act charged (as at 73. 2–5) there is good reason to counter the objection and round off the defence by reasserting the legitimacy of the act; it would be pointless for the prosecutor to do anything of the kind here. Instead the move towards generality heralded in the handling of the counterposition as a common topic (92. 2) is further developed through the thesis (90. 9), for which see *67. 13–18. In a case which turns solely on the interpretation of a legal instrument, this turn from particular facts towards generality is not surprising.

D. *Exploitation*

The concluding stages (90. 9) are handled as in definition; see *61. 6–18 for quality and intention, and *61. 18–20 for common quality.

4 Illustrations

In Libanius' *Declamation* 44 a general has executed a foreigner who illegally entered the assembly. In doing so he was acting in strict accordance with the law; but the foreigner claimed before his death to have some secret to reveal, and shortly afterwards a tyrant seized power. The suspicion arises that the general was deliberately preventing the disclosure of a conspiracy to which he was party. After the tyrant is deposed the general is prosecuted for complicity; he denies the charge, so the issue is conjecture. The underlying structure of the case is similar to that at Hermogenes *56. 26–57. 11: a killing which pre-empts the disclosure of a conspiracy raises suspicion about the motive behind the killing.

If it is concluded that the general killed the intruder in a deliberate attempt to silence the foreigner, he will be found guilty. He must therefore establish an alternative intention, i.e. that he was upholding the law which required the general to kill any foreign intruder in the assembly. This law is therefore the crux of the defence; presumably the prosecution would claim (in its objection to the counterplea) that it was an abuse of the law to apply it in the given circumstances, but Libanius makes no attempt to counter this argument. Contrast the treatment recommended for a similar theme at *RG* 5. 147. 9–20:- Exiles have arrested a man they suspect of conspiring to establish a tyranny, and brought him home; the general, who is required by law to execute exiles caught in home territory, puts them to death and frees their prisoner; the man does seize power, and after his overthrow the general is charged with complicity.[1] To counter the transposition of cause ('I acted in order to uphold the law') the prosecutor will argue that the law on exiles, being designed to

---

[1] Another related theme appears, without analysis, at *RG* 8. 407:- Young men who suspect a conspiracy apply to the general for weapons; because the law forbids the carrying of arms at night he refuses; the tyranny is established; and the general is prosecuted after its overthrow.

protect and not to endanger the security of the state, was not meant to apply in situations of this kind; this point will be argued out on both sides using the heads of letter and intent, so that the case interlinks conjecture with one of the legal issues. Zeno 335 treats a variant of the theme in the same way, and *Sopater 220–3 takes a similar approach to a related counterpositional case.

Libanius' declamation follows the standard division of conjecture very closely.

1–5 **Prologue:** The general's prologue dovetails with the peroration of the imagined prosecutor's speech. As we know from Hermogenes (52. 8–10), the prosecution will include in the epilogue a common topic against tyranny; by endorsing the condemnation of tyranny (1 f.) the defendant begins to establish his democratic credentials. He also directs the jury's attention towards the amplificatory part of the prosecution, and away from the argumentative base which gives it cogency and point.

In the second prologue (3 f.) the general invites the jury's sympathy for his misfortunes. By representing these misfortunes as a continuation of the sufferings of tyranny he deftly turns this common topic against the prosecutor, who is now placed in the role of tyrant himself. This move engages the jury's concern to uphold the democratic constitution with the defence's request for a sympathetic hearing.

The third prologue (5) shows how the verdict will affect the city's reputation: how wisely does it choose its generals? This invokes one of the heads of purpose (honour) on the side of acquittal. The jury can only find the general guilty if they are willing to admit to a gross misjudgement in electing him; but this will expose the city to ridicule.

6–12 **Preliminary statement:** To launch directly into the facts of the case at the beginning of the narrative was seen as lacking in artistry; it is better to begin with a preliminary narrative or preliminary statement which will set matters in a context.[2] Here the speaker picks up from the prologue the point about the city's choice of generals, developing it into a vivid picture of his own election (6–8) and then into a sketch of his performance in office. He emphasizes both his military service (9) and his devotion to the laws (10); in particular, the law on which his defence will

---

[2] See [Hermogenes] *Inv.* 108. 20–119. 19; cf. Anon. Seguerianus 58. Preliminary statement was defined by Apsines (242) as 'a way of approaching, or preparation for, the arguments'; cf. Troilus *PS* 52, and the metaphorical use of the term in *RG* 7. 500 for the preparation of an argument. (Apsines is quoted by Syrianus 2. 64, who however sees preliminary statement as a brief preview of the narrative proper.) Sopater 58. 1–7, 80. 22 f., associates preliminary statement especially with cases involving pathos.

turn is shown to have a crucial bearing on his military responsibilities (11 f.). Thus the speaker prepares his defence by presenting himself as someone concerned to uphold the laws in general, and as having a particular *ex officio* commitment to the law under which he acted.

13–16 Statement: The crucial events and their sequel are explained. As pointed out in the note to Hermogenes *47. 8–48. 2, rhetorical narrative is distinguished by its slanted nature. Here note the unfavourable characterization of the foreigner ('boldness'); the foreigner is discovered by the crowd, which takes the initiative in calling for action (14); the legality of the killing is emphasized (15), as is the consent of the assembly (16); and the speaker carefully avoids conceding that the tyranny was a consequence of his act ('somehow').

17–67 Argument: A reference to the celebrations of liberty binds the beginning of the argumentative section to the prologue (3). In mentioning the paradox of his position—his crime is to have obeyed the law—the general touches lightly on an exception, identifying the 'peculiarity' of the charge which the counterplea will examine more closely (57).

17–29 Demand for evidence: This is carefully elaborated:

(i) 17–19: It is unreasonable and undemocratic (18: as in the prologue the charge of tyranny is turned back against the prosecutor) to ask a jury to convict on so serious a charge on the basis of an unsubstantiated assertion; so where are the witnesses? This section uses three of the techniques of development recommended in Syrianus 2. 70 for the demand for evidence: parallel cases (17); circumstances (the list of persons in 18); lesser cases (the argument *a fortiori* in 19).

(ii) 20–7: In this case, unlike some others, it is unreasonable to appeal to probability (20); the crime by its nature requires collaborators, some at least of whom would have a strong motive for informing against the general (24). So the absence of witnesses is particularly significant in this case.

(iii) 28 f.: If there had been witnesses, the jury would have weighed their motives and credibility with care; *a fortiori* it is unreasonable to accept the prosecutor's unsubstantiated claim in the absence of witnesses.

30–49 Motive and capacity: The speaker has argued that it would be unreasonable to convict him on the basis of probability alone (20); now he argues that probability in fact acquits him (30). He develops at length his lack of motive for the crime (30–7), and briefly dismisses his evident capacity as irrelevant in the absence of motive (42–4: this use of motive to counter capacity agrees exactly with the recommendations of Sopater 10. 5–23). In 45–9 the fact that he was not one of the beneficiaries of the tyranny is brought in to substantiate his lack of motive. It may be observed that the speaker retained his office under the tyranny (49); this is a potentially damaging point, and the speaker treats it with due caution, but Libanius is apparently willing to assume that the prosecutor would have made no particular capital out of it.

50–6 **Sequence of events:** The speaker's analysis dwells on his own failure to expose the conspiracy. The prosecution would argue that this is a suspicious circumstance, since a conspiracy known to a foreigner should have been known to the man charged with protecting the city's security. The general shows that his ignorance was only to be expected (52–6); but he begins with some misdirection, responding in 50–2 as if his failure to expose the conspiracy were a grounds of complaint rather than of suspicion. For the argument here cf. Hermogenes 69. 3–13; and compare Hermogenes *69. 13–16 with the mitigation at 59–61. The general is using lines of argument characteristic of counterplea based on act and contingency because a powerful counterplea is at the heart of his defence; and he immediately invokes this counterplea in reply to the final and crucial step in the sequence of events, which is the killing itself.

57 f. **Counterplea:** The killing was required by law; the speaker dwells on the paradox (cf. 17) that he is being tried because he obeyed the law.

59–64 **Transposition of cause:** This head too is carefully worked out. First a set of motives is constructed (59): respect for the law; anger at the illegal intrusion; suspicion of the foreigner's motives—in elaborating this point the speaker tries to show how the foreigner's behaviour could reasonably have been interpreted as harmful to the city (59–61). Thus the general acted in accordance with the law, and under a reasonable misapprehension; the transposition of cause therefore rests in part on mitigation. But the counterpositions commonly keep each other company, and there are also elements of counteraccusation, since the foreigner's behaviour was suspicious (62 f.: the speaker perhaps takes a risk in encouraging the jury to wonder why the foreigner chose not to take his information to the general's office), and of transference, since the onlookers—who could have prevented the killing—did not intervene and so consented to and furthered the general's act (64).

65–7 **Persuasive defence:** Strictly speaking, this head is not available to the general: if he was a conspirator he had to kill the foreigner in self-protection (cf. Hermogenes 51. 3–11). But he can point to his behaviour during and after the counter-revolution as proof of his innocence: if he was implicated in the tyranny he would not have remained in the city.

68–81 **Epilogue:** After a brief recapitulation (at the end of 67; cf. Hermogenes 52. 15 f.) the general introduces the common topic against malicious accusers to discredit his prosecutor (68–71). At the end of this section he reintroduces the head of purpose already used in the prologue, pointing out the implications of the jury's verdict for the city's reputation (71, cf. 5). In 72–5 a further head of purpose is explored (cf. Hermogenes 52. 19–53. 1): the consequences of condemning a general for upholding the law will be extremely damaging to the city. In 76–9 the speaker excites pity (cf. Hermogenes 52. 16 f.). He pointedly avoids the parade of weeping relatives (76, cf. Hermogenes 52. 17 f.: note how even in referring to his children he sustains the emphasis on his respect for the laws), so that he can strike a soldierly pose and remind the jury of his military services (77). But this leads into a pathetic apostrophe to his disheartened comrades (78 f.: stylistic devices such as the anadiplosis 'bear up, men; bear . . .' reflect the heightened emotional tone), which ends by emphasizing his misfortune. The speech ends (80 f.) with a piece of self-portrayal which neatly brings back into focus the central point of the defence.

LIBANIUS *DECLAMATION* 44

> There is a law that any foreigner seen in the assembly is to be executed by the general. A foreigner was seen in the assembly; when placed under arrest he claimed to have a secret to disclose; the general executed him. Subsequently a tyranny was established in the city. After the tyrant's overthrow the general is charged with complicity.

1   The evils of tyranny, gentlemen, and the fact that this is the worst of all the adversities that afflict mankind, have I think been set out clearly enough by the prosecutor, whose speech was equal to our misfortunes. But as for my being an accomplice in any of these conspiracies against you, or the despot's having been imposed on the city with my support—

2   by god, I do not see that he has done anything at all to prove this. As for yourselves, if you regard the gravity of the matter as a grounds of complaint against me, and if you think it right to punish those who have

done you no wrong for what you suffered at the tyrant's hands, then do what you will. But if what you suffered at his hands has no bearing on my being disloyal to the city, then do not allow me to be ruined by speeches against tyranny, and do not direct the anger you feel on that account against a man in whom you have placed your trust.

I must be one of the most unfortunate men in the city. Everybody else   3
is celebrating and wearing garlands and rejoicing in the change of government; I alone experienced the afflictions of tyranny and yet am deprived of the blessings of freedom. In fact, it seems to me that those   4
who claim to be great supporters of democracy and warriors against tyranny are prolonging the hardships of tyranny and opposing the blessings that come from freedom. To resort to malicious abuse and seek to kill a citizen by the verdict of a jury that you have deceived—this is worse than when such things are suffered on a tyrant's word of command. In the latter case, it is in keeping with the times; one who is enslaved is used to suffering injustice. But when the rule of law is apparently established and there is a semblance of democracy, illegal execution is a greater misfortune for the victim and brings greater shame on those who voted for it; the one suffers and the others imitate the crimes of tyranny in a time of liberty. So if you are concerned for the genuine reinstatement of our constitution, listen sympathetically to the defendant's speech as well.

I think I would not be wrong in saying that while my life is at stake,   5
so too is the reputation of the city: is one to suppose that it is sensible and prudent, or not? For the generalship, unlike the right to address the assembly, is not granted to everyone who wishes;[3] it is the man you choose because you judge him qualified to administer the most important of your affairs who is appointed to command your forces. So if you recognize the justice of my case the defendant will be saved, and the city will gain glory from being seen to entrust itself to men of integrity. If, on the other hand, you prefer the abuse of malicious informers to the just defence, I will die, and you will gain a reputation for outstanding stupidity, since you choose as generals people you are going to execute as the worst kind of criminal.

I want to call to mind, gentlemen, the day on which you held the elec-   6
tions to official posts, and appointed me to lead your forces in preference to many other candidates. The assembly had convened; the election of generals was under consideration. There was not a little uproar, an abundance of speeches; and this was the kind of thing the speakers said: 'Our

---

[3] Alluding to the formula by which a topic is thrown open for discussion at the assembly (cf. 13 below).

security lies in our army; the army's security lies in the general above all.

7 He should be no ordinary person, but someone tried and tested.' One man spoke in favour of so-and-so; you paid no attention. Another expressed admiration of someone else; you would not hear of it. The same, I think, with the third and fourth nominations: there were supporters, but others were unconvinced. You found fault with the ancestry of some, others were poorly educated, others lacked military experience, others were not quick to discover the necessary course of action, others

8 lacked the capacity to implement their decisions. But when someone mentioned me, you all, gentlemen—even if it is somewhat vulgar to say so, I will not keep silent: you all agreed. The whole assembly broke into applause and reacted as if it had heard the name it had been seeking all along; and it made the election with joy and with good hope.

9 So I took charge of your affairs and tried not to disappoint the expectations of those who had elected me. I had no intention of reaping the benefits of power for myself and increasing my own wealth; my sole concern throughout was to neglect nothing which could serve the common interest. The troops know of my labours, the sleep I lost, how often I trained them in exercises, how I honoured those who performed well and disciplined those who did not, deployments, positions seized, caution in defence, alertness in attack, ambushes, stratagems, exhortations,

10 battles, the foundations of victory. But I believe that the best general should not give thought for mastery outside the city while ignoring what happens within the walls. So, although I was by no means ignorant of the laws before, I took pains to know them better, and especially those whose preservation is the responsibility of the generals. I knew that the city is superior to its enemies because of the laws by which it is governed, but is thrown into confusion if they are disturbed. So victory over our

11 enemies should lie less in force of arms than in the rule of law. So I saw all of them as advantageous and worthy of protection, but above all the law which forbids a stranger to take any part in our assemblies. Why? Because, gentlemen, the confidentiality of one's plans is a matter of great moment. The same resolution brings advantage to those who voted on it if it is kept secret, but if it is made public before being put into effect

12 it is futile, and may indeed do harm to those who passed it. I knew, then, that while this law was in effect there was military advantage in it, while military action was pointless if it was set aside. So I took care during meetings of the assembly that the gathering consisted purely of citizens, who would of necessity be loyal to their country, and that no one should be present who might readily disclose the decisions reached there to our

adversaries. I myself looked in every direction, as did those to whom I assigned this duty—and they were numerous. For I placed my hopes of victory in the assembly's meetings; and that no one outside should learn our secrets was, one might say, of more use to us than allies. This, I suppose, is the reason why the legislator summoned the general, not the other officials, to take action against the foreigner; he knew that the man who stands to gain most from the law's not being infringed would take most care to apply it strictly.

On other occasions foreigners submitted to our laws, and no one was 13 found whose boldness overcame his caution. But on one occasion we took our seats; there was intense concern, and the debate was about matters of the utmost importance; the herald asked 'Who wishes to speak?' When those who had considered the matter stood up, I looked at each in obedience to the law, and made a tour of those who had been assigned this task. Suddenly there was a shout and an uproar: 'This foreigner is 14 forcing his way in and finding out what is said, what is decided, what is approved, and what is rejected; and, wherever he comes from, he is going to get away with a knowledge of the city's affairs. The general is doing nothing, there is no sign of punishment; is there no sword here at all?' That is what was seen and what was said; and what should I have done? 15 Commended the man and awarded him a crown and told him to look on the law as empty verbiage? Thrown the assembly open to foreigners? No one will say that. What is left? To make an arrest and uphold the law by action. So I did what it would have been criminal to have left undone. To be sure, he said what those who are detained for execution always say; but everyone agreed to ignore it, and he suffered the prescribed penalty for this crime. After this you admired the care and dedication with which 16 I scrutinized meetings and the vigour with which I took vengeance on those who despised our city. But somehow accursed tyranny made its way into the city. You know that I was at one with you in hating it. At any rate, whatever was my duty in word or thought or plan or deed for putting an end to these evils—all this was, so I myself believe, a tribute which I paid you with loyal devotion.

The time of lawlessness has passed; we are a democracy again. You 17 offer sacrifices and libations, and everybody is in good spirits—except for me. The general is brought to trial, and (what is strangest of all) for being the tyrant's accomplice in subverting the laws. What is my reply? Straightforward and just. You say that I knew about the tyranny and had a hand in it? Very well; then let anyone who knows this come forward, give evidence, reveal himself to the jury and persuade those who have

taken the juror's oath that they will not be breaking it if they put me to death. That is the proper way to bring a prosecution. 'This man is a thief.' What is the proof? So-and-so gives evidence. 'The accused has committed adultery.' How are we convinced of this? By the evidence of
18 witnesses. Let this then be my salvation now. 'The general was the would-be tyrant's accomplice.' That is the charge; so call witnesses in support of the charge, free or slave, whoever you are able to call, archer or heavy infantryman or cavalryman or slinger or citizen or foreigner. This is the difference between democracy and tyranny: there the master just has to give the order, and you are dead; but here the death penalty cannot be inflicted until the man charged is proven to have committed
19 capital crimes. Do you think you are making a reasonable request when you demand that I be put to death on the basis of an unsubstantiated accusation? If you had charged me with assault or outrage or slander would it not have been just even then for you to be asked in whose presence I committed the outrage, in whose presence I struck the blow, who was present when I uttered the insult? Then when you charge me with the most serious of crimes, one that exceeds anything in human power—for what greater impiety could there be than tyranny? When you bring such a charge against me, do you think you will convince the jury by offering them signs and shadows?

20 Some crimes, gentlemen, need only one malefactor; others gain their strength from the collaboration of many. For example, suppose someone plotted to kill his enemy as he goes home from dinner at night. He could do this alone; he would have no need to summon assistance for the murder, nor to reveal his plan to those whose help he did not need. Or again: a doctor poisoned so-and-so, either out of personal hostility or because he was paid to do so. If he was tried on the basis of probability he could not reasonably object and insist that a witness should be present to give evidence against him. Why not? Because his hands and his skill were enough for the crime, just as in the case of the man who killed his enemy
21 his hands and his sword were enough. Even so, we see these people too shouting out, 'Are we to die without witnesses?'—and many think their complaint reasonable. But tyranny is not like that. A man with that ambition must communicate his intention to many others; and an accomplice, gentlemen, must share his complicity with many others. For the general to be an accomplice without the others knowing is com-
22 pletely impossible. Consider: assuming he told me what he intended to do and disclosed his aspirations, he would not have told me because he thought that my being informed of what was going on was in itself of

any use to him, but to gain the advantage of my orders presenting no obstacle to him if he were detected. So a general who was collaborating 23 should have discussed with the whole army the need to let so-and-so subvert the laws, and should have explained that he favoured the enterprise; or, if not to the whole army, to the senior officers and those others whose job it would have been to restrain the troops in the moment of crisis. If I knew, but they did not and would have interfered if they became aware of the plot, what good would my involvement have been to the tyrant without that of the men I commanded?

Why have I gone into this? To make it clear to you, gentlemen, that 24 if there is any truth in these charges the very nature of the affair would make available many witnesses. Even if they kept quiet then, out of deference to my distinction and the honour in which you held me, now that I am on trial and subjected to abuse they would give their support, encouraged by the situation. A general often makes himself unpopular with his followers by ordering them to work hard, criticizing those who hold back in battle, and discriminating against such people in the distribution of booty. Some of them should have stood by the prosecutor and 25 testified that the charges are true—and not a few of my servants as well, by god. An affair of this magnitude would have needed much discussion and much time; every day we would have needed to get together in person for consultations, or else confer with each other through intermediaries and send and receive messages about the affair. That, I think, is obvious to everyone. If the prosecutor claims that those who performed these services were members of my household, why does he not call them as witnesses? If friends of mine, why does he not make use of them? You 26 see those who supported the tyrant and maintained his power; some were bodyguards, some guarded the acropolis, some gave whatever assistance he ordered. If you ask them whether they knew about each other before the tyranny, they will say they did know. No individual would have dared if he could not look to collaborators. So if I was a member of 27 the conspiracy, and they knew that, as they knew each other, why do you not bring them forward, as well as the others? Because, gentlemen, there cannot be witnesses to what was not done. It is not surprising that the prosecutor has no evidence; but it is reasonable for me to demand it, and for you to join me in requiring it and to force him to provide it. For diligence over witnesses will save me, and will exempt you from the curse.[4] Come, if he had bribed people to come here and proclaim that I was an 28

[4] The jurors would place themselves under a curse if they were to break their oath by returning an unjust verdict; cf. 68 below.

accomplice, that I was implicated, would that have been enough for you? Would you have thought that you had to find me guilty? Would you not have looked into who was saying these things—whether they were my enemies, whether they have often given false evidence? Since you would have distrusted witnesses had they been present, will you trust the pros-

29 ecutor's assertions in their absence? In that case you will raise up a profusion of people willing to bring malicious charges. As things stand they sometimes hold back because if they come into court without witnesses it is thought they are talking nonsense. But if they know that there is no need of evidence, that punishment is directly annexed to the charges, there will be no end to the ruination of one citizen or another. It is the easiest thing in the world to act shamelessly in bringing a charge; it follows that they will accuse, you will condemn, and no defendant ever will go free.

30 Before now someone at a loss for witnesses has given the impression of saying something sensible by turning his attention to the defendant's motives, and showing that they are open to criticism. But in the present case that does not strengthen the charge so much as undermine it, and I am freed from the charge both by the lack of witnesses and also because probability suggests that I am loyal to the city. Who does not know that the people who try to change the existing constitution and are attached to some other are those who do badly out of the present state of affairs

31 and hope to do better out of a change? Those expelled from a city ruled by a tyrant long for laws and equality of political rights, and they try to restore them. But someone who is disadvantaged by the rule of law tries to subvert the laws. So who are those who fight against the laws? Those whose fathers were punished under them, those who owe money to the treasury, those disfranchised by the courts, those whose way of life debars them from public speaking, those who know that while the laws stand they cannot avoid being punished for their many crimes.

32 In which class do you place me, informer? What has made me an enemy of the constitution? Was I in prison? Was I a state debtor? Was I legally deprived of my right to speak? Was my property confiscated? Had I been caught in some vice? Was it suffering some severe penalty that made me want to overturn everything? Or is none of that so, but being a man of integrity I displayed my character among people of a very different sort? Was I not praised? Was I not admired? Was I not put in charge of the army? Did I not command the forces? Was I not envied, prosperous, and renowned among you? Was I not feared by our enemies?

33 Is there anyone who would deprive himself of such advantages? By god,

only a madman. Why should a man in possession of his senses do so? What would he be aiming at in place of what he has? I had been thought worthy of the generalship; did I impose a despot on the constitution to which I owed my position? Do I choose to be, and to be thought, ready to stop at nothing, so that someone else could gain unjust power? If I had been going to be the tyrant myself, would I have wanted to be tyrant instead of general, something impious in place of something lawful and constitutional? To what end? To be honoured? What is nobler than honours from the people, free of compulsion—which alone deserve to be called honours. A tyrant is flattered, but not honoured in the least. A man who is cursed by those who bow down to him—will anyone class him among those who receive honour? Or so that I could live in luxury, molest women, and plunder property? That was not the character in which I was brought up, nor was I trained to love such vices. You are witnesses to that by the generalship. By this one thing you testify to integrity, ancestry, superiority to pleasure, the pursuit of excellence in all things, schooling in the finest occupations, and everything that a man might pray to have himself. The generalship is an unmistakable sign that I have practised virtue from childhood. Would someone who held it already and had received the highest honours turn from the rewards of virtue to crime, and make the prize of his nobility the beginning of his depravity? It is not in the nature of honours to have that effect; they turn worthless men into good men, they do not turn a good man the other way. So the generalship was the reward for my previous life and an encouragement to hold still more firmly to virtue. Do you think a man who would have refused to be tyrant himself would have chosen to attach himself to a tyrant in the role of a satellite? Which is better: to be the leader of so many noble men, or to be the slave of one corrupt man? To be crowned after victories, or to satisfy the shameful lusts of a drunkard? To be named in proclamations, or to prostrate oneself before a despot? You there, you who bring others to judgement so lightly, if you had received at the people's hands what I received would you have committed the crimes you attribute to me? I am glad you are indignant at the suggestion. Then don't imagine that you act justly towards those who honour you while I, in the midst of my honours, betray those who trusted me.[5]

You heard the prosecutor making the utterly fatuous claim that the tyrant would have bought my allegiance for a great price, and that it was

34

35

36

37

38

---

[5] Compare Aristotle *Rhet.* 1398ᵃ3–8.

in my power to help him if I wanted. Who does not know that those who wage war, whoever their opponents are, would be delighted to purchase the other side's generals? Does that make all generals traitors, all bribed, all betrayers of their kith and kin? No. Those who are depraved by nature sell themselves, but people who would like to pervert the judgement of good men can effect no change; despite attempts to corrupt them they

39 retain their integrity. The other party's aims should not be used in evidence against good men. Suppose that, when I was serving blamelessly against the enemy, someone had brought forward enemy deserters and charged me with treason, claiming that the deserters knew it had often been said on the other side, 'If someone persuaded the enemy general to turn traitor, he would be very welcome.' If someone said that and demanded that I be punished, is there anyone who would have been con-

40 vinced? No one is so gullible. So the person who would not have been thought to favour the enemy, just because the enemy would have valued that, is he to be thought an accomplice in tyranny, just because gaining my support would have been a great coup for the tyrant? A man who falls in love with a chaste woman does not, by his mere desire, compromise her honour, if she does not even know of her admirer. Do not say, then,

41 that he would have wanted to have me as partner in crime, but prove that I chose to become his partner in crime. Do not bring me to court and accuse him. My wickedness is not to be inferred from other people's wishes; the general's intentions should be judged on their own account—and if you cannot show that they are corrupt, do not base malicious charges on the intentions of the tyrant.

42 As for his claim that I had the power to help the tyrant, a brief reply is sufficient. If men do automatically whatever it is in their capacity to do, then I collaborated with the tyrant, I am a criminal, I should be punished, convict me. But where the will does not give the lead to action, capacity is of no avail. Without the will, no crime is committed; so how is it just for the man who had only the power to be brought to account?

43 A helmsman can easily wreck his ship on the rocks; does that mean helmsmen actually do so? No. Why? Because they do not want to. Priests can easily live luxuriously off dedications. Do they commit this crime—those who are not corrupt—just because they have the power? By no means. Jurymen can easily record unjust verdicts, but because they

44 respect justice they cast their votes justly. What need is there for other examples? Does it take much effort and forethought to murder one's servant in his sleep, suffocate one's son, and kill oneself? What is easier, gentlemen? Does that mean each of you has done one thing, or another,

or all of them? It would have to be so, if the capacity leads to the action. But it is not capacities which make people will; capacity is the servant of the will in every case.

Because he cannot say that I am corrupt, he will babble about capa-   45
city. This is nonsense not because I declare myself innocent of the charge, but because of the actual facts. Does anything done after he had seized power bear witness to my having taken pleasure in the outrage? Did I live on the acropolis? Did I have a bodyguard? Was I party to his plans, his concerns, his secrets, his words, his deeds? Did I persuade him of this or give way to him in that? Was anyone sent into exile on my account? Or stripped of his property? Or deprived of his wife? Or made to drink poison? Did any of those who brought down orders say 'This is the tyrant's order, this is the general's'? Did I hand over to him the heavy infantry, or any of the archers? Did I make any use of the lawlessness under the tyranny? Is there anyone so wretched that he would take a   46
share in the impiety of a matter in which one could enjoy the utmost pleasure—and then have no more part in it? As if a man broke into a house with someone else, and after he had undergone the frightening part and it was possible to share out in safety the property for which all the risks had been run, he were to decline. Why, you idiot, did you com-   47
mit the crime for nothing? Why did you take a share in the hardships, but not continue it as far as getting some advantage? Is that what you see the associates of traders doing, gentlemen? Does anyone undergo the sea and the perils of the sea, and then on getting into harbour go off home with empty hands, resigning the profits to someone else? Am I the only   48
person in the world to set up a tyrant with a view to having no part in the pleasures of tyranny? Who would believe that? It would be more sensi-ble to be willing to profit from a despotism that one had no hand in bringing about once it had been established, than for someone who had laboured to establish it to shun involvement when there was an oppor-tunity to enjoy the results. As it is, I used the generalship to weaken the   49
tyranny so far as was possible, but I did not take the fruits of tyranny in return for the generalship. Is it not absurd that the tyrant's associates should be punished for that very fact, but someone who shunned associ-ation with him should get no credit for that, but earn the same reputa-tion as those who did the opposite?

What, then, is the proof of my complicity? 'Someone else', he says,   50
'came to expose the tyranny, and a foreigner at that; you said nothing.' It was not possible, sir, to proclaim what I did not foresee. And the fact that the plot was not perceived is the fault of the skilful criminals, not of

those who were ignorant. If this is my fault, why mine alone, by the gods? Am I the only one whose duty is to care for the city, and the rest of the citizens need have no concern? But why do I talk about the citizens? These speakers here, who put themselves forward and bring charges and are so persuasive; the people who claim that the security of everything lies in their voices, and who are upset if they are not awarded crowns—why are they not brought to trial on these counts? They too did not perceive the plot, but are influential among you. But I leave the orators aside; what about the magistrate here, and the executive committee, and the council which manages most of our affairs—why are they not summoned on the same charges? It is not wrong that these people are free of the charges—no, by god! But it is wrong that I should not be free. How many people, since cities were first inhabited, have arrogantly set themselves up against the laws? Innumerable. How many have been caught before achieving their ambition? Not a few. Were they all detected by the generals before anyone else? No. This one was detected by the general, that one by an orator, another by one of the market-traders, another by a servant, another by his wife, another however it chanced to happen. The people who find buried treasure are not the ones who deserve to be rich, but those—whoever they may be—who are lucky; in the same way, one of the masses has had the good fortune to discover this sort of plot before men of distinction. It stands to reason that matters of this kind are perceived by people of no great worth rather by than those in prominent positions. The criminal tries to escape the notice of those he fears; but he relaxes his vigilance a little towards someone he is able to despise. If he hears the general, he shudders; if he hears some nameless individual, he is confident. So in the one case he is cautious, in the other a little negligent—and in that way one of his secrets is laid bare. The same happens with dishonest servants. Those who are trying to steal their masters' property are often informed on by people one would not have expected, while the steward was aware of nothing. By god, even one of the neighbours knows of the plot before the fellow-slaves. So is it surprising if the same happens in the city's public affairs, too, and someone plotting against the laws manages to elude the person he thought would prevent him, but is seen through by someone he did not imagine would be interested?

'A foreigner came to speak.' Naturally. If someone is plotting against a city he does not make his preparations for seizing power in that city; that would be suicide, not the act of someone aspiring at tyranny. Who would not be suspicious, seeing the number of men gathered together, the quantity of arms in store, the parties, the conferences, the messengers, the flatterers—everything, in short, that is necessary to those who intend to set themselves above the people? This is why, when they plot against one set of people, they get ready what they need for action elsewhere; and why, though they escape the notice of the people whose masters they want to become, they are observed by those among whom they are making ready. So do not say that what by the nature of the matter is usually the case counts against the generals. 56

'You killed the foreigner,' he says, 'although he was bringing us a secret.' Add that the law required it. And ask these people here who it is that sets up a tyranny: those who think the existing laws should be upheld, or those who bring to court the upholders of the law? Could there be anything more peculiar than this? The indictment says that I was an accomplice in tyranny; the proof is that I obeyed the laws. They call the same person an ally of the tyrant and a guardian of the law. I could reasonably have been charged, I would rightly have been hated, if knowing the law and seeing the foreigner I had given what he said precedence over the law. What is the point of making laws at all, if we casually override them when faced with the situation for which they were passed? Is it not absurd that in the same court some should be punished for neglecting the laws, and others for adhering to them? 57 58

He said he was bringing a secret? Agreed. I paid no attention? Agreed. For first of all respect for the law, and secondly anger at the sight of a stranger in the midst of us learning of our affairs—this induced me to punish him, rather than to pay attention to what he said. And then, by the gods, I became suspicious: this fellow has come with hostile intent and has taken a risk in order to get away with knowledge of the city's affairs; and now he has been caught he is making up the usual thing. And what is that? Someone who knows for certain he is going to die makes up stories to cause delay and he tries to distract his captors by making false accusations against them. So those who are ill-disposed towards anyone have them arrested, bound, racked, tortured; they apply every kind of evil from which civil conflict is prone to arise, and which civil conflict brings with it. People in this situation believe that public disturbances will either save them, or postpone their death; and dragging innocent people down with them brings a kind of consolation to those who are dying. I supposed the foreigner was one of those, and I quickly took care, as the law enjoins, for the city's well-being, to prevent some sudden lie throwing everything into confusion. If that was the wrong decision, I was mistaken, but I committed no crime. There is, I think, a 59 60 61 great difference between making a false assumption and supporting a tyrant; and I do not believe that being a loyal general is the same as being a prophet. The fear which I felt was the product of loyalty; to know the future required a different skill.

62   The man himself gave me grounds for suspicion. He ignored me and the executive committee and the other officials, and illegally observed the assembly and heard what was said and ratified there. What would a genuine informant, as distinct from an impostor, have done? He would have gone to the general's office and said that he wanted a meeting with the general: he would have met him alone, talked to him, told him what he knew, explained how the plot began, what progress it had made, who the tyrant was, who his collaborators were. He would not, before giving assistance to the people, have harmed them by showing contempt for the law; nor, when he said he was concerned for the laws, would he have begun his service by subverting the law—which surely he knew was in force, unless, by god, as a foreigner he was ignorant of the constitution

63   he was so anxious about. 'But he arrived when the assembly had already convened.' Let him restrain himself, and wait a little. Let him approach the officials. For surely he was not intending to blurt out the secret in front of the assembly. That would not have been the act of a man handing over the quarry to us, or acting to prevent the evil, but of one trying

64   to throw us into instant turmoil. This is what you yourselves believed; you thought the same as me. And when you saw him being arrested, although it was possible to object and to tell me not to kill him, you let me do it, you encouraged me. By not preventing the killing you expressed your approval; by not criticizing the man who made the arrest you judged it right that the man arrested should suffer that penalty. If you had wanted to save him, what prevented you? Was it not enough to speak a couple of words, and say just this: 'Let him be'? The general is not stronger than the whole people. In that you allowed the execution, so far as was in your power, you conceded that the killing was no bad thing.

65   If this was everyone's will, I should not be the sole defendant. And even apart from the time before the tyranny and what happened during it, my loyalty to the people is proved by what I have been seen to do since the restoration. I did not go into exile, as an old accomplice would have done, nor was I in fear of prosecution if I stayed. I did not think my

66   safety depended on emigration. And yet while the attack was being made on the tyrant, when freedom was being recovered and the whole affair was still in ferment, I could easily have taken my wife and children and

gone to live somewhere else, beyond the reach of your laws and in complete immunity. But I had committed no crime against you, and nothing is sweeter to me than my native land; so I stayed here with confidence, because no fear drove me out. Gentlemen, do not suppose 67 that a lawful killing, done in ignorance of the future, is a clearer indication of dishonesty than my equanimity in the face of the tyrant's overthrow is a token of your general's integrity. Since there are so many things which disprove the charge—my dedication in office, my hatred of the enemy, the concern for the laws which I showed on your behalf, the fact that I stayed with you during the revolution—do not give more weight to the prosecutor's eloquence than to the actual facts.

It is a hateful species, gentlemen, that of malicious accusers, which is 68 nurtured in cities to the detriment of the laws, of decent people, and of sworn jurymen. They tear apart people who have committed no crime, and in so doing they annul the laws and inflict the heaviest penalties on those who are empanelled under oath, as much as on those who are judged. For the latter die; the former live under a curse and bequeathe the damage to their children. Just as we repel our enemies by force of 69 arms, so too the shamelessness and violence of malicious accusers should be warded off by successive juries. Because of them, innocence carries no less risk than a life of crime; the most upright man and the most corrupt are alike subjected to the jury's vote, and in fact more good people perish than bad. The latter think out what they will say when they commit their crimes; the former rely on their previous life, and are delivered unprepared into the hands of practised speakers. You, gentlemen, must 70 make their practice vain, their eloquence impotent, their shamelessness fruitless. As things stand, they have abandoned the other trades by which good citizens live, and live off the law-courts, sharpening their tongues instead of their swords. A man gives them something out of fear: 'Splendid fellow, decent, praiseworthy.' He refuses to pay up because he has done nothing wrong: 'Wicked man, tyrannical, guilty of every crime.' Every member of the jury should realize that he may soon be in the dock, 71 and should leave the vote he cast in others' cases as an example to those who succeed him on the jury, teaching them not to submit to these animals who try to persuade you that the man you praised so recently and who you placed in charge of all your affairs is to be handed over to the public executioner. What could bring more disgrace on the city than when even the generals perish by the verdict of a court, although their aspiration is to die under arms? Do you not realize that, as well as its being unjust to kill the innocent, it makes your enemies despise your generals, on the supposition that it was not for their virtues that they were promoted to that rank?

72   I know that you have been provoked by the word 'tyranny', which the prosecution has bandied about, but you must reflect that before now people have condemned a defendant to death and have regretted it when the mistake could no longer be put right, and the only thing left was self-blame. Do not fall into that trap yourselves. For if you were going to lose only a general, perhaps that would be no great matter; but in reality,

73   gentlemen, what is at stake is the rule of law. How is it that I am brought to trial for keeping the law, the law which grants you victory over your enemies through the concealment of your plans? If I am punished for that guardianship, anyone will be able to annul the laws on religious or military affairs, those concerning treason, those concerning self-control, those concerning temple-robbery and burglary—I say nothing of the

74   rest, gentlemen. Will any foreigner fear to enter our assemblies? Anyone will be able to slip in and make a list of the proposals which prevail when we are seeking our advantage. All our decrees will be published everywhere by land and sea. What secret, by god, will give the city victory over its enemies when they know the plans with which we go out against

75   them to battle? Many will send spies here, and there will be no shortage of people to perform that service; but there will be no one to punish them. Tell me: what general, in the light of my punishment, will fail to understand, whoever he may be, that it is easy for a prisoner to say that he came on the city's behalf, while the same things will attend the law's upholder as did me: prosecutor and indictment? Who is so foolish as to want to be killed by the people he tries to serve?

76   I am going to say to you now what I said to my friends when they advised me to appeal to my children's tears in seeking acquittal. I do have children, gentlemen, brought up in accordance with your laws, whom I have always told to live as the laws require. But I have forbidden anyone to bring them onto the rostrum. A general should not be saved out of pity for his children or his tearful wife or his weeping mother or the grey hairs of his weeping father or his friends and family standing by. Each man should be acquitted or punished for his own deeds. If he is childless but honest, he should go free; if he is the father of many but corrupt, he

77   should die. So who do I ask you to turn your attention to, if not my children? To the good discipline of the troops; the expeditions, the battles, the stratagems, my deeds. Send secretly to the enemy. Find out whether they hate me, and accept that it is a mark of the same spirit to hold no

78   converse either with the city's external or with its internal enemies. Why

do the officers and the troops look gloomy and downcast? Are you calling to mind the infantry battles and the cavalry engagements we won?
Do you miss your commander? Do you remember our concern, our
schemes, our grief when the tyranny was in power? The temples in
which we prayed, the processions in which we took part, the mysteries
we shared, the labours we underwent, the hopes we had? Bear up, men;   79
bear this present trial. No city is free of malicious accusers. And if the
verdict is my death, bear that too. Consider that I have fallen to an
enemy's weapon. Another general will take command of you in my place:
not a better one, perhaps, in other respects, but more fortunate.[6]

I depart having some consolation for my death. I have seen the city   80
free, I have seen the laws in force, I have seen the people convening. I see
trials properly constituted. I go, leaving my children in that secure state.
One thing only disturbs me: the worry that the generals may become
negligent of the laws out of fear, and conclude that it is more in their
interest to please this man than justice. But I say to my successors (suc-   81
cessors in office, I hope, and not in unjust judgements): be less afraid of
any indictment than of failing to do your duty by the laws, and do not
throw the assembly open to foreigners. There are two things above all by
which you will keep the city safe: by force of arms, and by protecting the
established laws.

4.2 DEFINITION

There are many attested declamation themes in which the tyrannicide's
right to claim a reward raises a question of definition (see on
Hermogenes *59. 18–60. 4): what must a claimant have done to qualify?
This section illustrates a number of approaches to a theme of this kind.

(a) Lucian

In Lucian's *Tyrannicide*[7] a man who set out to kill the tyrant in the event
only killed the tyrant's son; but the tyrant committed suicide in consequence, and the man accordingly claims the reward. His case has three

---

[6] An allusion to Euripides *Alc.* 182.
[7] Replies to Lucian's declamation were composed by Erasmus and Thomas More (text
in Erasmus *Opera Omnia* i/1, Amsterdam 1969, 516–51, tr. E. Rummel in Erasmus *Collected
Works* 29, Toronto 1989, 71–123; text and translation in More's *Complete Works* iii/1, New
Haven, Conn. 1974, 94–127). On humanist declamation in general see van der Poel 1987.

main thrusts: that the son was himself a tyrant; that bringing about the father's death indirectly was a way of killing him; that someone who planned and, at his own risk, achieved the death and overthrow of the tyrant has in effect done just what the law on tyrannicide was intended to encourage.

The date of Lucian's birth is uncertain,[8] but is likely to have been a little before AD 120. He claims to have abandoned rhetoric when he was 40 (*Bis acc.* 32); his declamation must therefore have been composed not later than the middle of the second century, antedating Hermogenes. But he was working in the same tradition, and his treatment of the theme is in close agreement with the Hermogenean division.[9]

1–3 **Prologue:** The opening words state concisely the core of the claimant's case: the son was a tyrant; the father was killed. The indirect means by which the father's death was achieved, which the opponent will use to undermine his claim, are presented as a peculiarly appropriate innovation, in anticipation of the climax of the speech's peroration. By stressing his own sole responsibility for the tyrant's death the claimant establishes himself as the jury's benefactor, facing unfair treatment at the hands of an opponent whose motives are vulnerable to prejudicial attack.

4–6 **Preliminary statement:** The claimant prepares for the narrative of the liberation by amplifying the evils from which it freed them. The amplification is carefully focused: what made this tyranny unbearable was the part played in it by the son (for the characteristics of young men see Hermogenes *29. 19–22); so the killing of the son was the greater part of the liberation. An emphatic reference to the demoralizing effect of the tyranny's seemingly inevitable prolongation allows the claimant to begin the narrative proper with a dramatic antithesis stressing his own unique bravery.

7–8 **Statement:** The brief narrative lays the foundation of the argument. First the difficulty of what the claimant did is stressed, and the omission on which the opponent's case rests is trivialized: the father was old, unarmed, and helpless. Then the suspicion that the father's death was an unforeseen consequence for which the claimant can take no credit is excluded; characterization (see p. 16) is used to make the claimant's rea-

---

[8] Baldwin 1973, 10 f.

[9] The treatment of counterplea in Lucian's *Disinherited Son* is somewhat simpler than Hermogenes' division, and is in fact closer to Zeno; see the analysis in Berry and Heath (forthcoming).

soning vivid. The foregrounding of the claimant's sword as co-agent in the act prepares for the epilogue.

9–18 Argument

9 **Presentation:** The claimant begins the argumentative section of the speech by setting out the advantages won through his act; he is careful to remind the jury that he himself has brought about the opponent's freedom to challenge the reward in a court of law. This should ensure an unreceptive response to the suggestion that his act is 'incomplete' (note the allusion to the technical definition of definition: cf. Hermogenes 37. 1).

10 **Definition:** The opponent's definition is introduced as a counter-position,[10] solved by the counterdefinition. This is not explicitly formulated, but implied through a series of questions in which the speaker acts out an unsuccessful search for the alleged incompleteness in his act.

11 **Assimilation:** The assimilation is introduced by a counterposited objection based on the manner of the killing (see Syrianus 2. 108. 19–23 for objection as a standard response to assimilation: the speaker here anticipates and pre-empts this response). The claimant briefly asserts the equivalence of killing and causing death,[11] and at once moves on to substantiate his assertion by appeal to the legislator's intention.

11–13 **Legislator's intention:** The law on tyrannicide aims to secure political liberty; the tyrant's death is only a means towards that end, and its manner is indifferent. This position is elaborated in three ways. First (11) a series of examples illustrates the indifference of the means. Secondly, a parallel law is cited (a technique suggested by Syrianus 2. 109. 18); note how this is introduced with a deft reminder of the interruption of the legal process which the speaker has brought to an end. Finally, a parallel case is cited: if someone who forced a tyrant into exile without killing him was honoured as a tyrannicide, *a fortiori* there should be a reward where the tyrant is killed. Lucian is here making a tongue-in-cheek allusion to another familiar declamation theme; we know from the case of the philosopher's non-violent tyrannicide (Hermogenes *59. 18–60. 4) that the reward in such a case does not go uncontested. There

---

[10] A. M. Harmon, the Loeb translator, is wrong to say (p. 445 n. 1) that the opponent has already spoken; it is standard doctrine in the rhetoricians that a petitioner speaks first (p. 141).

[11] On 'killing' and 'causing death' see Nörr 1986, esp. 36–48, 52–62 (on declamation), 63–77 (on the background in Greek law); Quintilian discusses a case turning on this concept in 7. 3. 30–4.

is another such allusion in 14; the man whose attack put the tyrant to flight, giving someone else the opportunity to kill him, was a standard example of definition involving rival claims (see on Hermogenes *64. 5).

14–18 **Importance:** Lucian introduces an elaborate amplification of the claimant's act with an explicit use of the technical term 'sequence of events' (cf. on Hermogenes *60. 15–18). The steps of the amplification are: I intended to kill a tyrant (14); I acted on my intention (15); I killed someone (16); and the tyrant died (17); indeed, he died a particularly terrible death (18). The last step in the sequence, showing how the indirect way he brought about the tyrant's death makes it a more fitting and painful end than if he had killed the tyrant outright, illustrates the use of relative importance to bring the amplification to a climax.

19–22 **Epilogue:** The speech as a whole reaches its climax with a further round of amplification, more imaginative and using more overt devices of emotional arousal. First is the apostrophe of the claimant's sword (19, picking up a theme introduced in 7). Then techniques of description and characterization learnt in the preliminary exercises are used to bring the tyrant's last moments vividly before the jury's mind (20–1; see p. 16). Theatrical imagery is introduced here, and the finale draws this motif together with the sword, listing the three actors in the claimant's drama, and the sword as their common instrument (22).

(b) Choricius

The same theme was treated in the sixth century by Choricius of Gaza. His *Declamation 7* is too long for inclusion, but it is worth summarizing its structure, which is very different from that of Lucian's declamation and resists analysis according to the Hermogenean division.[12]

After a prologue (1–6) and brief statement (7–17) there is a neat transition to the opposition to the speaker's claim for the reward ('two tyrants have been killed so gloriously; but now, it seems, a third has arisen, who twists the laws . . .'). The argumentative section itself consists of a series of counterpositions with solutions:

18–36 **Definition:** The law specifies the killing of a tyrant, not of a tyrant's son. The reply makes a string of points, but lacks the lucid internal structure of the Hermogenean and similar schemes. Some of the

---

[12] Kustas 1973, 5 n. 3, remarks on the school of Gaza that 'Hermogenes, though probably known to its representatives, is not central to their views as he is in other circles of the Byzantine world.'

arguments are new; e.g. if the tyrant is blamed for the deaths of those victims of his cruelty who committed suicide, then the claimant should take the credit for the tyrant's suicide (35); even if you refuse to call the son a tyrant, he was going to be tyrant, and prevention is better than cure (36).

37–50 **Objection** (based on manner): The reward is a compensation for dangers undergone, and your exploit was not dangerous. The speaker responds by counter-representation (avoidance of risk would not make the achievement less valuable: 40–4) and refutation (the enterprise was in fact extremely dangerous: 45–50).

51–72 **Conjecture:** By killing the son you could have provoked the tyrant into harsher rule. The response is, as theory requires, by motive and capacity; specifically, the claimant analyses the tyrant's state of mind to establish that the suicide was predictable (52–9), and shows in detail why the tyrant's situation was not comparable to that of other fathers who had managed to endure the loss of their children (60–72). Choricius identifies this as a major problem for the speaker in his introductory comments (*theoria* 6), and in the prologue he prepares for this argument by portraying the tyrant's devotion to his only child (4–6).

The next section plays a similar game to Lucian, alluding to the theme in which a tyrant is persuaded to abdicate and asserting *a fortiori* a claim to the reward conceded in such cases (74). Here the speaker argues in some detail for the superiority of the tyrant's death to his voluntary abdication (75–80); these points are not perhaps of great relevance to the case in hand, but provide an interesting pointer to lines of argument for the opposition in the abdication theme. If the tyrant abdicates:

(i) there is a risk of his seizing power again;
(ii) the deterrent to others is removed;
(iii) justice has not been done (any more than if a thief simply returns the stolen goods, without further punishment);
(iv) his victims are deprived of consolation.

The epilogue considers the consequences of refusing the reward (80–2) and amplifies the benefits the claimant has bestowed on the city (83–90)—using as a concluding device a description (cf. p. 16) of the publicly exhibited painting of his exploit which will be the only reward he desires (91–3).

(c) Sopater

Sopater's *Division of Questions* is a collection of declamation themes classified according to their issue, with more or less extensive outlines of the recommended treatment. Sopater allows us to see behind the declaimer's finished product, taking us 'into the very workshop of the rhetor'.[13] Unfortunately, workshops are rarely aesthetically pleasing places, however elegant the products that come out of them, and Sopater is not fun to read. The extract translated here is a variant of one of Hermogenes' examples of definition (*59. 18–60. 4); an orator (instead of a philosopher) persuades a tyrant to abdicate and claims the reward for tyrannicide.

The orator's influence over the tyrant argues a degree of trust and intimacy, and the opposition will no doubt question the orator's motives: was it not an act of friendship on the orator's part to provide a tyrant who saw his regime crumbling with a safe escape? So the orator's association with the tyrant is identified as a point which will need careful handling in the statement. The characterizations which Sopater recommends (cf. Lucian *Tyrannicide* 8 for a speaker using characterization to portray his own state of mind) will provide a vivid way to make clear the orator's motives and the courage it took to face the tyrant and speak frankly to him.

On Sopater's terminology in definition see p. 106 above; since he is taking the claimant's role his usage here coincides with that of Hermogenes (i.e. definition belongs to the second, counterdefinition to the first speaker). In both counterdefinition and assimilation examples are used to illustrate the indifference of manner (cf. Lucian *Tyrannicide* 11). The legislator's intention is not given a convincing formulation; the orator seems to appeal to the simple letter of the law, although the reward is in fact laid down for tyrannicide.

The counterposited conjecture is an element missing in Lucian, and in the Hermogenean division; see p. 109. The argument that the tyrant's survival leaves open the possibility of his return to power is solved by motive (since he has been persuaded that tyranny is a bad thing, he will not want to return) and capacity (having destroyed his credibility by abdicating once he will not be able to recruit supporters); for motive and capacity as the only heads in incomplete conjecture based on person see Hermogenes *56. 14–20.

---

[13] Innes and Winterbottom 1988, 3.

The handling of the end of the case is simpler than Hermogenes' recommendation; the common topic on tyrannicide is introduced without the preparation of individual quality and intention. The head of purpose invoked is consequence, taking Demosthenes 20. 163–7 as a model. The concluding idea, in which the orator pledges to kill the tyrant if occasion arises, shows that the 'omission' in his act is one that he will make up if need be.

(d) Syrianus

Sopater gives us only the bare outline of a declamation; the extracts from Syrianus' commentary on Hermogenes illustrate some of the standard techniques for fleshing such a skeleton out. Syrianus uses the theme for piecemeal illustration, rather than giving a complete division. In Syrianus, as in Hermogenes, it is a philosopher who persuades the tyrant to abdicate.

Syrianus is not a gifted rhetorician. He tends to work through standard techniques, such as the use of the elements of circumstance for amplification, in a mechanical way; and his treatment of individual arguments can be clumsy. Lurking behind his assimilation is a workable argument: the opponent makes the reward depend on a homicide; but homicide *per se* is a bad thing, merely tolerated in the case of a tyrant for the sake of liberty. But Syrianus' attempt at a striking formulation ('if murders secured tyrannicide, one would have to honour murderers with the rewards given to tyrannicides') is inept. Likewise, importance is contorted in its expression. The contention is that the death of a tyrant does not in itself secure the rule of law (since someone else may make himself tyrant), but the rule of law does tend to eliminate tyrannical ambitions; so by re-establishing the rule of law the philosopher has created the conditions which will foster an abhorrence of tyranny; the death of the tyrant would have added nothing; if that is so, then establishing the rule of law is the more inclusive concept.

For Syrianus' additional head, request for intention, see p. 107 above.

LUCIAN *THE TYRANNICIDE*

A man ascended the acropolis intending to kill the tyrant. He did not find the tyrant in person, but killed his son and left his sword in the body. The tyrant came, saw that his son was dead, and killed himself with the same sword. The man who ascended the acropolis and killed the tyrant's son claims the reward as a tyrannicide.

1   I killed two tyrants, gentlemen of the jury, in a single day, one already advanced in years, the other in the prime of youth and the readier to succeed to his father's crimes. Yet I am here to ask a single reward for both—I, the only tyrannicide ever to have done away with two wicked men with a single blow, killing the son with my sword and the father with fondness for his son. The tyrant has paid us penalty enough for his crimes; while he lived he saw his son predecease him, and at last he was made (astonishing as it is) himself to become his own tyrannicide. His son died at my hands; but even in death he was my accomplice in another killing. Alive he shared in his father's crimes; dead he played his part in

2   his father's death. So then I was the one who put an end to the tyranny, and the sword which accomplished it all was mine; but I changed the order of the killings and devised a novel means of putting criminals to death. I myself slew the one who was stronger and better able to defend himself; the old man I gave over to my sword alone.

3   I assumed that you would award me some special distinction for this deed, and that I would receive rewards equal in number to those I killed. For I freed you not only from present ills, but also from the expectation of ills to come. I made your liberty secure, since no one remained to inherit the crimes. But as it turns out there is a risk that I who accomplished so much will be dismissed with no reward, and that I alone will be deprived of the recompense which the laws I defended bestow.

My opponent here is in my view doing this not, as he claims, out of concern for the common good, but because he grieves for the deceased

4   and aims to take vengeance on the man responsible for their deaths. But you, gentlemen of the jury, bear with me for a moment while I recount the facts of the tyranny, although they are familiar to you. In this way you will understand the magnitude of the service I have done you, and your joy will be the greater as you reckon up the things from which you have been freed.

It was not, as it has often been with others, a straightforward tyranny and single servitude that we endured; we were not subjected to the whims of a single master. Alone of all who have ever suffered such ill-fortune, we had two tyrants instead of one and had the misfortune to be torn apart by double injustice. The father was by far the more moderate, less extreme in his anger, less vigorous in his punishments, less impetuous in his whims; by now age restrained the intensity of his desires, and reined in his appetite for pleasure. And even at the start of his criminal career he was led against his will by his son, so it used to be said; he was not himself much inclined to tyranny, but gave way to his son. For he was extremely devoted to his offspring, as he has shown. His son was everything to him; so he gave way to him, committed whatever crimes he urged, punished anyone he prescribed, and served him in everything. In sum, the son was his tyrant, and he was the bodyguard of his son's desires.

The young man yielded the honour to him on account of his age and 5
gave up the title of ruler, and that alone; he himself was the substance and the sum of the tyranny. He gave the regime its assurance and security, and he alone enjoyed the fruit of its crimes. He was the one who held the bodyguard together and commanded the garrison. He was the one who terrorized the victims of their tyranny and purged conspirators against it. He was the one who abducted young men and violated marriages; it was to him that young women were carried off. And whatever executions, whatever banishments and confiscations of property and tortures and outrages there were—all these things were done with the boldness of youth. The old man went along with him and shared in his crimes, and had nothing but praise for his son's misdeeds; and things became intolerable for us. When the spirit's desires acquire the licence of power, no bounds are set to wrongdoing. But worst of all was the knowl- 6
edge that our servitude would be long, or rather unending, that the city would be handed down in succession from one master to another, and that the people would be a criminal's inheritance. Others have derived no small encouragement from thinking and telling each other 'It will soon be over,' and 'Soon he will be dead, and we shall be free.' But these men left us no such hope; we saw the successor to power already in place. For this reason none of the brave men who shared the same objective as myself dared even to make the attempt. Liberty was given up as hopeless and the tyranny seemed invincible when the assault would have to be made against so many.

But I was not deterred. When I reckoned up the difficulty of the deed 7
I did not shrink from it, nor did I play the coward in the face of danger. I alone, I alone, went up against a tyranny so strong and so numerous— no, not alone: with the sword which was my partner in the struggle, and in its turn my partner in tyrannicide. Death was before my eyes, but still I sought to purchase liberty for all by the shedding of my own blood. I encountered the first guard-post and routed the guards, hard though

that was; killing everyone I met with and overcoming every obstacle in my path I pressed on to the very crown of my deeds, to the sole strength of the tyranny, to the foundation of our sufferings. I came upon the guardian of the acropolis; I saw him defend himself bravely and hold out

8   against many wounds; and yet I killed him. So the tyranny was overthrown now, and my enterprise had reached its consummation; from that moment we were all free. Only the old man was still left—unarmed, without his guards, deprived of that great bodyguard of his, alone, unworthy of a noble arm. At that point, gentlemen of the jury, I reasoned to myself as follows: 'I have enjoyed complete success; all is done, all is accomplished. How is the survivor to be punished? He is not worthy of me or my right hand, least of all if his death comes after so glorious, dashing, and courageous a deed, and dishonours that killing as well. We must find an executioner worthy of him; but after this loss he must not have the benefit of the same end.[14] Let him see; let him suffer; let him find near to hand this sword—to which I entrust the rest.' On reaching this decision I myself withdrew, and he brought what I had foretold to fulfilment; he killed the tyrant, and supplied my drama with its final act.

9   I am here, then, to bring you democracy, to make a public proclamation that your fears are at an end now, to declare the good news that you are free. You are already enjoying the fruits of my deeds. The acropolis, as you see, is emptied of criminals; no one dictates to you. You are free to award honours, to hear cases, and to speak in opposition in accordance with the laws; and all this you have gained through me and through my daring, and as a consequence of that one killing after which the father could not bear any longer to live. On these grounds I ask you to give me the reward that is owing to me. It is not that I am acquisitive or pettyminded, nor was it my intention to serve my fatherland for profit; but I want what I accomplished to be confirmed by the reward, and my undertaking not to be belittled or rendered inglorious on the grounds that it was judged incomplete and unworthy of the prize.

10 But this man opposes my request. He suggests that I am acting unreasonably in wanting to be honoured and to receive the reward. He denies that I am a tyrannicide, or that my action amounts to anything in the eyes of the law; he says that what I did was somehow not enough to establish a claim on the reward. Well then, I ask him: what more do you require of me? Did I not form the intention? Did I not ascend the acro-

---

[14] The text of this sentence is corrupt.

polis? Did I not kill? Did I not liberate you? Is anyone dictating to you now? Is anyone issuing commands? Is there any despot uttering threats? Did any of the criminals escape me? You cannot say so. On the contrary, everything is at peace; all the laws and liberty are assured; democracy is secure; marriages are inviolate; boys are without fear; young women are safe; the city holds festival to celebrate the public good fortune. Who, then, is responsible for it all? Who put a stop to what is past and provided you with all of this? If there is anyone at all who deserves honour more than I do, I concede the prize, I resign the reward. But if I alone brought all this to pass by my boldness and the risks which I took, ascending the acropolis, killing, punishing, taking vengeance on them one through another—why do you belittle my achievements? Why do you try to make the people ungrateful towards me?

'Oh, but you did not kill the tyrant himself, and the law grants the 11 reward to a tyrannicide.' Tell me, what difference is there between killing the man in person and furnishing the cause of his death? In my opinion, none. The one and only thing the legislator had in view was liberty, democracy, and an end to terror. That is what he honoured, that is what he supposed worthy of recompense; and you cannot deny that this has come about through me. I killed a man whose death he could not bear to outlive; I myself accomplished his death. The killing was mine, though the hand was his. So do not quibble any more about how he died, and do not scrutinize the manner of his death; ask only whether he no longer lives, and whether it is through me that he no longer lives. Otherwise I expect you will extend your enquiries further and bring malicious charges against your benefactors if someone inflicts the fatal blow not with a sword, but with a stone or a piece of wood or in some other way. Tell me: if I had besieged the tyrant and brought about his death by starvation, would you still have insisted that I should have killed him by my own hand? Would you have said that I fell short of the law's requirements in any way—even though the criminal had suffered a crueller death? Ask after one thing, demand this alone, concern yourself about this alone: which of the criminals survives? What expectation is there of future fear? What reminder is there of past misfortunes? If everything is purged and peaceful, it is malicious to use the manner in which something was done to try to take away the reward for what was won with toil.

I remember another thing stated in the laws—or have I forgotten 12 what they say because of our long servitude? They state that there are two kinds of responsibility for death, and whether someone kills in person or whether someone does not kill in person nor do the deed with his own hand, but compels it and instigates the killing, the law holds that this man too should suffer the same penalty. And this is just. The law would not allow itself to be thwarted by the deed because of his immunity;[15] consequently enquiry into the manner of death is superfluous. So if you think it right to punish the man who kills in this way as a murderer, and refuse absolutely to acquit him, should you not hold a man who has served the city in the same way as him worthy of the same treatment as your benefactors? For you cannot even say that I did one thing, and some other result followed which happened to be beneficial without my intending it. What else had I to fear once the stronger was dead? Why did I leave my sword in the corpse if I did not foresee exactly what would happen? Unless you claim that the dead man was not a tyrant and did not have that title, and that you would not gladly have given many rewards for his death; but you cannot say that. Then with the tyrant dead, will you not give the reward to the man who caused his death? How petty! Do you care how he died, so long as you enjoy your liberty? Do you have any further demand to make of the man who gave you back democracy? 'And yet', you say, 'the law enquires into the end result of what is done, ignoring all that is incidental to it and raising no quibbles.' Well? Has not a man who drove a tyrant into exile been honoured as a tyrannicide before now? And rightly so. For he too gave liberty in place of servitude. But what I have brought about is not exile and the anticipation of a second coup, but thorough cleansing, the complete elimination of the whole family, the whole evil cut out by the root.

14   By the gods, consider the whole sequence of events, if you like. Has anything the law requires been omitted? Is anything missing which should be present in a tyrannicide? First of all there should be a prior intention that is noble and patriotic, prepared to run risks for the public good and to purchase by one's own death salvation for many. Did I fall short in this respect? Was I faint-hearted? When I had set my objective did I shrink from any of the intervening dangers? You cannot say so. Dwell on this one point a little longer, and imagine that in return for simply wishing and planning these things, even if the result had not been a success, I had presented myself and asked on the basis of the intention itself to receive a reward as your benefactor. If I had not been able to do so, but someone after me had killed the tyrant, tell me, would it have been unreasonable or senseless to grant me a reward? Especially if I said,

---

[15] The text of this sentence is corrupt.

'Gentlemen, the will was there, the desire, the attempt, the endeavour. I deserve to be honoured for the intention alone'—what would you have answered then?

But as it is, that is not what I am saying. I went up and I ran the risks 15 and I performed countless exploits before the young man's death. For you should not imagine that it was a straightforward or easy matter to get past the guard-posts, defeat the bodyguards, put so many to flight on my own; that is in fact pretty well the greatest thing in tyrannicide and the sum total of the action. It is not the tyrant himself that presents such a great obstacle to conquer and subdue, but the defences and apparatus of the tyranny. Anyone who defeats that has won complete success; the rest does not amount to much. Reaching the tyrants would not have been possible for me if I had not overpowered all the guards and body-guards that surrounded them and beaten them all beforehand. I add nothing more, but insist once again on this point: I overpowered the guard, I defeated the bodyguards, I left the tyrant unprotected, unarmed, naked. Do you think that I deserve honour on this account, or do you also demand of me the killing?

Well, if you want a killing, that is not lacking either. I have shed 16 blood. I accomplished a great and glorious deed in killing a young man in his prime, feared by all, who kept the other safe from plots, who was the sole ground of his confidence, who was the equal of many body-guards. Am I not worthy of reward, sir, am I to receive no honour for such deeds? What if I had killed a single bodyguard, or one of the tyrant's henchmen, or a valued servant—wouldn't that have seemed a great thing, going up and in the middle of the acropolis, amid all those weapons, killing one of the tyrant's entourage? But as it is, look at the man I killed. He was the tyrant's son, or rather a crueller tyrant, an inexorable despot, whose punishments were harsher and whose oppression was more violent; above all he was the heir and successor to it all, who could have prolonged our sufferings. Suppose that this is all I did, and 17 the tyrant himself escaped and survives. I ask a prize on these grounds. What do you say? Will you refuse it? Did you not fear him too? Was he not a despot, cruel, beyond enduring?

And now consider the chief point of all. The very thing this man demands from me I brought to pass in the best possible way. I killed the tyrant by killing someone else, not straightforwardly nor with a single blow, which would have been too good for him after such crimes; but first I tortured him with extreme grief, and set before his eyes what he most loved in a pitiful state, a son in his youth—evil I agree but nevertheless in his prime and like his father—covered in blood and gore. These are the wounds which fathers feel, these are the swords which just tyrannicides wield, this is the death worthy of cruel tyrants, this is the fitting punishment for so many crimes. To die at once, knowing nothing, seeing no such sight—that contains nothing worthy of a tyrant's punishment.

18   For I was not unaware, sir, I was not unaware, nor was anyone else, how much affection he felt towards his son and that he would not have wished to survive his son even for a little while. All fathers, perhaps, feel that way towards their sons; but he felt so more than the rest—not surprisingly, since he saw in him the one guardian and defender of his tyranny, the one person who ran risks for his father and gave the regime its security. So I knew that he would die at once, if not through affection at any rate through despair, reckoning there was no longer any point in living deprived of his son's protection. So I set about him all this throng of troubles—his natural feelings, grief, despair, fear, anxiety for the future. I enlisted these things as my allies against him, and drove him to that fatal resolution. He died childless, in misery, in mourning, in tears, having endured a grief short-lived, it is true, but painful enough for a father; and (worst of all) he took his own life, the most wretched of deaths and far crueller than if he had died at another's hands.

19   Where is my sword? Does anyone else recognize this? Did this weapon belong to anyone else? Who took it up with him to the acropolis? Who made use of it, before the tyrant? Who dispatched it against him? Sword, you were partner and successor in my accomplishments; after so many dangers, after so many killings, we are disregarded and deemed unworthy of reward. If it were on behalf of this sword alone that I was seeking the honour from you, if I said, 'Gentlemen, when the tyrant wanted to die and found himself at that very moment unarmed, this sword of mine served him, and helped in every way towards the goal of liberty; consider it worthy of honour and reward'—would you not have recompensed the owner of a possession so loyal to the people? Would you not have enrolled him among your benefactors? Would you not have dedicated the sword in the temples? Would you not have reverenced it along with the gods?

20   Now, please, imagine what the tyrant must have done, what he must have said before his death. When I killed the son and inflicted many wounds on him in the visible parts of his body, so that I should give greatest pain to his father and break his heart at the first sight, the son cried out pitifully, calling on his father not for help or assistance—he

knew he was a feeble old man—but to behold his own sufferings. When I departed, I had composed the whole tragedy, and left for the actor the corpse, the stage, the sword, and all that remained of the play. He came up and saw his only son, scarcely breathing, covered in blood, steeped in gore, his many wounds packed close together and fatal; and he called out: 'My child, we are slain, we are killed, we have fallen victim to the tyrannicide. Where is the killer? What is he keeping me for? What is he preserving me for, when I am already slain through you, my child? Does he despise me as an old man? By delaying when I must be punished, is he drawing out my death and making my execution longer?' So saying he 21 began to look for a sword—for he was unarmed, because he placed all his trust in his son. But that was not lacking, either; far in advance I had provided that as well, leaving it behind for the bold deed to come. Drawing the sword from the bloody wound he said: 'A little while ago you killed me; now, sword, give me rest. Comfort a grieving father, and assist the hand of an old and unfortunate man. Kill me, slay the tyrant, and set me free from my grief. If only I had come upon you first, if only I had preempted the sequence of deaths. I would have died, but as a tyrant only, still believing that I would have an avenger; but now I die as one childless, as one scarcely able to find someone to kill him.' And as he said this he tried to effect his death, trembling, incapable, longing for death but lacking the strength to bring that enterprise to fulfilment.

How many punishments were there in this? How many wounds? 22 How many deaths? How many tyrannicides? How many rewards? And at the last you all saw the young man lying dead—no small or simple achievement—and the old man embracing him, their blood mingled, that libation to liberty and victory. You saw what my sword achieved, and the sword itself between them, proving that it was not unworthy of its master and bearing witness that it served me faithfully. If this had been done by me in person, it would have been less; the novelty adds to its glory. I am the one who overthrew the whole tyranny, but the action is divided among many, as in a play. I played the leading role, the son the second, the tyrant himself the third. The sword served us all.

SOPATER *DIVISION OF QUESTIONS* 95. 21–98. 11

An orator in a city ruled by a tyrant persuaded the tyrant to abdicate his tyranny. He asks for a reward as a tyrannicide.

The *statement* contains the constitution and the blessings of democracy; then the sudden conspiracy, and the evils of tyranny with amplification; then his association with the tyrant, and how he persuaded him to abdicate the tyranny. The statement also contains characterizations of the orator speaking to himself, exhorting himself to address the tyrant, and such like.

96   Then the opponent's *definition*: 'But you did not kill the tyrant.' Then a *counterdefinition* belonging to the person who is the subject of the exercise: 'Tyrannicide is not just a matter of putting him to the sword, but of freeing the city from tyranny, giving liberty back to the citizens, establishing democracy inviolate for the city. Why are you so concerned about the manner, and fail to consider the outcome of the act?' Uphold this with examples: 'It is as if someone were to call a doctor to account because he did not use surgery or cauterization to heal the illness, but diet and advice; or a soldier who has defeated the enemy, because he freed the city from siege without a pitched battle and without being wounded.' Then *assimilation*: 'Persuading a tyrant to abdicate is equivalent to putting him to the sword; both free the city from his ill-treatment. If you were captured by pirates, or fell into some other danger, you would not be concerned who saved you; in the same way, deposing the tyrant by the sword and by persuasion are equivalent, since they both equally free the city from tyranny.' *Legislator's intention*: 'The democratic legislator did not specify a manner or a form for the act, but simply said that the man who frees the city from tyranny is to receive the reward.' *Importance*: 'It is a great and marvellous thing to overthrow a tyranny in this way, and worthy of your admiration, whether you look to the orator and his speech, or to the one who was persuaded. Let us take account of the good fortune which ensured that he was not enraged by the orator, which made the tyrant so docile that he was persuaded by the

97   speech and set aside power, bodyguards, wealth, authority, the freedom to do as he wished.' *Relative importance*, by comparison with the other form of tyrannicide: 'This is greater than killing the tyrant. I did not come into danger nor did I commit a murder, and yet I have set him far from his tyranny.'

Counterposited conjecture: 'But it is likely that he will become tyrant a second time.' This always arises in cases of definition arising out of a request for a reward if a tyrant or the enemy survives. If the tyrant had been killed it would not be possible to say that it is likely he will attempt to recover the tyranny—how could someone once killed be tyrant? So a counterposited conjecture always arises in cases of definition arising out of a request for a reward, if in such an issue the enemy or a tyrant survives. You will solve it conjecturally; of the heads of conjecture only motive and capacity occur in such subjects (for you learned in incomplete conjectures that there are only two heads relevant to person, motive and capacity, and the discussion here is about the person). So you will solve conjecturally: 'It is not likely that he will be tyrant a second time, having once given up willingly, and not under compulsion, and knowing by reason that this is a better life than that of tyrants. It is impossible or hard for one who has voluntarily and of his own will abdicated tyranny to want to subject himself a second time to those same misfortunes, having once learned the reasons why tyranny is unnatural. Nor will he be able to hold the acropolis, having once deceived and cast aside his bodyguards,' and so forth.

Epilogue: 'It is noble to honour a tyrannicide, so that everyone will be inspired to emulation of his service to the city.' You can take ideas for the epilogue from *Against Leptines*: 'If you do not honour him, no one will be willing to run risks for the security of the city; no one will thrust himself into danger to defend the constitution, knowing that he will receive no reward from you, whether for taking the risk or success.' After that you will say: 'I will protect the people, I will guard the acropolis, I will   98
pledge myself again as security for the future; and if—which god forbid!—someone again should rage against the constitution, I shall speak the same words a second time. I will make him hate tyranny and love equality before the law again. And before I embark on that discourse I shall say to you all, "It is on your behalf, gentlemen, that I arm myself with words; it is on behalf of the constitution that I bear the panoply of education; it is on account of the laws that I go up to be a hero. And if he should not be persuaded thus, then I have my sword; I have a right hand armed on the city's behalf; I shall use weapons against the man who does not yield to persuasion." '

SYRIANUS *COMMENTARY ON HERMOGENES ON ISSUES* (EXTRACTS)

[101. 21–102. 18] The *presentation* contains amplification of the acts performed. It is expanded using the elements of circumstance, as (e.g.) in this definitional problem:- The law states that a tyrannicide is to receive a reward. A city is ruled by a tyrant; a philosopher persuaded the tyrant to abdicate the tyranny and asks for the prize. He will say, making use of

expansion on the basis of the persons: 'By applying myself to philosophy
I overthrew the tyranny, making the tyrant see reason by arguments and
not by murder, and I freed the citizens, whose birth-right is liberty and
democracy, from their existing troubles.' Thus he will cover the ground
by way of persons, and also by place: 'The acropolis seized, the whole city
enslaved, the countryside laid waste by the oppressive weight of taxes.'
By manner: 'By the knowledge I gained from philosophy I put an end to
the impiety of his thinking'; here there will be extensive praise of philosophy, as stronger than weapons, money, and every power. By cause:
'Seeing the temples shut up, the sacred rites despised, women outraged,
men put to death without trial, and no one with the courage to put an
end to these crimes, I dedicated myself to this concept.' The presentation is always expanded by the prosecutor with these and similar considerations inspired by the elements of circumstance.

[104. 18–24] The *counterdefinition* is expanded using the circumstances,
the acts performed, and examples; as in the case of the philosopher who
ended a tyranny: 'This is tyrannicide: to ascend the acropolis, to persuade
the tyrant to drive out his own party, to deceive his bodyguards, to save
the laws, to make the enslaved free.'

[107. 21–108. 28] The *assimilation* is expanded using the topic of purpose,
and description. The topic of purpose, as in the case of the philosopher:
'Consider, what is the overthrow of a tyrant? Is it to commit many murders, or to make the city free of the hardships that arise from tyranny?
The latter, in my opinion. For if murders secured tyrannicide, one would
have to honour murderers with the rewards given to tyrannicides; but as
it is they are subjected to punishment by the laws, while those who liberate peoples are everywhere held in honour—and that is what you will
find that I have dared to do.' Then you will attach a description, describing all the blessings the city has as a result of the tyrant's abdication:
'Consider that good fortune encircles the city, in place of its previous ill-
fortune. Temples and precincts of the gods are tended fittingly by people who have lived pure lives; the council consults over the city's interests
and makes the people vote on measures advantageous to the law-
abiding; those who do well by their homeland are celebrated with honours, and those who love wickedness are subjected to the punishments
they deserve by the laws, and so make those of like aspirations more self-
controlled. Do you say that someone who has filled the city with such an
abundance of blessings is not worthy of reward? Is that not absurd?'
The defendant solves the assimilation by an objection: 'But winning a

tyrant over by arguments is not to be called tyrannicide. For if he is removed by death he undergoes the just penalty for his crimes against the citizens and leaves the city free of fear for the future; but if he survives he proves that wickedness goes unpunished, and before long he will recruit bodyguards again and turn his gaze towards the acropolis', and so forth.

[110. 1–111. 12] In *importance* the prosecutor always insists on the acts performed and will try to show that the action is more inclusive than the omission, and he will attach the greatest importance to it. The defendant, on the contrary, diminishes the act performed, and will try to show that in fact the omission is more inclusive. E.g. the philosopher will say (he takes the place of the prosecutor in a request for a reward, by virtue of speaking first): 'Consider, gentlemen: does tyrannicide entail the rule of law and liberty? Or is it not rather the securing of the laws and the freedom of judgement of loyal citizens that ensures that a lust for tyranny does not even begin to enter into the inhabitants? The latter, I think. For if the tyrant had been killed, there would perhaps have been many who, through kinship or association, would have harboured similar thoughts against the homeland; but since he has seen reason and recognized the injustice of his crimes he will not be so reckless as to try himself to seize the things he regards as ultimate ills, nor will he look on if someone else commits such crimes.' The philosopher will use these and similar considerations to show that the act he performed is important and inclusive; his opponent will develop importance by means of diminution, and try to show that the omission is more inclusive than the act performed: 'You did not take up arms; you did not kill the tyrant; you ran no risk in defence of the fatherland—and you ask for a hero's reward? Is that not senseless? If, fearing those citizens who lay in wait for him and distrusting the fickleness of fortune, he pretended to be won over by your arguments that does not give you the right to reap the prize that belongs to a tyrannicide. Since they cut the lawlessness out of the city and free it from an *Iliad* of woes,[16] it is right that they should come proudly to the rostrum and seek a reward that matches the greatness of the risks they ran. But you, who exempted from punishment the public demon of our country and procured our destroyer's escape—do you think you have done anything distinguished?'

[113. 1–3, 11–23] After relative importance occurs a *request for intention*, raised by the prosecutor and solved by the defendant by means of a gloss . . . The philosopher, too, will raise the question of intention (I have

111

[16] Cf. Demosthenes 19. 148.

already mentioned that in requests for reward the first speaker takes the place of the prosecutor, the opponent that of the defendant); the philosopher, then, will raise the question of intention thus: 'But if I had not meant to overthrow the tyranny, why take so little care of myself as to go to the acropolis and try to drive the tyrant out by argument—a man against whom to that day so many phalanxes of citizens had done nothing?' The opponent will suggest a gloss in reply to this, based on the following intent: 'Knowing that the tyranny was already on the point of collapse you dared to persuade a man who already believed that exile was preferable to the ultimate penalty.'

4.3 COUNTERPLEA

Libanius' *Declamation* 36 is a counterplea arising out of an act and its contingent consequence.[17] An impoverished orator whose tongue had been cut out wept when he saw the rich man who had inflicted that injury address the assembly; the rich man was stoned to death in the ensuing riot. (For conflict between rich and poor see on Hermogenes *57. 14–58. 2.) The riot was not an act of the poor orator, but the prosecution maintains that he must bear responsibility for it as a consequence of his act; the defence (conducted, for obvious reasons, by an advocate) dissociates the poor man from the riot, while stressing that his tears were natural, and therefore not blameworthy.

Substantially the same theme provides Zeno with his example of counterplea (344 f.). After a less elaborate definitional exception, the defence produces the counterplea proper; the prosecution's objection is made by refutation (it was not legitimate for the defendant to weep) and counter-representation (even if it was, not to this effect), and is developed by sequence of events (see on Hermogenes *67. 3–5). The defence responds (in effect, although this terminology is not used) with two counterpositions, transference and counteraccusation; i.e. responsibility is first transferred to the people, over whose actions the poor man had no control, and then turned back on the victim, who deserved to suffer what the people did to him.

For another theme in which a man is prosecuted for violence occasioned by his display of grief see Seneca *Contr.* 3. 8. Compare also *RG* 4. 469, 5. 147:- A disfranchised man follows someone who has committed

---

[17] This declamation is briefly analysed in Schouler 1984, 215 f.

adultery with his wife weeping; the adulterer is stoned to death, and the man is charged with causing a public disturbance. The key point here is that the defendant's disfranchisement barred him from access to legal redress against the adulterer; there are clear grounds for suspecting, therefore, that his unusual action was a deliberate attempt to incite violence against the victim, and the case is analysed as a combination of counterplea with conjecture on the basis of intention. Intention is crucial to all counterpleas (see on Hermogenes *67. 3–5; Libanius addresses the question in 34–42), but in this case will require a more explicit and elaborate treatment.

Libanius gives a vivid account of the rich man's activities; some of the things mentioned are very useful to the case, but are not implied in the theme as stated. It is, of course, legitimate for the declaimer to attribute secret machinations to the opposition; speculative slander is free. But one wonders whether Libanius is not exercising a little too much licence in his account of the rich man's public dealings.[18]

1–6 **Prologue:** The advocate begins by explaining his own commitment to the case (cf. Anon. Seguerianus 42), quickly moving on (2) to draw the jury into the same network of obligations towards the defendant. The jury is bound to the defence, too, by a sustained evocation of pathos, and by the argument (5) that the killing of the rich man was an act of the whole people (cf. 43–8). The prosecution will, of course, have given an exactly contrary account of the killing, as a factional attack on a public benefactor. The defence must therefore disarm the prejudice in favour of the rich man which arises out of his success in raising the siege; the undertaking to show that this was part of a conspiracy (6) is taken up in the narrative section.

7–9 **Preliminary statement:** An apostrophe to the poor man, portraying his political career as a struggle, at immense personal cost, to defend the city against the rich man's machinations.

10–19 **Statement:** The statement itself begins by viewing the poor man's political career, sympathetically described in the preliminary statement, from the rich man's perspective: frustrated in his evil plans by a persistent and incorruptible opponent, he was driven to desperate expedients to rid himself of this obstacle to his ambition. Thus the preparation in 7–9 makes the defence's hostile interpretation of the raising of the siege

[18] For the principle that declaimers should keep to what is stated in or can legitimately be inferred from the theme see Sopater 60. 6–8, 115. 13–17; Quintilian 7. 2. 54–6; [Quintilian] *Decl. Min.* 325. 2, with Winterbottom's note to 316. 3; Seneca *Contr.* 10. 5. 18.

seem plausible; inherent implausibilities in the prosecution's favourable interpretation are drawn out in 15–17. Note that the actual excision of the poor man's tongue is reserved for the emotional climax in the epilogue (53); here the speaker limits himself to the rich man's tyrannical demand and the poor man's loyal acquiescence, reinforcing the portrayal of each man that has been unfolding since the prologue. Since the defence has to be careful that its hostility to the granting of the rich man's request should not appear anti-democratic, this section carefully dissociates the people from their decision to grant the request; the account of the rich man's death (18 f.) picks up from the prologue the corr -ponding idea that in condemning the rich man's death the prosecutor is condemning an act of the people.

20–49 **Argument**

20 **Presentation:** The portrayal of the poor man as a defender of the law against the rich man's evil machinations is exploited to make the prosecution seem paradoxical: how can the guardian of the laws be a lawbreaker? This paradox is systematically worked out in the following sections.

21 **Part of right:** A series of rhetorical questions is used to introduce the argument that the defendant has done nothing that would make him liable to the charge; this argument is next worked out positively in terms of person and act.

22–3 **Person:** The defendant cannot be guilty of the crime he is accused of: a man with no tongue, since he is of necessity silent, cannot disturb the peace.

24–7 **Definition:** What the defendant did is not an instance of the crime he is accused of. This is argued by refutation and counter-representation: since the people acted with one accord, what happened was not civil strife (24 f.); but even if it was civil strife, the poor man's act was not an incitement to it, since it omits the essential element of specific, verbal encouragement (26 f.).

28–33 **Counterplea:** The crucial head is elaborately developed. First the defendant's weeping is identified as one of a range of natural responses which are not in fact, and in principle could not be, accountable (28 f.); this point is then turned on the prosecutor, who is not immune to the kind of emotional display for which he is blaming the defendant (30); finally (30–3) a focused conclusion for the claim to legitimacy is achieved by challenging the prosecutor to identify the law which forbids the defendant's acts.

34–41 **Mitigation:** One obvious response to the counterplea is that the poor man's crime was not weeping *per se* but weeping in order to provoke violence against the rich man. The defence mentions this possibility (34), and uses a counterposition to establish the innocence of the poor man's intentions; since the counterplea was based on nature this takes the form of a plea of mitigation, showing that the poor man's reaction was in the circumstances beyond his control.

42 **Mitigation** and **exception:** A second line of argument against the counterplea would be that, irrespective of intention, the poor man's weeping had the effect of inciting violence. At this point the prosecution has been driven from the act to its contingent consequence, and so the special form of mitigation which Hermogenes recommends for that category of counterplea (*69. 13–16) becomes relevant: the poor man could not have foreseen this contingent consequence, and therefore cannot be blamed for it. The same consideration brings in the characteristic exception (Hermogenes *68. 18–69. 13): if the prosecutor himself failed to foresee the outcome, he cannot reasonably blame the poor man for failing to do so; if he did foresee it, he is at fault himself for taking no steps to prevent it.

Hermogenes places this mitigation before the counterposition (69. 13 f.). In this case there are two counterpositions, and Libanius has placed it between them. The first counterposition refers to the poor man's weeping itself, the second to the ensuing riot; since the special mitigation serves to introduce the argument from contingent consequence, it appropriately precedes the latter.

43–8 **Counteraccusation:** The blame for the violence attaches to the rich man himself; it was his brutality which incited the people (cf. 2) to violence against him, and which (along with his contrivance of the siege: 48) justified that violence. The prosecutor's good faith is called in question by his willingness to side with the brutal would-be tyrant against the people (43, 47).

50–6 **Epilogue:** The epilogue has a standard structure. The arguments are recapitulated (49 f.); the quality of the poor orator restated (50); pity is invoked by a vivid description of the cutting out of his tongue (52 f.); the adverse political consequences of conviction are mentioned (54). Where in other cases wife and children might be called to the rostrum to excite pity, here it is the poor man himself who is summoned (55 f.) in a conclusion which links sympathy to the theme of his public spirit.

LIBANIUS *DECLAMATION* 36

It is a capital offence to cause riot and civil strife. A poor orator was the political enemy of a rich man. During a famine
under siege the rich man promised victory if the poor man's
tongue was cut out; this was granted. He went out at night
and drove off the enemy. The next day the poor man was
present as he made a speech, and wept. The people stoned
the rich man. The poor man is accused under the law.

1   The man who has spoken so much from this rostrum, gentlemen, often
bringing criminals to judgement and giving aid to the victims of injustice—now he stands in silence, placing his hopes of salvation in other
people's tongues. And we, whose power of speech survives still, who are
still allowed to speak by the rich, we must as far as lies within us join
forces to prevent the defendant's speechlessness impeding the force of
justice—not only because this is something for which one should always
be concerned, and because those who are free of misfortune should
always defend the helpless; but also because when we too were the victims of malicious accusers this man who now looks to us stood by us and
2 helped to save us. It would be utterly despicable if we were to fail to
return those services now, in so desperate a situation. And it is right that
you too, members of the jury, out of respect for justice and compassion
for his suffering should not add to the poor man's woes the reputation of
having broken the law.

3   The poor man himself has no fear of death; indeed, he would very
much wish to pass away. The man who owed his distinction to eloquence, and who had in his political career a consolation for poverty,
now that he is deprived of the power to offer advice would think death a
gain. But because life is burdensome to the defendant, it does not mean
that you should condemn him to death. He is on trial before you
unjustly, and because of the disaster that has come upon him he longs for
death; so from your hands he should receive acquittal—after that, he can
take counsel with himself about the other. Your verdict, I believe, should
have no regard for the desires of the contending parties, but should be
based on justice.

4   I do not know, gentlemen, what this wretched man must do to escape
maltreatment at the hands of the well-to-do. When he used his eloquence on your behalf, he was deprived of his tongue by his enemies to

prevent him doing them any further harm; but now that he is silent he is brought to trial as a criminal. If he is to be beset by accusations and troubles whether he speaks or does not speak, where must he look to secure himself from fear? Members of the jury, those who suffer griev- 5
ously at every turn and who are allowed no respite have one refuge—your humane temper. It is right that this man should profit from that now, especially because, although it may be thought that the poor man is on trial, in reality it is the people which is being brought to account. The rich man's fate was the people's work, and whatever the verdict may be on the defendant, the people must share it too.

None of you should suppose that a public benefactor was pelted with 6
stones, or be taken in by the encomia which the prosecutor went through to give the rich man an air of majesty. He declaimed tragically about the siege, he marvelled at the astonishing sortie, he extolled the swiftness of the victory. But if you listen quietly to what we have to say, I believe that I will prove that he was no public benefactor, but a villain who concocted the war himself and put an end to dangers which did not arise of their own accord.

Allow me, members of the jury, first to speak briefly to the poor man 7
himself—for that is all that is left to him, to listen to others speaking. This is what your political career has reduced you to, poor fellow. This is the degree of calamity to which your ignorance of fortune has brought you. From your noble decrees this terrible grief has come about, from your advantageous laws, from your democratic freedom of speech. It was 8
a glorious thing to give the best advice, to convince the city of what should be done and prevent what was inexpedient from being done— glorious, but fraught with danger. It was just to share the city's labour and take care of its liberty and expose the rich man's machinations—just, but unsafe. You trusted in the laws to assist you. Did you not know that the laws are often overpowered by money? Had you not heard the poets singing of the power of wealth, and how it directs the affairs of men as it wills? Did you expect that the integrity of your way of life would pre- 9
vail over riches? That you, who could hardly afford a second-hand cloak, would prevail over a rich man? Would it not have been better to set your sights lower, accumulate money and increase your household? But no, you were too meddlesome and did not know your station; you came into conflict, you hated, you provoked a man who could easily make himself tyrant. So you paid the penalty with the voice you had used to cause him pain; you are compelled to be silent because you would not consent to hold your tongue.

10   For, members of the jury, although the rich man had tried everything and stopped at nothing, he could not catch this man by malicious prosecution nor could he bribe him to change sides and become one of his own paid hangers-on. He wanted to break the law, but this man would not let him. He knew that while the city enjoyed peace and prosperity he could never wreak his revenge on the poor man. So to launch his attack he had to imperil the commonwealth and bring public affairs to such a pitch of desperation that the people would yield everything and disre-

11   gard the laws out of fear. What, then, did he do? Consider how cleverly he draws down war upon our country and sets an army in motion against us. It is not at all hard for generals and senior officers to persuade someone to take up arms, by spending money and promising co-operation of other kinds. So when war fell suddenly on our country we, as brave men do, had it in mind to march out and intervene and drive them off, and such like. But he, putting up a pretence of anxiety and grief at what was happening, came to the rostrum and held the people back with his long speeches, saying on one occasion that the matter needed much deliberation, insisting on another that the invader's forces were invincible, and the next day the same and things of similar vein. And they came right up to the walls while we were listening to speeches; the opposition was

12   curbed; the food-stocks were exhausted. And when this noble fellow knew that we had sunk to the utter depths of despair and considered that his plan was as good as achieved, this man who had feared with us and feared for us and had been so cautious was suddenly bold; manliness took the place of that familiar decadence.'What is it you seek?', he said, 'The lifting of the siege? I give you that; I preside over victory; it is in my

13   power to free the city from trouble. But I must have a reward.' We listened; and when he stood to make his claim, what—oh ye gods, what a word he spoke! The guardian of our bodies and our laws, who promised us victory—he did not ask for acres of land, not for maintenance at state expense, not for a statue in bronze; these things are at home in a democracy. It would have been moderate had he asked for the poor man's death. For cruel and bestial though that would have been, yet the deceased have no perception of what they have suffered. But that was not enough for him. No, by all the gods. Oh, what a novel punishment! His prize was the tongue of a single citizen. He asked as the wages of his heroism that the orator should lose his power of speech, mingling the semblance of democracy with the savagery of tyranny. The reward was a vote of the people, but the outrage was that of a tyrant. He presented his request to you as if the laws held sway; but he asked to receive what the

laws forbid. The people, when it heard what was said, was horrified; we   14
looked at each other, loathing the claim but oppressed by the siege. We
were at a loss, caught between an unnatural gift and a situation beyond
endurance. And as we hesitated, this great-hearted man who lives only
for the public good, although he could have spoken against the motion,
chose to keep quiet. He surrendered himself to the knife with great
courage, and having no money he donated to us his tongue.

And when that noble reward had been given, we waited for the vic-   15
tory and wondered what form it would take. 'Will he take the heavy
infantry and sally forth? Will he assign the task to the archers? Will he
set an ambush? What has he devised that will strike terror into an army
buoyed up by its successes?' That is what we said. He strolled about
within the walls until dusk; then in the middle of the night he went
beyond the gates, encountered the enemy, and they were gone, as if at
their general's command. Does this not speak for itself? Does it not cry   16
aloud that the whole thing was contrived and managed by the rich
man? That they came and went away as he willed? I have given the
matter some thought, but I cannot see how I could call this a victory.
A whole army is routed by one man? The victor by the vanquished?
The besieger by the besieged? An army is routed by a rich man—pam-
pered, soft, and effete? A man who has had neither training nor education in anything straightforward or noble, but has squandered his life
on mean-spirited quarrels? The rest of you are warriors; you have   17
trained hard in the arts of war from childhood. But none of you saw
that a night attack was needed, or were so daring. And yet the money-
grubber, who devotes all his efforts to that, like a god turned the
besiegers' blockade into a rout. It is not possible. But it was necessary
for the enemy to sit before our walls until disaster had overtaken the
poor man; and when he had suffered what he did, the rich man saw
fit—and they were gone.

But I shall let that be, in case anyone should think that I am not   18
speaking to the matter in hand. What followed was that he summoned
us all to the assembly, priding himself on his glorious victory; many convened in haste, and among them this orator came to see the meeting.
When he saw you and you saw him, he wept and you took pity; calling
to mind what gift you had given, you punished those who had forced you
to do it. Then I saw a lawful assembly, a free people, a casting of stones   19
becoming to our constitution. The man died on the rostrum which he
had shamed by his proposal. You gave a fine defence of yourselves before
the Greeks with your stones; you dispelled the disgrace contracted under

compulsion by deeds performed in freedom. You proved that the vote was the product of the moment, not of the city's character.

20   We rejoiced together at our anger, our just wrath; we went on with our lives in the belief that the most holy thing possible had been done. But the poor man's troubles are not at an end. He is indicted and brought to trial and accused of breaking the law on riot and civil unrest. This is the one thing that remained: for the guardian of the laws to be counted

21   among the lawless. But what, sir, did he say to incite riot? Did he propose the confiscation of some rich men's property, so that civil strife broke out? Did he propose that poor people should be deprived of their right to speak, and cause civil strife that way? Did he set the infantry at odds with the cavalry, the archers with the slingers, the generals with the officers by slandering each to the other? What bill did he move that split the city? What opinion did he express that divided the people?

22   Are you not ashamed, by god, to accuse a man who cannot speak of disturbing the peace? It is as if someone had charged this same man with supplying the enemy—you lunatic, a destitute man's only thought is to supply his own daily needs. So look now at the orator's tongue, and give up your accusations. What you are doing is almost as if you were to

23   blame statues for causing a disturbance among the people. You malicious accuser, such charges are for those who speak and take part in politics and move proposals; it is to such people that the law addresses itself, because it holds the policies of some of them in suspicion. A disadvantageous speech that is plausibly constructed can sway the audience's judgement and induce them to think that what is harmful is good, and what is good is damaging; and so the city is at war with itself and the people is carried away into civil strife. Then the person who provided the occasion must be called to account for what has been done on the people's part. Since things they would not have done if those words had not been spoken have been done because of those words, the speaker of them bears the responsibility. How can someone who is excluded from speech be guilty of things which only those who speak can do? Did the man who now conducts his case through others stir up the people? The man who is silent? The man who does not open his mouth?

24   And how can what was done be worthy of the name 'civil strife'? The people punished the evil gift, reaching for stones with one accord, unanimous, sharing a common anger. There was no disturbance, with this party having one view and that party having another; all felt hatred, all

25   cast stones. It is civil strife when different desires divide the people against itself; when divided opinions lead one party to seize the high

ground while another holds the harbour; when they build fortifications; when they call in allies against each other; when the city is no longer united. But punishing a bestial fellow—what kind of disturbance is that? What kind of civil strife?

But suppose that what happened in the rich man's case was distur- 26 bance and civil strife. Even so, this man is not guilty. Did anyone hear him saying, 'Citizens! Pelt the tyrant's head, pelt the rich man who took advantage of the crisis. The danger has passed; take vengeance!'? He said nothing of the kind; indeed, he could not have done so had he wanted. How can he be prosecuted under this law for silence? By the gods, if, 27 though he was silent, someone else had used these words to incite the people to the deed, would they not have laid great emphasis on what he said when they brought the charge against him? Since they would have brought the man who spoke these words to trial, they declare the man who did not speak them innocent.

'But', he says, 'he came to the assembly.' What law forbade him? 'And 28 he stood by and wept.' Is lamentation a crime? An unfortunate citizen took part in the assembly, and wept. I do not know of these things being tried among us or among our neighbours, among us now living or among our ancestors. Laughter is permitted; weeping is allowed. It is not possible to call nature to account. To breathe, to be hungry, to be glad, to laugh, to be gloomy, to be unwell—no such state is a crime; nor is it possible for lamentation and tears to be subject to judgement. You see those 29 who follow the dead to their graves. They weep; they are not taken to court. You see those on whom surgeons operate. They weep; they are not charged. How many orators, calling the misfortunes of allies to mind, have shed tears as they spoke? How many peoples, hearing of disasters that have befallen their colonies, have been moved to lamentation? If you count weeping as a crime, there are many criminals you are not prosecuting. If in other cases the deed is not called to account, you are over-zealous in the present case.

Tell me, are you above feeling grief when you suffer? Or if you feel 30 grief, would you like to be penalized for it? You are not, in fact, superior to nature or immune to emotion yourself. So do not try to deprive another of the freedoms you think you should enjoy. You have not come here to make laws, but to adhere to the laws that are established of old. So show that tears are counted as a crime in the statutes. Do we not dis- 31 tinguish criminals from the law-abiding in just this respect—that the former do what is forbidden, the latter what is allowed? For example, we bring the thief, the adulterer, and the murderer to court. Why? Because they do what it is enacted should not be done. But we do not take to court or bring to trial someone who talks or walks or moves his hands or

32 shouts or frowns. Why? They do not break the law. So you must show that this stands written: 'If anyone cries, let him be punished as other malefactors are.' If you cannot do that, your behaviour is insolent; you are making those who are accustomed to bring malicious accusations worse by teaching them and showing them how to make any occurrence

33 the pretext for a charge. If not in the laws, show that this is defined in the decree which made the reward: 'The poor man is not to appear in the assembly, and is not to lament his suffering, and is not to be grieved by his misfortune.' Not even the rich man, unscrupulous though he was, tried to deprive him of that. You are making yourself out to be more oppressive than the rich man.

34 If he had suffered nothing and had no cause to groan, but had deliberately wept to stir the people up, I would have found fault with him myself. As things are, he could hardly stop himself weeping however much he tries. Because the suffering afflicts his tongue, it moves him to copious tears. Can the orator turn to examples and find comfort in sim-

35 ilar cases? No. He has not lost a child, nor been deprived of his civil rights—things which happen to many. He has not had his hand cut off in accordance with a vote of the people, leaving his tongue as consolation for his loss. The very thing in which we differ from animals, the use of speech towards one another, that is what he has lost to serve another's whim. And now he stands here as speechless as marble statues, who only the other day was in full flood on the rostrum. What is one to call him?

36 His art says 'orator'; his tongue does not allow it. 'No more pitiful suffering has ever there been in all of time. I am punished because of my zeal for the people. The tongue with which I served the common good has been taken from me. In return for loyalty, I have silence. My tongue is cut out at the rich man's command. Even the least loss is unendurable to me when it is inflicted by my enemy; but when the fine is my tongue,

37 what is to become of me?' Add that he is an orator. That makes a vast difference. An orator is nothing but his voice. For such a man the loss of his sight is easier to bear than the loss of his tongue. A layman might bear that loss with resignation, since it is not in his tongue that his distinction lies; but for an orator to lose his tongue is like a wrestler losing

38 his arms. Are you surprised, then, that an orator unable to speak weeps? He weeps at home because he uses a nod for every purpose. He weeps in the market-place because he cannot speak to his friends. Is it any wonder that the man who suffered this weeps, when we are moved to tears

by the sight of him? He wept out of longing for his voice. What is 39
strange in that? Each copes with his present circumstances without it
being held against him, and this man can feel no joy. If he had not wept
before, would the assembly not have moved him to tears? The orator saw
his old love—the rostrum, the seats of honour, the counsellors, the people, the president, and the executive committee; he saw his enemy raise
his hand; he heard him shouting; he heard the herald proclaim 'Who
wishes to speak?' He sought for his voice—and could not find it. He
compared his previous eloquence with his present silence, and discerned
his own loss more clearly in the rich man's address to the people; and at
the sight of the role in which he once exulted the memory of things past
shook his very soul. If you maim a racehorse's leg and take it to see a race, 40
when it sees the course and the state of its leg it will weep copiously. If
you cut off the right hand of a brave general and take him to see a battle, comparing the loss of his hand with the work of spears he will not
bear the sight without a tear. If you break an artist's fingers and show
him a canvas, the memory of his skill will move him to lamentation. A
place, an object, an action—all can bring previous happiness to mind,
and that brings on tears. The tongueless orator saw the assembly, and 41
was reminded of what he did when he had his voice. He thought to himself, no doubt: 'I used to go forward and mount the rostrum; I used to
make proposals and receive applause; it was through me the city used to
manage most of its affairs. And now I stand here like a statue, a witness
to other people's success.' You yourselves, members of the jury, are
weeping; what was he supposed to feel?

Suppose that he did not weep for himself, but had devised some 42
advantageous policy which he was unable to express, and wept for the
advice of which the city was deprived. Should he pay a penalty to the city
for that? What are you demanding punishment for? For his tears? Tears
are permitted. Because he moved the people? He was not a prophet and
did not know the future; ignorance is not actionable. Who is punished
for not foreseeing what is to come? If you knew that anger would be
stirred up why did you not quickly drive him off, before the people were
affected? If you did not foresee it, why are you imposing a penalty rather
than paying it? But it is clear what you are doing. You are making this 43
man a pretext, but it is the people you are accusing. What do I mean?
The people was going to do what it did even if the poor man had not
come and had not wept. People who are compelled to give what they do
not want to give, when they have the power demand vengeance for their
unwilling concessions, enemies of the recipient because of what they

gave. What chance of war, what grievous adversity has forced a decree such as this to be passed in the city? 'The tongue of a citizen is to be cut out.' Why? Because, although his property was small, he was a rich man's

44 political rival. This decree, members of the jury, was the overthrow of democracy, the overthrow of law and religion and all that is holy. The earth was defiled, and the all-seeing sun. The basis of our constitution was overturned, and that noble thing, equality of speech, was transformed into despotism. The city was filled with pollution, and took a share in the savagery by its vote. So it was obvious that when affairs were restored the time of peace would be a time of vengeance too against the rich man. The poor man's tears and the people's judgement were in one

45 accord. You were not wrong, members of the jury, when you used stones against a man who had luxuriated in your troubles; you could not have wiped out the shame had you not picked up those stones. How could you have approached the temples? How could you have offered sacrifice? How could you have celebrated the festivals? How could you have asked for blessings from the gods when the rich man joined in placing his vile hands on the sacred offerings? What ally would have answered the sum-

46 mons to share your deeds? Are you unaware that the character of a city is known from the decrees it passes, and is inferred from their qualities and defects? How would your way of life have been judged if you had stood by the gift and not purged yourself by a killing? More savage than barbarians, I am sure. But now it has been proved to all that the gift was not the city's, and what went before is overshadowed by what came after. A man is dead who in a time of liberty surpassed the brutality of tyranny. A man is dead who had learned to transgress the norms of democracy. A rich man has been stoned who turned his wealth against the laws. And is someone indignant at his death? Does someone bring charges and go

47 to court? Members of the jury, I distrust the prosecutor. A tyrant is dead, and he grieves. Did he join you in casting stones, or not? If he took part in the stoning, how can he prosecute things which he did? If he alone stood aside, he accuses the people of madness.

48 And if you speak to me of the night of the victory, you are speaking of craft; you are speaking of fraud; you are speaking of money's work. If he had been so mighty that his mere appearance caused a rout and that he alone could do more than the whole city, rumour of his courage would have reached the enemy; they would never have attacked a city in which such a warrior lived. He has paid the penalty for two crimes: for the siege he contrived, and the gift he demanded.

49 And you, members of the jury, do not renew the shame of that decree

by your votes; do not put the victim of injustice to death as a criminal; do not repudiate the casting of stones by your verdict. The law speaks of a man who causes riot and civil strife; this man is innocent, for he was silent. He came to the assembly, and he wept. Both of these are lawful. His suffering compelled his tears. He had no knowledge of the outcome. So save the victim of malicious prosecution, members of the jury, the man who has done no wrong but has suffered extraordinary ills. If a foreigner had been reduced to this plight, you would certainly have felt pity when you saw it. This gathering is a token of your humanity. 50

This orator is a democrat; he caused pain to the rich by defending the laws; he suggested many policies; he proposed many decrees; he went on many embassies; he brought allies over to our side; he found sources of revenue; he passed good laws; he undermined the wicked; he was in charge of many matters, but remained poor. This is the man to whom we used to look in times of need. Show your gratitude to him in his misery by saving him, and do not make it obvious that those who serve your interests are fools. To whom will you ever give aid if you have no pity for this man? To whom will you be merciful if you pay no heed to him? You will never find a man more devoted to you or more wretched. The prodigies of myth are made credible by this man's sufferings. The rich man led him out of the assembly, and he followed like a captive. Gathering his cronies about him, he reminded them of the poor man's freedom of speech; he displayed the decree and said, 'Well then, put out your tongue—the tongue I hate, the democratic tongue that did not fear wealth, that did not know its station.' The one gave the order, the other obeyed; and the voice that guided the city's affairs aright was struck out. Will you condemn a man who has suffered such things, and add to the miseries of one even now inconsolable? And who will that harm more—this man or the commonwealth? Members of the jury, the poor are already intimidated by the decree concerning the tongue; that has shown clearly enough how dangerous a station loyalty to you is. If they see this man condemned in a court of law as well, when will they devote themselves to your affairs? Who will speak? Who will serve on embassies? Who will be just when he sees that such are the prizes awarded to justice? Will they not change their allegiance and conclude that it is good policy to take their stand with the rich, who will be able to assault the constitution with impunity? This is what destroys democracy; this is what brings in oligarchy. From such seeds grows slavery for the people. In this one individual the common good is at stake. 54

Come up here beside me and make your contribution. You still have 55 hands, you still have tears. Openings for supplication are not all denied you. And if you will not use those, show your tongue. You see how the jury are moved? Have confidence in the verdict, and do not blame the people. It voted the gift with groans, overwhelmed by the crisis. Many have given themselves on many occasions to die for the fatherland; and you too, by the cutting out of your tongue, put an end to the siege. I shall inscribe your sufferings among the public benefactions. Forget the decree, remember that noble assembly and the stones. Hold to your old policy and keep to your resolution, I beg you, even though you are silent. Give your advice on public affairs in writing; I will read it out. And if I think of any policy I will tell you; you nod and shake your head, and practise politics by nodding. Compose a defence of the people—it befits you, despite your sufferings, to glorify the city. Compose an address to the poor to encourage them; drive out their fear, confirm them in their loyalty. And the city, taking consolation, will keep you at public expense, an orator speechless and poor.

56

4.4 COUNTERPOSITION

A man charges his father with conspiracy, and the magistrate disallows the case because it is illegal to bring an action against one's father other than for insanity; the father establishes a tyranny; after his overthrow the magistrate is charged with harming the public interest. (The same situation occurs in Fortunatianus 95. 5–7, where the father himself challenges the action.)

The scenario is similar to the one we met in *Libanius Decl. 44; here, too, an official has furthered a tyrannical conspiracy by obeying the law. But the different charge entails a change of issue. Since there is no suggestion of witting complicity on the part of the magistrate in the present theme there is no crime to be inferred from his ruling; the ruling itself is alleged to be criminal, since it was against the public interest. Sopater therefore analyses the case as transference, the blame being shifted to the law which required the magistrate to reject the son's suit.

Sopater's sketch of the statement shows how to give a narrative the desired slant. The magistrate's election to and conduct in office are used to establish his loyalty and his respect for the law; this provides a context in which the controversial ruling can be explained as the product of his law-abiding temper. The approach is similar to that of *Libanius in Decl. 44. 6–16; and (as there) the unfortunate consequences of the defendant's act are passed over lightly, while the restoration of liberty is celebrated at length—further evidence of the speaker's democratic outlook, while his focus on the rule of law as the key element in the restoration continues the statement's leading motif.

When he reaches the argumentative section, Sopater's division has a similar overall shape to Hermogenes', although it is somewhat simpler and his terminology is slightly different. The presentation is not separately identified, although there is in fact a brief presentation at the beginning of the definition (for Sopater's variant term cf. on Hermogenes *65. 22–66. 6). After the definition a closer analysis of events from a hostile perspective is counterposed in the sequence of events (cf. on Hermogenes *72. 12–18), to be solved by the transference itself (although Sopater does not use the term here). By contrast with Hermogenes, intent is here made to follow the transference; Sopater in fact treats the order as variable (intent precedes at 190. 27 ff., 210. 21; follows at 199. 13, 224. 26). The elaborate series of heads which follows the counterposition proper in Hermogenes is radically simplified in Sopater; the defence retains only its tendentious recharacterization of the act (the forcible definition), the prosecution only the objection (without which there would be no case).

Since the defendant's case rests on the constraint placed on him by the law, a legal question arises incidentally; an appeal from the letter of the law to its intent is counterposed and solved before the objection is tackled.

SOPATER *DIVISION OF QUESTIONS* 220. 11–223. 11

> No suit may be brought against one's father, except for insanity. A man accused his father of conspiring to establish a tyranny; the magistrate disallowed the suit. The son withdrew from the city; the father established a tyranny. After his overthrow the magistrate is charged with harming the public interest.

In general the headings of counterpositional issues are (as I said earlier) the following: definitional exception (this is relevant if the charge is generic, e.g. harming the public interest, impiety, etc.);[19] then

---

[19] If the terms of the charge apply only to a single kind of act (e.g. theft, homicide) definition does not arise; but if the term may subsume a variety of different acts it can be

sequence of events, which is the charge itself; then the transference; then one or even two objections. The objection is as indispensable in counterpositionals as the gloss in conjectures when there are actions.[20]

The quality of the magistrate is well-disposed towards the people; he takes the laws seriously, as his election and action show. So the *statement* of the problem is as follows on the magistrate's part: his election to office, because of his loyalty; his judgement of cases, by way of defending the laws; the fact that no one had ever criticized him for making a judgement contrary to the law. Then the son's suit against his father, and his disallowing it on legal grounds; you will develop this at greater length, e.g. 'The law, which forbade him a hearing, prevailed upon me', and so forth. Then the action itself, the son indicting his father for treason, which seemed incredible. Then, in passing, the tyranny and the son's departure, and the overthrow of the tyrant at greater length and solemnly: 'The laws were enforced', and so forth.

Definitional exception: Then: 'This is how I defended the laws when I held office; and he says that I have acted against the public interest of the city' (for you will speak this head directly for the magistrate) 'although I destroyed none of the city's property, [no law, no gift, no place, no city];[21] so how have I harmed the city's interest, when I myself have done nothing?' And: 'It is absurd that I should be brought to trial although I have done nothing', and so on.

After the definitional exception you will place in order the *sequence of events*, which is the charge itself; e.g.: 'You did not receive the boy when he tried to bring the suit for tyranny.' The solution is based on the law: 'The law is to blame, since it clearly forbade me to allow any suit except that for insanity.' Then *intent*: 'If that had not been the case, why should I have disallowed it—a man with no convictions against me?'—and similar material based on intent (you have the technique from the first examples).[22] Then hypothetically: 'If I had allowed the suit and the father had been acquitted, as he very likely would, would I not have been held to account before you under the law?'

221

---

argued that it applies more properly to one of the others (as the speaker argues below that harming the public interest means destroying public property). Cf. 199. 4–7 and the note to Hermogenes *72. 10–12.

[20] i.e. in conjectures that are not based only on person (cf. Hermogenes *29. 12 f.).

[21] The text is corrupt; examples standardly include ships, defences, etc. (e.g. Hermogenes 66. 6).

[22] Sopater discussed intent in more detail in his first examples of counterposition (esp. 191. 28–192. 20, 199. 13–23, 202. 14–20).

Then use the *forcible definition*: 'This, of all things, is not to harm the public interest—protecting the laws', and so forth.

After that you will place a counterposition arising out of the law's intent: 'But, he says, the law applies to private matters, not public ones. In private cases the law does not allow children any suit other than for insanity, but it does not prevent the magistrates granting public suits. It would be absurd if the legislator had completely excluded children from a hearing concerned with treason or tyranny, and if he had forbidden children access to the law-courts even if someone is able to lay information concerning the subversion of the democracy.' The solution to this: 'The law expressly forbade me to allow any suit other than that for insanity.' And: 'If the legislator had wanted to allow a public suit, he would have included that provision in the law. But he did not include that provision: he explicitly excluded any accusation being brought.' And: 'Reasonably so. He knew that children are often mean-spirited, and this gives rise to false suits and charges and danger; so he forbade any accusation being brought, agreeing only to that of insanity, which would be self-evident to all observers, both members of the jury and members of the public.'

Next you will place the *objection*: 'But, he says, you should have placed the matter before the assembly.' The solution: 'Since it was accepted that it could not be allowed, there was no point in placing the matter before the assembly. It is proper to consult the people on controversial matters, but it is pointless to do so on a matter of common consent.' Then: 'Also, I did not think that the suit was genuine, because he approached me— and I was restrained by the law. If he had genuinely wanted to make a denunciation he would have gone before the judges, he would have gone before the assembly. What prevented him? But since he in fact approached me, I assumed that his suit was no more than a display.'

After that the *epilogues*. Those against the magistrate are somewhat aggressive, and try to arouse a suspicion of complicity. Those of the magistrate are based on the city's good fortune: 'It watches over the laws and makes away with the wicked.'

4.5 PRACTICAL

When the Thebans sent news to Athens of their crushing victory over Sparta at the battle of Leuctra in 371 BC, with a request that the Athenians assist in the punishment of their former oppressors, the response was frosty (Xenophon *Hell.* 6. 19 f.); whatever their feelings about Sparta, Athenian interests would not be served by the growth of Theban power. Aelius Aristides' sequence of five *Leuctrian Orations* assumes that Sparta and Thebes are both seeking an alliance with Athens in the aftermath of the battle, and considers the problem of policy from a variety of perspectives. The pro-Spartan and pro-Theban positions are presented alternately in the first four speeches; the fifth argues for neutrality.[23]

Aristides' style is condensed and difficult, as is his manner of argumentation; he disdained improvisation, preferring (as he put it) to polish rather than to vomit his declamations (Philostratus 583). This density of thought and expression is offset by a tendency to formulate a point in several different ways—which is not to say that Aristides repeats himself uncritically, for he passes over some of his weakest points with deft rapidity.

1–5 **Prologue:** The first part of the prologue (1–3) is oriented on the speaker, who strikes a pose of self-sacrificing loyalty to the public good: a partisan speaker retains at worst the goodwill of his party, while the advocate of neutrality risks alienating everyone and can hope at best for the goodwill only of the uncommitted. The second part moves from ironical praise of the opposing speakers to an attack on their good faith, and a preliminary formulation of the idea (developed at greater length in 25–8) that their arguments in fact support neutrality. The prologue ends with a reminder that the speaker alone has the interests of Athens at heart. (Compare the beginning of Demosthenes 16, *On behalf of Megalopolis.*)

There is no narrative section; it was standard doctrine that narrative is usually out of place in deliberative speeches, because they are concerned with future events (Aristotle *Rhet.* 1414ª38 f., 1417ᵇ12–16; Quintilian 3. 8. 10 f.; Syrianus 2. 170).

The argumentative section is organized, as one would expect, around the heads of purpose.

6–11 **Custom:** Since the case is non-documentary, the argument begins with custom rather than law (see on Hermogenes *76. 12–77. 2). This takes the form of a counterposed appeal to the tradition of active intervention in defence of the weak that was crucial to the Athenians' idealized self-image (cf. Heath 1990, 394). After flirting briefly with a highly

---

[23] There are many interconnections between the five speeches, which can be read as a complete sequence in Behr's translation (1986).

sophistical response (6), the speaker solves the appeal to custom with an argument from justice, a quality crucial to the interventions hallowed by tradition and absent (he claims) in the present situation.

11–16 **Advantage:** By neutrality Athens can at no cost to itself inflict damage on both of its rivals while remaining on friendly terms with both; intervention would be a costly way of inflicting damage on one side only while incurring (because of the bad faith of its ally) the enmity of both.

17–28 **Justice:** This topic is introduced by a counterposed appeal to the services rendered by one or other side; justice demands a recompense. The response is a caustic review of the harm inflicted on Athens by both sides (17–20); an even-handed approach precludes both injury to either side (both being benefactors) and help to either side (both being hostile). The section concludes with a demonstration (adumbrated in the prologue) that the opposed arguments of the Spartan and Theban partisans collapse into the speaker's case for neutrality (25–8).

29–32 **Feasibility:** The first speaker had recommended as a model the Persian policy of keeping the strongest Greek power in check by supporting its weaker rivals (*First Leuctrian* 59); the second speaker objected to the moral basis of this policy (*Second Leuctrian* 33). The advocate of neutrality echoes this objection and adds a warning about the difficulty of what is proposed: unlike the king of Persia, Athens would be unable to avoid costly direct involvement.

33–42 **Consequence:** This leads into an exploration of the consequences both of entering and of keeping out of the war. Non-intervention would not (as might be feared: cf. *First Leuctrian* 2) give one side a quick victory (33), while intervention would embroil the city in many difficulties, as the Argives once found (34). It would be foolish to expose Athens to the instabilities of war (35) when there is an opportunity to rebuild its prosperity in peace (36), and thus to restore its hegemony (37). There is nothing to fear from neutrality (38–40), while involvement in the war entails risk and harm whatever the outcome (40 f.).

43–4 **Epilogue:** The speech ends with a summary of the policy proposed, and a brief reminder to the audience of whose interest their deliberations should be serving.

4. ILLUSTRATIONS

AELIUS ARISTIDES *FIFTH LEUCTRIAN ORATION*

1   If I too, men of Athens, am allowed freedom of speech, I shall try to give my opinion of the present situation; and I ask you not to interrupt until you have heard me out. It is not easy to submit your interests to an unbiased scrutiny. The speakers who have supported one side or the other enjoy the favour both of those they have chosen to support, and also of those among you who share their views. But those who dissociate themselves from that and are neutral have no opportunity to speak for the gratification of either of those parties, nor to tell you what you want and expect to hear. Partisan speakers who fail in their aim gain far more than the neutral one does by winning the argument. They have the friendship of the side for whom they contended, but he gets no gratitude from you.

2   But I will not shirk this matter, despite its drawbacks. For it is my view that those people here who have spoken on either side are still in need of someone who will speak on your side. If you will regard me as that man, I will show gratitude to you on your own behalf. For those who have spoken for others will enjoy the favour of the people they chose to support even if they are defeated by the opposition. But a neutral speaker has deprived himself in advance of the favour of both parties, and it is

3   unclear what kind of reception he will receive from you. It is by no means the same thing to support what is advantageous to others and so retain the goodwill of those among you who share the same view, and to stand up for you and so provoke you. In that case, one has in defeat forfeited the goodwill of three groups, while victory and success leave one in the same position as those who have been defeated; but they have others in place of you whom they have chosen to support and whom they have made their friends.

4   Now, it seems to me shameful, unstatesmanlike, and totally unfair that when there is a debate in Athens speakers can be found to support Thebes and Sparta, but there are none to support you. Even so, I commend the speakers on both sides, since they have found many admirable arguments against each other and so between them have helped me to see the position that I should adopt about them. I think that even if I had been completely devoid of ideas of my own, I would be able to discern the best course by following what these people have said. And yet I find fault with them in one respect: although they have disguised themselves and sought to conceal the fact that they are speaking to please one side or the other, the one thing they could not avoid revealing was that they

were seeking to conceal it. For what is the point of saying 'I have not now   5
come forward to gratify the Thebans', and then telling us to go to their
aid? Or 'It is not my intention to gratify the Spartans', and then ordering you to expose yourselves to danger on their behalf? If this pose is
genuine on both sides, and you should accept what they say (and that is
what I myself say you should do), then my argument for non-involve-
ment has a place on both sides. But as things are, it is as if you were seeking someone to declare war on and it were not your duty to seek the
course of action that is in the city's best interest; one side is telling you
to go to war with these people, the other with those, as if you would lose
out by exposing yourselves to no risk. But a middle way was open to
them: to advise you to associate with neither side and to get on with your
own affairs. There is nothing which will bring greater gain to the city,
nothing that will do more to keep our young men safe and be a safeguard
to our ships, our resources, and us all.

They say that you and your ancestors have taken upon yourselves   6
many dangers on behalf of others; and they are right. But if you take such
thought for others that you are not deterred even by the need to go to
war on their behalf, will you not take enough thought for yourselves
to prevent you running unnecessary risks? Surely it is inappropriate to
secure other people's advantage even at some risk to yourselves, and to
neglect our own advantage when it costs us nothing? And if anyone cares   7
to consider why our forefathers were renowned—was it just because of
their naval and military exertions and their love of danger? Or was it
because of the character of their deeds and the reasons for them, which
were sensible and compelling?—he would not, I think, say the former.
He would be ascribing to them praise more appropriate to pirates and
buccaneers if that was what he admired, and if he thought that one
should emulate the incessant exposure of oneself to danger. In my view   8
what made them deservedly glorious was defending the Greeks against
the barbarians and never deserting the cause of justice for the sake of
ease. But the present war has no such status, such as to give you a part in
it either out of necessity, or as protector, or for some such just cause. For
this very point is irresolvable: which side ought we to aid? Why? For one
thing, if the fact that you have helped many in their affairs should be
grounds for being active now as well, this applies to both sides. So the
grounds for joining one side justly will be grounds for seeing your disregard of the other side as an error. Secondly, if we should bear in mind   9
the injustice that we have suffered at the hands of each party, we will
attach ourselves to neither; but if we remit the blame, we surely will not

do so for one side and not the other, but for both alike. This being the case, there is no side to which we can show preference, since they both
10   have the same claim. And more generally, is it not strange, supposing that we should help one side in accordance with the principle of not bearing grudges, that we should join them in the deliberate destruction of the other side? So if we should give aid, but cannot give it to both sides, the principle of amnesty is neutral: we should not aid the one side (because we ought to aid the other side as well), nor the other side
11   (because we would be obliged to do it for the first side too). So because we should bear no grudges, we should give no aid.

What has come about is the thing one would most have prayed for. Thebes and Sparta have clashed; you have been given an opportunity for rest and recreation while they are embroiled in unremitting warfare. This in my view is due to some god's protection and providence for the city. If we had wanted to punish them, it would have involved trouble and risk; if we did nothing, they escaped with impunity. But now fortune's stratagem has brought things to a point where we can stay at home
12   and use them to punish themselves. This opportunity must be exploited prudently and with caution. It is not the victory of one side over the other to which you should give thought, but your own freedom from the interference of either. It would be strange if, when each side has sought its own advantage—not yours—in sending envoys here, you should place their interests ahead of your own.

13   Consider, by god, who is making the better and more moderate case. Those who urge you to put yourselves to trouble, to avenge yourselves on one side, and to do this as an enemy? Or the man who advises you to run no risks, to punish both sides, and to do so without coming into conflict with either? If you do march out to battle, it is far from clear that you would be treated in good faith by those who have fought alongside you. But if you stay at home, quite apart from ensuring your own security, it
14   is transparently clear that both sides will be grateful to you. Neither side will blame you because they did not win you over to fight on their side; they know that this is not possible. But both sides will be grateful (and rightly so) because they experienced no injury at your hands; they know that this is the only course open to those who have decided to harm nei-
15   ther side. Is it not better to grind both of them down while winning gratitude from both than to attach ourselves to one side and make friends of neither, but have first one and then the other as our enemy? That my suspicions are reasonable has just now been demonstrated, in the case of Sparta by the advocates of Thebes, and in the case of Thebes by the

advocates of Sparta. And the point is clear even aside from their argu- 16
ments. In the past they have always conspired and co-operated with each
other in everything more closely than any one people participates in its
own affairs; but now that they have come up against each other with such
commitment and passion they want to be friends with you, whom in the
past they treated unjustly. Clearly their attitude to you in future will not
be straightforward or just, especially since their invitation stems from
need, not goodwill. Indeed, when they see us sitting to one side and still
are at each other's throats, how can we doubt that once we had destroyed
one side the survivors would turn against us in the knowledge that, if
they conquer us, no one will be left to oppose them?

'But, my dear sir, on other grounds it is just to take the risk, even if we 17
have to endure such arrogance. It would be terrible to disregard the
Spartans—or the Thebans—men whose services to our city are so many
and so great.' In my view, the number of services on each side makes it
impossible for me to decide which has conferred more or greater benefits on us. First I reflect on the friendly zeal with which they both
invaded our territory annually for almost thirty years in succession;[24]
then again, on the untroubled ease with which they fortified Decelea
against us and obstructed us in Sicily, and were on hand everywhere even
before they were summoned. As for the destruction of Plataea, I think
they both will yield the honour to the other. 'Yes, by god, but the 18
Thebans did not fight badly at Delium.' Will anyone say that the
Spartans fought worse at Amphipolis? As for their other services, there
are so many I cannot give an accurate list. That is how they have treated
Athens turn and turn about. 'But the Thebans attached themselves to
the king of Persia in the past.' So did the Spartans later, despite the tro-
phies which they set up with us.[25] Do I not have good reason to be
uncertain which are responsible for greater good towards our city? 'Yes, 19
by god, Sparta voted for our city's survival.' True. 'And didn't Thebes

[24] During the Peloponnesian War (431–404 BC) Sparta invaded Attica repeatedly
(although not annually) with the support of their Theban allies. The speaker goes on to
mention other incidents in this war. In 413 the Spartans established a permanent base in
Attica at Decelea, and at the same time aided and encouraged Syracusan resistance to the
Athenian expeditionary force in Sicily. A Theban attack on Athens' ally Plataea was one
of the opening moves in the war; Sparta co-operated in the siege, and the city was razed
after its surrender in 427. Athenian armies were defeated by Thebes at the battle of Delium
(424), and by Sparta at the battle of Amphipolis (422).

[25] Thebes went over to the Persian side during Xerxes' invasion (480 BC); Sparta
and Athens jointly led the Greek resistance. But in 386 (in the 'King's Peace') Sparta
secured its hegemony in Greece by recognizing Persian control of the Greek cities in Asia
Minor.

ignore the Spartan summons?' That is also true. So should we be grateful to the Spartans for not destroying the city in the same way they did Plataea, and to the Thebans for refusing to invade?[26] Or should we be angry with the Spartans for reducing us to a state of dependence on them, and find fault with the Thebans for joining in all their previous invasions, rather than owe gratitude to the former for saving us and to the latter for failing to join the invasion on one single occasion? We should not be more bitter towards the Thebans for voting for our destruction than we are towards the Spartans for giving them the opportunity to cast their vote about us as they saw fit; nor should we be more angry with the Spartans for their campaign against Plataea than we are with the Thebans because of the reason for their desertion—if we are allowed to consider that precisely, we will find that it was the failure of their vote to carry the day.

But why do I go into these details? If anyone wants to count these things as outstanding services, I do not dispute it. But I will tell you what I think. If we are to consider whether they have done Athens any good, I do not believe that we should mention the services of Thebes and Sparta's acts of injustice, nor *vice versa*. We should state what good both sides have done. And if we are to examine their arrogance we should not publicize that of one side and conceal that on the other side behind their good deeds. But since there is both on both sides, there are two alternatives: either we injure neither since both are our benefactors; or we conclude that both are hostile to us, and help neither. In fact, if both are to receive what they deserve, because of the injuries they have done us let neither receive help, and because of the good they have done us let neither suffer harm. In this way you will have adopted a good policy with respect to them both. But if you incline to one side or the other, you will be treating neither justly. You will be doing good to one side despite their injustice and destroying the other despite their services, although it is possible to be good stewards of justice and to moderate your commitment to either side to the extent that excessive hostility towards the other is inappropriate. And, if it has to be said, I think we have already shown the Thebans sufficient gratitude for refusing to join in the invasion and for giving Thrasybulus refuge, by killing Lysander and co-operating in all the other acts with which you are familiar; and we should now show

20

21

22

23

[26] After Athens' surrender in 404 BC Thebes urged the city's destruction, but Sparta refused. Subsequently Thebes gave refuge to the Athenian democrats in exile, and declined to join in the Spartan intervention after the restoration of democracy in Athens. For the destruction of Plataea see n. 24.

our gratitude to the Spartans for their vote by passing over the opportunity we now have to join the Thebans in their destruction.[27] Our alliance with the one side should have sufficient force to prevent us attaching ourselves to the Spartans; and the Spartans' past kindness should prevail on us to the extent of our not now siding with the Thebans. This point 24 too makes them equal: it is unreasonable to help either the Spartans, since they have broken their pledges, or the Thebans, since they have already inflicted a severe punishment. We cannot honourably join in trampling on the former, nor hinder the latter in their just indignation.

I shall question separately those who have spoken on each side. 25 Gentlemen, you who have spoken for Sparta: what is it you are aiming for? Do you want to prevent the Thebans gaining the alliance, and to ensure that the Spartans suffer no unkindness at our hands? That is what I advocate as well. Very well. Gentlemen, you who have spoken for Thebes: is it your wish that no impediment is put in the way of the Thebans, and that we should not incline to the Spartans? I cast my vote with you. So why do we shout aimlessly and squabble, when there is an impartial and just mediator in view? But neutrality in the war is not enough for these people—whether or not it is for you is another question. But if there are three things which you are aiming at between 26 you—first, that the side you have chosen to support should suffer no harm; second, that their opponents should receive no help; and third, that you will be able to strengthen those you support—and if of these three I dispense with the last and retain the first two, do I not share your opinion twice as much as I dissent from it? And I should add that I share your view in those respects in which you yourselves would admit that your case is stronger. For of course the shared pursuit of the city's interest is preferable to private involvement in partiality or animosity. What each of you criticizes the other side for doing, you are doing yourselves. You forbid mention of services rendered—but you yourselves run through those of the side you support. You offer a defence on the charges that have been brought—and then take on the role of accuser.

Well, men of Athens, I do not contradict myself and am moreover in 27 agreement with these people; but they—on both sides—manifestly contradict both their own arguments and those of their opponents. And perhaps I too, since I disagree with neither side to the extent that I share their opinion, should be allowed my turn? For there is no way that 28

---

[27] See n. 26. Thrasybulus was the leader of the exiled Athenian democrats. Athens allied itself with Thebes in 395; the Spartan general Lysander was killed at the battle of Haliartus (in fact before the arrival of the Athenian contingent).

advocacy could contrive to urge you to help both sides: how could you? So the advocate's position turns out to be to attack neither side; for each of these two parties objects to joining in the other's campaign. So my argument is nothing other than (so to speak) something read out by a clerk who has strung together each side's speech and made a single speech out of two.

29   Moreover, the point about the king of Persia (I am sure you remember) that was made just now forbids us to help either side, rather than enjoining us to help one or the other. Let me explain what I mean. It is not possible, according to this argument, to help the Thebans, since they collaborated with Persia; nor the Spartans, because they too emulate the king of Persia's evil ways.[28] Nor is it at all fitting for you to be heirs to his malice and duplicity. Surely you would deny hating Greece so much that you would seek to weaken it as he did; nor is it tolerable that you should show yourselves to be fickle. But there can be no objection to letting the combatants reach a decision by themselves, and no

30   one would resent your doing that. Furthermore, the king of Persia did not come here in person or run any physical risk. His contribution to the troubles was financial, given his great wealth; and he sent one of his many subordinates. That was the way the king made war: Pharnabazus, Pissouthnes, Tissaphernes, deceit, gold, and so forth. But if we incline to either side, we shall suffer exactly what the king was guarding against

31   by these means. He took care never to run risks on his own account, and so he spun out the troubles from a distance. By contrast we will put at risk our lives, our land, and (in a word) all our resources. We cannot make war by proxy; nor can we stay remote from the war and foment troubles; nor can we learn about them by report; nor can our participation in events be an undemanding supplement, kept within bounds set by our own discretion. We have to be on the spot and share in the labour; we have to expose ourselves to no less risk than the original parties to the conflict; and we cannot send a subordinate whenever

32   we so choose. Even if we could wage war with money, our resources are certainly not such as to allow us to divert them to a commitment of this magnitude. And even if we could contribute to one side or the other in this way, it cannot be said that there is Susa or Ecbatana, or that they must put the sea a year's march out of sight behind

---

[28] i.e. the policy of supporting the weaker of two parties against the stronger to ensure that neither becomes a threat to oneself, recommended by the first (pro-Spartan) speaker (*First Leuctrian* 59, cf. *Second Leuctrian* 33). For Spartan complicity with Persia see n. 25.

them.[29] It is one or two days' travelling for those we harm to invade, ravage, and plunder us; so this course of action will inevitably result in hand-to-hand combat—that is, in misfortune.

I would myself have urged you to come to the aid of Sparta because of the excessive power of Thebes, if I did not believe that the Thebans' advantage in numbers and strength will be counterbalanced by the Spartans' training. If they had been equal, I would have feared for Thebes as the weaker side; but since the Thebans have (I am glad to say) gained superiority I conclude that the war is evenly balanced. The Spartans can overtake them despite their slower start. The war will be long-drawn-out because the Thebans, keyed up by their successes, will seek outright victory, while the Spartans' belief in their superior courage and resolution will prevent their tolerating any advantage on the other side.

If we should imitate anyone's behaviour, that of the Argives is a fine model.[30] During the war between ourselves and Sparta they kept quiet and their youth, the condition of their land, and everything of theirs flourished. But when they got involved in the troubles they lost their existing prosperity, their democracy was overthrown, and other ills ensued. War, one might say, begets everything: the overthrow of constitutions, strife, an unpredictable variety of harms, which we (of all people) because of our experience of them would rightly guard against.

I understand that our ancestors who lived in those days ceded Salamis to Megara for a time, and passed a decree that anyone who proposed its recovery should be put to death.[31] Since it is sometimes necessary and advantageous to withdraw from and surrender what is one's own, how can it be right to take over someone else's problems? How can it be right to resent it if it so happens that either of the parties now calling on us invaded Attica in the past, while we recklessly impel ourselves into war and confused instability, although we know that it is easy to start a war and hard—harder than anything—to stop it? Most men choose danger when they are their own masters, and avoid it when they are at another's mercy; but neither course is the behaviour of sensible men.

Our land has been ravaged continually; our bodies have long wasted

33

34

35

36

[29] According to Herodotus 5. 50–4 the Persian capital Susa was just over three months' march inland—far enough for the Spartan king Cleomenes to dismiss the idea of attacking Persia as absurd.

[30] Argos was neutral during the first part of the Peloponnesian War. Her alignment with Athens after 421 led to defeat at the battle of Mantinea (418) and subsequent internal conflict.

[31] See Demosthenes 19. 252, Plutarch *Solon* 8.

away; the massive funds we once accumulated on the acropolis have been expended; there is a shortage of men of military age. The city is just now recovering; let us do it no damage. While these people treat each other with hatred, anger, aggression, and threats, let us sit by as umpires in the war and take care of our city. Let us husband its money, horses, and ships and in general build up its affairs like those who restore ruined house-

37 holds. If you take my advice and restrain yourselves, embassies will come a second time from both sides; they will come, I assure you, when all your affairs are in such manifest good order and good repair. And I think that not only these, but (by the favour of the gods) many others will send embassies to seek our friendship if you are patient and are willing to use these people's conflict to establish your hegemony.

38 No one will say that he is afraid that the two sides will unite, and leave each other alone to turn on us. I do not mean that either side is well dis-posed towards us, but the logic of the situation is against it. On what grounds, by god, will they unite? 'Because, by god, we did not join either side's campaign.' The more angry they are, the more impossible it is for them to unite. When both sides are furious because they were unable to use us to harm their opponents, how will they leave them alone? How will they join each other, when each side knows that the other is angry

39 because it did not have you as allies against them? And aside from that, as things stand they could not spare the time and effort. The Thebans are pressing on in the belief that there is a chance of their destroying Sparta; the work they are now engaged in they would not abandon for the king of Persia's empire. As for the Spartans, they would all die happy if they can avenge themselves on Thebes. That is how angry they are— and it is no wonder if those who think they suffered an undeserved defeat

40 are resentful out of shame. In sum, their hatred of Thebes and their exas-peration have overshadowed their hostility towards Athens; as if a cloud had intervened, they see nothing that bears on us.

If we are afraid of them now, despite doing them no injury, will we not have good reason to be much more afraid that if we join one side the other will win? As things are, we have nothing to fear if the victors make some new move. Exhausted and weary, they will soon realize that they have won a Cadmean victory[32] if they pit themselves against us, unharmed and fresh. But if we join one side, either it will turn out that

41 we win; in that case we will inevitably have taken an equal share in the trouble and harm, so that we will be in no better state than they are if

[32] Proverbial for a self-destructive victory (e.g. Herodotus 1. 166); cf. Libanius Or. 28. 18, 30. 47.

they subsequently treat us unfairly. Alternatively, if affairs go badly the danger is self-evident. As things are, the victors will win the victory for us; but in the other event one side will prevail (if it so happens) through our exertions. Moreover, our affairs are unlike theirs in other ways. The Spartans live on the far side of the Peloponnese, well protected from war and trouble. The Thebans are at a distance beyond Cithaeron. But our city is on the route of war, and neither side will have any access to the other before invading our territory, so ripe for destruction. 42

In general I do not see that we have any cause to go to war if we will not fight with either side to destruction, or if we sit in the middle sparing both adversaries.[33] It is possible for us to avoid the appearance of harming either one side or the other, making no provocative statement to the ambassadors, but in this gentle and moderate fashion to tell both that if they were calling us against others we would have paid ready attention, but since they call us against each other we are unwilling to be involved, not out of a reluctance to help one side, but out of reluctance to injure either. 43

This is what seems to me reasonable, whichever way I view the matter. But I am afraid, men of Athens, that you may be better at putting right the affairs of others than at managing your own well. 44

4.6 OBJECTION AND THE LEGAL ISSUES

A husband who catches another man in bed with his wife may lawfully kill them both (see on Hermogenes *43. 3–8); but what if a wife catches her husband in bed with another woman? Sopater offers two different analyses of a theme based on this scenario.

The theme is first treated as objection. The defence claims that the charge is invalid because the law explicitly allows the killing of an adulterer; the prosecution does not deny that the killing of an adulterer is lawful, but in this instance objects to one circumstance of the killing—the fact that it was done by the injured wife, not the injured husband. Sopater comments on the treatment of both sides of the case (discussing the defence's case first, although the prosecutor would in reality speak first). He begins by noting that an advocate speaks for the woman (who would not normally be eligible to speak in a Greek court), although he seems to slip into the first person at some points.

[33] The text here is corrupt, and the interpretation most uncertain.

His division of objection differs slightly from Hermogenes', although the strategy is substantially the same. At 248. 6–8 Sopater says that the defendant uses intent to solve the objection: 'for every counterposed verbal instrument (ῥητόν) is . . . solved first on the grounds of intent (διάνοια).' At first sight this seems to be the standard opposition between letter and intent; but since the woman's exception assumes that the law gives explicit licence for the killing, she should not need to appeal to the implied meaning of the law here. In fact 'intent' has a broad sense (any meaning ascribed to a verbal instrument) as well as a narrow sense (the implicit as opposed to the explicit meaning of that instrument); thus in Hermogenes 83. 2 f. both parties in letter and intent use the heading intent. Sopater's point, then, must be that in reply to the prosecutor's objection, which makes a distinction as to the person or persons permitted to kill an adulterer not explicit in the law, the defence offers its own account of the law's intent, in which the person makes no difference—a point elaborated in the following series of definitional heads leading up to an assimilation: 'So it is just the same to receive the fatal blow from a man and from a woman' (248. 17–19). Note that Sopater includes importance among the definitional heads (see p. 140), using it as a point of entry to the counteraccusation against the dead husband. At the end of the wife's speech, note the reference to preliminary exercises supplying material (249. 21 f.)—here, the common topic against adultery.

The analysis of the prosecution's speech presents a serious problem of interpretation. The prosecutor solves the defence's intent γνωμικῶς: 'for every intent is solved by γνώμη' (250. 18 f.). γνώμη may mean 'maxim'; but it is not true that intent is always solved by citing maxims, and there is nothing of the kind in this context. Innes and Winterbottom (ad loc.) conclude that the text is corrupt, and suggest that intent ought to be solved by the letter; but (as explained above) that opposition does not seem to be in question here. Another possible sense of γνώμη is 'intention', as in legislator's intention (γνώμη νομοθέτου). It would not be absurd for the prosecutor to respond to the defence's account of the law's intent by exploring the intention of the legislator; and this is, in fact, what the ensuing argument amounts to ('knowing who suffer most from this outrage . . . it is to them that he conceded the right of vengeance').[34]

Subsequently Sopater (or some later annotator) rejected the analysis of the theme as objection, and treated it afresh as assimilation. On this view the defence does not maintain that the law explicitly invalidates the

---

[34] But the adverbial form γνωμικῶς can hardly bear this sense, and is perhaps best deleted as a gloss on οὕτως.

charge, but nevertheless argues that there is an implicit warrant for the killing of an adulterous husband by his wife. This technical difference expresses a substantive difference in strategy. The second approach is more cautious and, given ancient Greek attitudes to marriage and adultery, more prudent. Faced with a law on the killing of adulterers most Greeks would assume that it applied to the injured husband; the idea that it applied to wives as well would be neither self-evident nor (in view of precedents like Clytaemnestra) appealing. The defence therefore does not present at the outset its claim that the law gives the injured wife a licence to kill her husband; instead it argues towards this interpretation of the law by the strategy of assimilation. The stronger claim might provide a more effective defence if successful, but risks seeming simply impudent if it miscarries. In evaluating different strategies of argument the rhetorician has to balance opportunity against risk (see, on a different level, Hermogenes 49. 3–6 and the note on *48. 3–9).

In Hermogenes' paradigm of assimilation the letter was possessed by the defence and the prosecution argued for the equivalence of the act performed to that specified in the law; here, it is the prosecution which claims possession of the letter (assuming that the law's explicit reference is only to husbands) and the defence which attempts the assimilation.

Sopater begins (383. 25–7) by restating his doctrine that in the legal issues an initial enquiry based on the verbal instrument will be followed by a second enquiry divided according to one of the logical issues (see 348. 21–349. 9, and e.g. 344. 18–25). This two-part structure is identical to that of documentary objection in Hermogenes (79. 19–80. 3); in his division of the legal issues themselves Hermogenes incorporates a logical component by placing a counterposition in the secondary stage of the argument, achieving the same effect in a slightly different way.

The legal enquiry is given in the most summary way, but has substantially the same structure as in Hermogenes. The defence counterposes the prosecutor's appeal to the letter, and offers a solution 'based on equality'; this is the assimilation proper, using the first of Hermogenes' four classes (89. 16 f.). Legislator's intention follows, explaining the rationale of the law as the defence understands it ('it is granted to me, above all . . .'), followed by the amplificatory heads of the definition-sequence. Sopater does not include forcible definition.

The associated logical enquiry is a counteraccusation. The prosecutor's response is an objection to the manner of the punishment; the defence in turn solves this by counterplea, appealing first to nature (see

p. 115) and then to the equivalent verdict of a hypothetical jury as evidence of the legality of the killing.

SOPATER *DIVISION OF QUESTIONS* 247. 8–252. 2

> It is legal for an adulterer to be killed summarily. A wife caught her husband committing adultery and killed him. She is charged with homicide.

The *statement* of the wife (obviously, an advocate speaks for her) contains her education by her parents, their frequent advice on self-control, that they said that this is what sustains the democracy: 'If you have this virtue, child, you will have everything that follows in succession. This is what preserves the laws, this is what upholds the constitution.' Then you will say: 'The woman was raised on these words and lived her life on these terms; and when she had the good fortune to obtain a companion to father her children, her desire and ambition was to keep these commandments, to seek to bring joy to her household by her chastity. But—how it came about I do not know—she saw her husband breaking the law, destroying the foundations of the constitution, annulling what is held lawful among you, corrupting family, succession, inheritance; and she came to the laws' defence,' and so forth.

Then introduce the *exception*; the wife will have this directly:[35] 'Then, for killing an adulterer, she is subjected to judgement and trial. The laws themselves had condemned the crime; but she is subjected to judgement. She is brought to account before you as if she had committed a crime, although the laws clearly granted permission to kill.' And such like exceptions.

After the exception you will place the *objection*, which always and necessarily arises, since it is what gives the issue its character. For the wife it is counterposed: 'But, he says, you are not the person the law allows to kill.' You will solve this first of all on the grounds of *intent*; for every counterposed verbal instrument is necessarily and invariably solved first on the grounds of intent. Then in the same way with other relevant solutions; e.g. 'But the law does not distinguish whether men or women should kill, but simply says that adulterers may be killed.' You will develop this using the definitional heads; e.g. first, *definition*: 'It makes

[35] i.e. not by counterposition; contrast the prosecutor's use of this head below (250. 8–10).

no difference whether an adulterer is killed by a woman or by a man; where the purpose is fulfilled and is the same, any other difference is completely pointless.' Then: 'Everyone looks to the purpose. Sailors look to coming to land; the manner is immaterial. Those who are ill look to be cured; whether they are relieved of their ailment one way or another is of no concern.' Then *assimilation*: 'So it is just the same to receive the fatal blow from a man and from a woman.' Then *importance*: 'It is immaterial whether he died this way or that; the point you should consider is whether he deserved to die.' Then, since he is an adulterer, a *counterposition* is relevant in accordance with one of the counterpositionals, I mean counteraccusation: 'He deserved to die, because he did harm to the family, corrupted the concord of wives towards their husbands and the inheritance of sons from their fathers, and would not allow the parentage of children to be known,' and so forth.

After the counterposition you will place the *second objection*. This does   249
not necessarily occur, but is derived from the circumstances, as in this case; e.g.: 'But, he says, you should have consulted the city on this matter.' You will solve this on the grounds of the law: 'There was nothing to be gained. If the law had been ambiguous, it would have been right to consult the people. But where the text expressly stated what was to be done, what need was there to trouble the people?' Then: 'If I had brought him before the people, they would certainly have judged him according to the laws, and in that case would have suggested a course of action in accordance with the laws. Since the people would have obeyed the laws, there is nothing untoward if she forestalled them in complying with the laws.'

The *epilogue* remains: 'Give the laws their strength, give democracy its due. Show that democracy is maintained by self-control, and that when husbands are away everyone will guard their wives—brothers, fathers,[36] relatives, and friends alike. Let everyone know that the law has chosen to arm wives with chastity, and has enjoined them too to preserve the glory of chastity.' Then the common epilogue, as in a common topic, since he was an adulterer; you can supply all the topics from the preliminary exercise.

The prosecutor's *statement* contains a mixed narrative, partly against the wife, partly in defence of the adulterer. For it is sensible to attack the wife for killing illegally and to speak as persuasively as possible in the husband's defence. So you will say that they lived together; the husband   250

---

[36] See Innes and Winterbottom ad loc.; the transmitted text ('wives') is obviously corrupt.

had never been condemned by the people; and that at the beginning even the wife admired him for his self-control. Then: 'She found her husband, how I do not know, with a woman; and at once, as if she had laid hold of some villain, she made no allowance for human nature and showed no pity for his mistake, but at once resorted to murder, at once resorted to butchery,' and so forth.

After the statement you will place the woman's *exception* by counterposition; e.g.: 'Then she says, I ought not to be brought to trial for killing an adulterer.' The solution is by *objection*; for this belongs to the prosecutor: '. . . as if we were claiming that he should not have been killed for being an adulterer. That is not what I am saying, but that it was not right for her to inflict the penalty, for a woman to use her right hand against adulterers, nor for a man's partner to use the sword.' Then after the objection solve the *intent* of the law; e.g.: 'Now, after breaking the law, she has the audacity to provide you all with explanations of the text. She claims that the law grants permission to kill adulterers indiscriminately to everyone.' Then adduce its solution thus (for every intent is solved by intention):[37] 'But I assert that the law has very clearly distinguished who may rightly kill an adulterer. Knowing who suffer most from this outrage—that the husbands are the sufferers—it is to them that he conceded the right of vengeance.' 'And knowing who it is that the disaster of adultery most afflicts, and that the sufferers are obvious to all, he ratified retaliation for them.' 'But if one grants that this distinction of persons is not made in the law, then retaliation is the right of the relatives, retaliation is the right of the family that is wronged, to prevent any member of the family being harmed in respect of succession.'[38] Then adduce the heads of *definition*: 'You, who are not related to the family in any way, but are a complete stranger to it, you planned to make yourself accountable to the law by taking vengeance.' Then: 'Who does not know that there is a great difference between a husband catching an adulterer with his partner, and your killing your adulterous husband?' Then the *assimilation*: 'It is obvious that the station of a husband and a wife are different; and their designation in the laws is not the same.' All this you should expand with examples, maxims, comparisons, and so forth. Then after assimilation you will place *importance*: 'This is a matter of the greatest import, a terrible and outstanding calamity, that a woman should kill

251

[37] See the preamble for the problem of text and interpretation here.

[38] The point is that if the distinction is not granted, any relative who might be adversely affected by the adultery is licensed to kill the adulterer; this consequence, the prosecutor implies, is absurd.

an adulterer.' Then from the converse: 'If it had been a man, whose legal right vengeance is, I would have said nothing after the killing. But since it is a woman who has brought this tragedy to fulfilment against her partner and has filled the house with disaster, I consider the atrocity fearful, unendurable,' and so forth.

Then after the heads of definition you will place the wife's counterposed *counteraccusation*: 'But he deserved his death.' You will solve by *objection*: 'You should have consulted the people.' E.g.: 'He deserved it, I say so myself: but he deserved to suffer at the hands of the people, to be killed by the laws themselves. You have robbed the people and the laws of their sovereignty, setting aside ⟨. . .⟩.'[39] Then you will state his desert in this way: 'An adulterer deserves punishment: but the public executioner should strike the blow, the people should pass judgement,' and so forth.

Then you will speak the *epilogue*, which is common; e.g.: 'Punish her for killing unjustly, for despising the laws'; and you will fill out the epilogue as in a common topic.

252

SOPATER *DIVISION OF QUESTIONS* 384. 16–385. 24

One might suppose that the problem is an objection, because only the person of the wife is in question: does the law grant permission to kill adulterers to her, or only to the husbands of the women involved? But the problem is not of this kind; the issue is assimilation, because of the claim that permission is granted equally to husbands and wives, and the enquiry is concerned with the verbal instrument; this is not the case in objection.

As I have said before, after the initial proposition based on the verbal instrument every legal issue[40] will be divided according to the incident issue; and this is exactly what we will do in the present question.

The first counterposition in it is that based on the law: 'But you are not the person the law allows to kill adulterers.' The solution is based on equality: 'Instructing husbands to kill adulterers and granting impunity to wives are equivalent. If the legislator had not obviously meant this, he would have specified that wives should not kill adulterers, or that only husbands should do this.' Next: 'It makes no difference whether the penalty is inflicted by a man or a woman.' Also: 'It is granted to me,

385

---

[39] The text is lacunose at this point; see Innes and Winterbottom ad loc.
[40] Reading στάσις (or ζήτησις, 'enquiry') for the transmitted διαίρεσις ('division').

above all, whom he wronged by his adultery.' And in general for the solution of the verbal instrument all the heads of definition as far as importance and relative importance.

After the legal enquiry and the definitional solution there arises a counterpositional issue, the counteraccusation, which follows on from the definitional heads and is developed in turn. The prosecutor solves it by counterposing[41] an objection to the counteraccusation; e.g., 'You should have brought a charge, or informed the assembly.' The wife will solve this on the grounds of distress, anger, occasion, and because if she brought a charge she might not have received full satisfaction; for the outcome of court cases is uncertain. Also: 'The jury would have done just the same, if they passed judgement in accordance with the law,' and so forth.

After that you will place the epilogues, containing intense indignation and arguments from advantage on behalf of women, so that husbands will show self-control and not commit two wrongs, outraging some by their adultery and grieving others by the fact of their outrages.

[41] The word is not used here in either of its technical senses. This passage neatly illustrates the convolutions to which rhetorical terminology can lead: one of the counterpositions (i.e. counteraccusation) is used directly by the defence and counterposed (i.e. cited as an argument on the other side) by the prosecution, which now counterposes (i.e. places in opposition) an objection to solve it.

Bibliography

*PIR*²	E. Groag, A. Stein, L. Petersen (eds.), *Prosopographia Imperii Romani* (Berlin and Leipzig 1933–87)
PLRE	A. H. M. Jones, J. M. Martindale, J. Morris (eds.), *Prosopography of the Later Roman Empire* (Cambridge 1971–92)
PS	H. Rabe (ed.), *Prolegomenon Sylloge* (Leipzig 1931)
RE	Pauly–Wissowa, *Realenzyklopädie der klassischen Altertumswissenschaft*
RG	C. Walz, *Rhetores Graeci* (Stuttgart 1832–6)
RLM	K. Halm (ed.), *Rhetores Latini Minores* (Leipzig 1863)
sch. Dem.	M. R. Dilts (ed.), *Scholia Demosthenica* (Leipzig 1983–6)
Spengel	L. Spengel (ed.), *Rhetores Graeci* ii–iii (Leipzig 1854–6)
Spengel–Hammer	L. Spengel and C. Hammer (eds.), *Rhetores Graeci* i/2 (Leipzig 1894)

ADAMIETZ, J., 1966, *M. F. Quintiliani Institutionis Oratoriae Liber III* (Studia et Testimonia Antiqua 2, Munich).

—— 1986, 'Quintilians "Institutio oratoria"', *ANRW* II.32.4, 2226–71.

ANDERSON, G., 1982, 'Lucian: A Sophist's Sophist', *YCS* 27, 61–92.

—— 1986, *Philostratus* (London).

—— 1989, 'The *pepaideumenos* in Action: Sophists and their Outlook in the Early Roman Empire', *ANRW* II.33.1, 29–208.

—— 1993, *The Second Sophistic* (London).

AULITZKY, K., 1917, 'Apsines περὶ ἐλέου', *WS* 39, 26–49.

BALDWIN, B., 1973, *Studies in Lucian* (Toronto).

BALDWIN, C. S., 1928, *Medieval Rhetoric and Poetic* (New York).

BARWICK, K., 1961, 'Augustins Schrift De Rhetorica und Hermagoras von Temnos', *Philologus* 105, 97–110.

—— 1964, 'Zur Erklärung und Geschichte der Staseislehre des Hermagoras von Temnos', *Philologus* 108, 80–101.

—— 1965, 'Probleme in den Rhet. LL Ciceros und der Rhetorik des sogenannten Auctor ad Herennium', *Philologus* 109, 57–74.

BERRY, D. H., and HEATH, M., forthcoming, 'Oratory and Declamation', in S. E. Porter (ed.), *A Handbook of Classical Rhetoric* (Leiden).

BOMPAIRE, J., 1958, *Lucien Écrivain: Imitation et Création* (Paris).

BONNER, S. F., 1949, *Roman Declamation* (Liverpool).

—— 1977, *Education in Ancient Rome* (London).

BOOTH, A. D., 1983, 'A quel âge Libanius est-il entré à l'école du rhéteur?', *Byzantion* 53, 157–63.

BOWERSOCK, G. W., 1969, *Greek Sophists in the Roman Empire* (Oxford).

—— 1974 (ed.), *Approaches to the Second Sophistic* (University Park, Ill.).

BOWIE, E. L., 1982, 'The Importance of the Sophists', *YCS* 27, 29–59.

BROWN, P., 1971, *The World of Late Antiquity* (London).

—— 1992, *Power and Persuasion in Late Antiquity* (Madison, Wis.).

BUCK, D. F., 1987, 'Prohaeresius' Recruitment of Students', *LCM* 12, 77 f.

BURGESS, T. C., 1902, *Epideictic Literature* (Chicago Studies in Classical Philology 3).

CALBOLI MONTEFUSCO, L., 1972, 'La dottrina del *KPINOMENON*', *Athenaeum* 50, 276–93.

—— 1986, *La dottrina degli status nella retorica greca e romana* (Hildesheim).

CLARK, D. L., 1957, *Rhetoric in Greco-Roman Education* (New York).

COLE, T., 1991, 'Who was Corax?', *ICS* 16, 65–84.

DINGEL, J., 1988, *Scholastica Materia: Untersuchungen zu den Declamationes Minores und der Institutio Oratoria Quintilians* (Berlin).

DOUGLAS, A. E., 1960, '*Clausulae* in the *Rhetorica ad Herennium* as Evidence of its Date', *CQ* 10, 65–78.

FAIRWEATHER, J., 1981, *Seneca the Elder* (Cambridge).

FATOUROS, G., and KRISCHER, T., 1983 (eds.), *Libanios* (Wege der Forschung 621, Darmstadt).

FORNARA, C. W., 1970, 'The Cult of Harmodius and Aristogeiton', *Philologus* 114, 155–80.

FORTENBAUGH, W. W., 1988, '*Benevolentiam conciliare* and *animos permovere*: Some Remarks on Cicero *De Oratore* 2. 178–216', *Rhetorica* 6, 259–73.

GLOECKNER, S., 1901, *Quaestiones Rhetoricae* (Breslauer Philologische Abhandlungen 8.2).

—— 1921, 'Zur Komposition der P-Scholien zu Hermogenes περὶ τῶν στάσεων', *Satura Viadrina Altera: Festschrift zum fünfzigjährigen Bestehen des philologischen Vereins zu Breslau* (Breslau), 1–11.

GRANATELLI, R., 1991, *Apollodori Pergameni ac Theodori Gadarei testimonia et fragmenta* (Rome).

GRUBE, G. M. A., 1959, 'Theodorus of Gadara', *AJP* 80, 337–65.

HÅKANSON, L., 1986, 'Die quintilianischen Deklamationen in der neueren Forschung', *ANRW* II.32.4, 2272–306.

HALLIWELL, S., 1991, 'Comic Satire and Freedom of Speech in Classical Athens', *JHS* 111, 48–70.

HEATH, M., 1989, *Unity in Greek Poetics* (Oxford).

—— 1990, 'Justice in Thucydides' Athenian Speeches', *Historia* 39, 385–400.

—— 1993, 'στάσις-theory in Homeric Commentary', *Mnemosyne* 46, 356–63.

—— 1994*a*, 'Zeno the Rhetor and the Thirteen *staseis*', *Eranos* 92, 17–22.

—— 1994*b*, 'The Substructure of *stasis*-theory from Hermagoras to Hermogenes', *CQ* 44, 114–29.

HOCK, R. F., and O'NEILL, E. N., 1986, *The Chreia in Ancient Rhetoric* (Atlanta).

HOLTSMARK, E., 1968, 'Quintilian on Status: a Progymnasma', *Hermes* 96, 356–68.

HUNGER, H., 1978, *Die hochsprachliche profane Literatur der Byzantiner* (Handbuch der Altertumswissenschaften xii/5, Munich).

INNES, D., and WINTERBOTTOM, M., 1988, *Sopatros the Rhetor* (BICS Supplement 48).

JAENEKE, W., 1904, *De statuum doctrina ab Hermogene tradita* (Diss. Leipzig).

JONES, A. H. M., 1964, *The Later Roman Empire, 284–602* (Oxford).

JONES, C. P., 1986, *Culture and Society in Lucian* (Cambridge, Mass.).

KASTER, R., 1983, 'Notes on "Primary" and "Secondary" Schools in Late Antiquity', *TAPA* 113, 323–46.

—— 1988, *Guardians of the Language: The Grammarian and Society in Late Antiquity* (Berkeley, Calif.).

KEIL, B., 1907*a*, 'Pro Hermogene', *Nachrichten von der königlichen Gesellschaft der Wissenschaften zu Göttingen, phil.-hist. kl.*, 176–222.

—— 1907*b*, 'Zwei Identifikationen', *Hermes* 42, 548–63.

—— 1913, 'Über Lukians Phalariden', *Hermes* 48, 494–521.

KEIL, J., 1953, 'Vertreter der zweiten Sophistik in Ephesos', *JÖAI* 40, 5–26.

KENNEDY, G. A., 1957, 'The Ancient Dispute over Rhetoric in Homer', *AJP* 78, 23–35.

—— 1963, *The Art of Persuasion in Greece* (Princeton, NJ).

—— 1972, *The Art of Rhetoric in the Roman World* (Princeton, NJ).

—— 1974, 'The Sophists as Declaimers', in Bowersock 1974, 17–22.

—— 1980, *Classical Rhetoric and its Christian and Secular Tradition* (London).

—— 1983, *Greek Rhetoric under Christian Emperors* (Princeton, NJ).

KOHL, R., 1915, *De scholasticarum declamationum argumentis ex historia petitis* (Rhetorische Studien 4, Paderborn).

KUSTAS, G. L., 1973, *Studies in Byzantine Rhetoric* (Thessalonica).

LAURENTIUS, G., 1614, *Hermogenis ars oratoria absolutissima, et libri omnes cum nova versione Latina . . . et commentariis Gasparis Laurentii* (Coloniae Allobrogum).

LIEBESCHUETZ, J. H. W. G., 1972, *Antioch: City and Imperial Administration in the Later Roman Empire* (Oxford).

LONG, A. A., and SEDLEY, D. N., 1987, *Hellenistic Philosophy* (Cambridge).

MACDOWELL, D. M., 1978, *The Law in Classical Athens* (London).

—— 1990, *Demosthenes Against Meidias* (Oxford).

MacKendrick, P., 1989, *The Philosophical Books of Cicero* (London).

Martin, J., 1974, *Antike Rhetorik* (Munich).

Matsen, P., Robinson, R., Sousa, M., 1990 (eds.), *Readings from Classical Rhetoric* (Carbondale, Ill.).

Matthes, D., 1958, 'Hermagoras von Temnos', *Lustrum* 3, 58–214.

Meador, P. A., 1964, 'Minucian *On Epicheiremes*: An Introduction and a Translation', *Speech Monographs* 31, 54–63.

Nadeau, R., 1952, 'The *Progymnasmata* of Aphthonius in Translation', *Speech Monographs* 19, 264–85.

—— 1959, 'Classical Systems of Stases in Greek: Hermagoras to Hermogenes', *GRBS* 2, 53–71.

—— 1964, 'Hermogenes *On Stases*: A Translation with an Introduction and Notes', *Speech Monographs* 31, 361–421.

Nitsche, W., 1883, *Der Rhetor Menandros und die Scholien zu Demosthenes* (Wissenschaftliche Beilage zum Programm des Leibniz-Gymnasiums zu Berlin 63, Berlin).

Norman, A. F., 1965, *Libanius' Autobiography* (Oxford).

Nörr, D., 1986, *Causa Mortis* (Münchener Beiträge zur Papyrusforschung und antiken Rechtsgeschichte 80, Munich).

Ober, J., 1989, *Mass and Elite in Democratic Athens* (Princeton, NJ).

Patillon, M., 1988, *La Théorie du discours chez Hermogène* (Paris).

Penella, R., 1990, *Greek Philosophers and Sophists* (Leeds).

Pernot, L., 1981, *Les Discours Siciliens d'Aelius Aristide* (New York).

Petit, P, 1956, *Les Étudiants de Libanius* (Paris).

Poel, M. G. M. van der, 1987, *De Declamatio bij de Humanisten* (Bibliotheca humanistica et reformatorica 39, Nieuwkoop).

Rabe, H., 1895, 'De Christophori commentario in Hermogenis librum περὶ στάσεων', *RM* 50, 241–9.

—— 1907, 'Aus Rhetoren Handschriften: 1. Nachrichten über das Leben des Hermogenes', *RM* 62, 247–62.

—— 1908, 'Aus Rhetoren Handschriften: 7. Georgios', *RM* 63, 517–26.

—— 1909, 'Aus Rhetoren Handschriften: 11. Die Dreimänner Kommentar WIV', *RM* 64, 578–89.

Radermacher, L., 1951, *Artium Scriptores* (SBVienna 227.3).

Reardon, B. P., 1971, *Courants littéraires grecs des IIᵉ et IIIᵉ siècles après J.-C.* (Paris).

Richter, P., 1927/8, 'Byzantinischer Kommentar zu Hermogenes', *Byzantion* 3, 153–204.

Robinson, C., 1979, *Lucian* (London).

Romano, R., 1989, 'Il commentario a Ermogene attribuito a S. Nilo di Rossano', *Epeteris Etaireias Byzantinon Spoudon* 47, 253–74.

Russell, D., 1978, 'The Pseudo-Dionysian *Exetasis* and *Mistakes*', *Entretiens sur l'antiquité classique* 25, 113–34.

—— 1983, *Greek Declamation* (Cambridge).

—— and WILSON, N., 1981, *Menander Rhetor* (Oxford).

RUTHERFORD, I., 1986, 'Technique and Innovation in Late Greek Stylistics: Six Studies in the Idea-Theory of Hermogenes and ps.-Aristides', Oxford D. Phil.

—— 1992, 'Inventing the Canon: Hermogenes on Literature', *HSCP* 94, 355–78.

RYCHLEWSKA, L., 1940–7, 'In anonymum Hermogenis Statuum interpretem . . . cum Nilo . . . collatum observationes criticae', *Eos* 41, 173–89; 42, 195–201.

SCHENKEVELD, D. M. 1991, 'The Philosopher Aquila', *CQ* 41, 490–5.

SCHILLING, L., 1903, 'Quaestiones rhetoricae selectae', *Jahrbuch für classische Philologie*, Suppl. 28, 663–778.

SCHISSEL, O., 1926/7, 'Lollianos aus Ephesos', *Philologus* 82, 181–201.

—— 1927, 'Die Familie des Minukianos' *Klio* 21, 361–73.

SCHMID, W., 1917, 'Die sogenannte Aristidesrhetorik', *RM* 72, 113–49, 239–57.

SCHÖPSDAU, K., 1975, 'Untersuchungen zur Anlage und Entstehung der beiden Pseudodionysianischen Traktate περὶ ἐσχηματισμένων', *RM* 118, 83–123.

SCHOULER, B., 1984, *La Tradition hellénique chez Libanius* (Paris).

—— 1990, 'La Classification des personnes et des faits chez Hermogène et ses commentateurs', *Rhetorica* 8, 229–54.

SCHRADER, H., 1902, 'Telephos der Pergamener περὶ τῆς καθ' Ὅμηρον ῥητορικῆς', *Hermes* 37, 530–81.

SOFFEL, J., 1974, *Die Regeln Menanders für die Leichenrede* (Meisenheim am Glan).

STEPHENS, S. A., 1983, 'The "Arginusae" Theme in Greek Rhetorical Theory and Practice', *BASP* 20, 171–80.

STURMIUS, J., 1570, *Hermogenis Tarsensis rhetoris acutissimi Partitionum rhetoricarum liber unus, qui vulgo de statibus inscribitur, Latinitate donatus et scholis explicatus atque illustratus a Ioanne Sturmio* (Argentorati).

—— 1575, *De statibus causarum civilium universa doctrina Hermogenis explicata a Ioanne Sturmio* (Argentorati).

SUSSMAN, L. A., 1974, 'The Elder Seneca and Declamation', *ANRW* II.32.1, 557–77.

—— 1978, *The Elder Seneca* (Mnemosyne Supplement 51).

SWAIN, S., 1991, 'The Reliability of Philostratus' *Lives of the Sophists*', *Classical Antiquity* 10, 148–63.

THOMPSON, W. N., 1972, 'Stasis in Aristotle's Rhetoric', *QJS* 58, 134–41 = K. V. Erickson (ed.), *Aristotle: The Classical Heritage of Rhetoric* (Metuchen, NJ 1974), 266–77.

THROM, H., 1932, *Die Thesis* (Rhetorische Studien 17, Paderborn).

WALDEN, J. H. W., 1909, *The Universities of Ancient Greece* (New York).

WINTERBOTTOM, M., 1970, *Problems in Quintilian* (BICS Supplement 25, London).

—— 1982, 'Schoolroom and Courtroom', in B. Vickers (ed.), *Rhetoric Revalued* (New York), 59–70.

WINTERBOTTOM, M., 1984 (ed.), *The Minor Declamations Ascribed to Quintilian* (Berlin).

WISSE, J., 1989, *Ethos and Pathos from Aristotle to Cicero* (Amsterdam).

WOOTTEN, C., 1987, *Hermogenes* On Types of Style (Chapel Hill, NC).

WURM, M., 1972, *Apokeryxis, Abdicatio und Exheredatio* (Münchener Beiträge zur Papyrusforschung und antiken Rechtsgeschichte 60, Munich).

Who's Who

This section is intended as an index to the Hellenistic and later rhetoricians mentioned in this book. Since many of them are unfamiliar figures I have included brief notes to identify the individuals in question, and to direct readers towards further sources of information on them and to texts and (where they exist) English translations. I have not attempted to provide a comprehensive prosopography of later Greek rhetoricians. The guide to sophists mentioned by Philostratus in Bowersock 1974, 35–40, may provide a useful complement; see too the indexes in Bowersock 1969, Penella 1990, and *RE* Suppl. VIII 731–77 (s.v. Zweite Sophistik).

Alexander Peloplaton: 2nd c. AD; sophist (the nickname means 'Clay-Plato'). See *Philostratus 2.5; *RE* I 1459, s.v. Alexandros (98); *PIR²* A 503: 68

Alexander son of Numenius: Early 2nd c. AD; author of an influential work on figures of thought and diction, and of a rhetorical treatise organized according to the parts of a speech. Neither work survives; the latter is known mainly from citations in the *Anonymus Seguerianus. See *RE* I 1456–9, s.v. Alexandros (96); *PIR²* A 505: 15 n., 23 n.

Anonymus Seguerianus: An anonymous third-century rhetorical treatise organized according to the parts of a speech; the main sources are *Alexander son of Numenius, *Neocles and *Harpocration. See *RE* I 2328–30; Kennedy 1972, 616–19. Text: Spengel-Hammer 352–98, cited by section; cf. J. Graeven, *Cornuti artis rhetoricae epitome* (Berlin 1891): 9 n., 10 n., 15 n., 23 n., 27, 82, 91, 103, 157 n., 195

Antiochus of Aegae: 2nd c. AD; sophist, See *Philostratus 2.4; *RE* I 2494, s.v. Antiochos (65): 12 n.

Antonius, M.: 143–87 BC; Roman politician and orator. See *RE* I 2590–4 s.v. Antonius (28); Kennedy 1972, 80–4: 19 n., 24

Aphthonius: Late 4th c. AD; pupil of *Libanius, and author of an extant treatise on preliminary exercises. See *RE* I 2797–800, s.v. Aphthonios (1); *PLRE* I 81 f.; Kennedy 1983, 59–66. Text: H. Rabe (Teubner 1926), cited by page and line. Translation: Nadeau 1952, partially revised in Matsen 1990, 267–88: 13–17, 82, 91, 95

Apollodorus of Pergamum: Late 1st c. BC; tutor of Octavian (later Augustus). His school (opposed to that of *Theodorus) applied rhetorical precepts strictly, insisting (e.g.) that every standard part of a speech must appear in all speeches. See *RE* I 2886–94, s.v. Apollodorus (64); *PIR*² A 920; Grube 1959; Kennedy 1972, 338–41. Testimonia and fragments: Granatelli 1991: 22 n.

Apollonius of Athens: Late 2nd c. AD; sophist. See *Philostratus 2.20; *RE* II 144, s.v. Apollonios (88); *PIR*² A 142: 12 n.

Apsines of Gadara: 3rd c. AD; his only surviving work is a treatise organized according to the parts of a speech. See *RE* II 277–83, Suppl. XIV 53; *PIR*² A 978; Aulitzky 1917; Kennedy 1972, 633 f. Text: Spengel-Hammer 217–329, cited by page and line: 9 n., 10 n., 15 n., 27, 76, 82, 84, 88 f., 91, 96, 118, 121, 125, 127, 129, 131, 138, 143, 157 n.

Aquila: 4th c. AD; Neoplatonist rhetorician cited by *Syrianus; he is usually paired with *Evagoras, although some detailed technical material is attributed to Aquila alone. See *RE* II 314, s.v. Aquila (6); *PLRE* I 90; Schilling 1903, 693–702; Keil 1907b (arguing that Aquila's reworking of Evagoras was Syrianus' direct source, Schenkeveld 1991 (dating): 10 n., 78, 92

Aristides (P. Aelius Aristides Theodorus): Sophist of the 2nd c. AD; his extensive works include numerous speeches (including a response to Plato's critique of rhetoric) and declamations. See *Philostratus 2. 9; *RE* II 886–94, s.v. Aristeides (24); *PIR*² A 145; Bowersock 1969, 36 f.; Reardon 1971, 120–54; Kennedy 1972, 582–5; Pernot 1981 (an analysis of the Sicilian declamations). Text: vol. 1, ed. F. W. Lenz and C. A. Behr (Leiden 1976–80); vol. 2, ed. B. Keil (Berlin 1898). Translation: C. A. Behr (Leiden 1981–6): 17 n., 69, 132, 211–23

A composite rhetorical treatise in two books transmitted under Aristides' name is not authentic. See Schmid 1917; Kennedy 1972, 628–30; Rutherford 1986. Text: W. Schmid (Teubner 1926).

Aristotle: On Aristotle's *Rhetoric* see (e.g.) Kennedy 1963, 81–114; Wisse 1989, 9–76. Text: R. Kassel (Berlin 1976). Translation: G. A. Kennedy (New York 1991): 4 n., 9 n., 10 n., 15 n., 19 n., 64, 74, 82, 87, 111, 133, 143, 167 n., 212

Athenaeus: 2nd c. BC; a contemporary and main rival of *Hermagoras. See *RE* II 2025 f., s.v. Athenaios (21); Heath 1993 identifies traces of the indirect influence of his system of issues in the Homeric scholia: 19 n.

[Augustine]: An anonymous Latin treatise of uncertain date, falsely attributed to St Augustine. See Matthes 1958, 104–7; Barwick 1961. Text: *RLM* 137–51: 7 n., 10 n., 11 n., 13 n., 82

Calpurnius Flaccus: Author of a collection of Latin declamations dating (probably) from the 2nd c. AD, surviving only in excerpted form. See *RE* III 1371–3, s.v. Calpurnius (40). Text: L. Håkanson (Teubner 1978). Text, translation, and commentary: L. A. Sussman (Mnemosyne Supplement 133, 1994): 67, 83, 97

Choricius of Gaza: 6th c. AD; his works include eleven declamations, with prefatory remarks. See *RE* III 2424–31, s.v. Chorikios; *PLRE* III 302; Kennedy 1983, 175–7; Russell 1983, 82–4, 102–5 (on *Decl.* 6). Text: R. Foerster and E. Richsteig (Teubner 1929): 178 f.

Christophorus: Commentator on *Hermogenes, possibly of the 12th c. AD. See Rabe 1895; Gloeckner 1901, 5; Kennedy 1983, 314: 129

Cicero: 106–43 BC; Roman politician and orator. Among his voluminous and varied works are a number of rhetorical treatises, from which (with the *Rhetorica ad Herennium*) much of our detailed knowledge of Hellenistic Greek rhetoric is drawn:

(i) *On Invention* (80s BC): a derivative technical handbook; text and translation: H. M. Hubbell (Loeb 1949);

(ii) *On the Orator* (55 BC): a dialogue in three books; text: K. Kumaniecki (Teubner 1969); translation: H. Rackham (Loeb 1942); commentary: A. D. Leeman *et al.* (Heidelberg 1981–);

(iii) *Partitiones Oratoriae* (*c.*54–52 BC): a short school-text for his son; text: A.S. Wilkins (Oxford 1903);

(iv) *Brutus* (46 BC): a historical survey of Roman oratory; text and commentary: A. E. Douglas (Oxford 1966); translation: G. L. Hendrickson (Loeb 1937);

(v) *Orator* (46 BC): on style; text: H. Westmann (Teubner 1980); translation: H. M. Hubbell (Loeb 1939); commentary: J. E. Sandys (Cambridge 1885);

(vi) *The Best Kind of Orator* (46 BC): introduction to a projected Latin translation of Demosthenes *On the Crown* and Aeschines *Against Ctesiphon*; text and translation: H. M. Hubbell (Loeb 1949);

(vii) *Topica* (44 BC): on arguments: text and translation: H. M. Hubbell (Loeb 1949).

See (e.g.) Kennedy 1972, 103–300; MacKendrick 1989 contains convenient summaries and bibliographical references; Heath 1994*b*, 116–21 examines some aspects of the evolution of Cicero's approach to issue-theory over the course of his career: 2, 5 n., 7 n., 8 n., 9 n., 10 n., 12, 15 n., 17 n., 19, 22 n., 23 n., 24 n., 70 f., 73, 76, 82, 88, 111, 116, 118, 143, 145, 153

Damianus (T. Flavius Damianus): 2nd c. AD; sophist. See *Philostratus 2.23; *RE* IV 2054, s.v. Damianos (2); *PIR*² F 253: 12 n.

Dionysius of Halicarnassus: 1st c. BC; historian and rhetorical critic. See *RE* V 934–71, s.v. Dionysios (113); *PIR*² D 102; Kennedy 1972, 342–63. Text: H. Usener and L. Radermacher (Teubner 1899–1929). Translation: S. Usher (Loeb 1974–85): 4 n., 7 n., 8 n., 9 n., 118

Included among Dionysius' works is a later composite treatise, including material on epideictic (see Kennedy 1972, 634–6; translated in Russell and Wilson 1981, 362–81), on figured speeches (see Schöpsdau 1975), and on declamation (see Russell 1978; 1983, 71–3): 10 n., 15 n., 22 n., 82, 122, 137

Eunapius: Late 4th-early 5th c.; his *Lives of the Philosophers* (an extension of *Philostratus' Lives of the Sophists*) is our main source of information on fourth-century sophists; he gives a particularly enthusiastic account of his teacher *Prohaeresius. See *RE* VI 1121–7, s.v. Eunapios (2); *PLRE* I 296; Kennedy 1983, 136–40; Penella 1990. Text: Giangrande (Rome 1956), cited by Boissonade's pagination. Translation: W. C. Wright (Loeb 1922): 12, 18 n., 20 n.

Evagoras: Late 3rd or early 4th c. AD; Neoplatonist rhetorician cited by *Syrianus, usually together with *Aquila. See *RE* VI 829 f., s.v. Euagoras (13); *PLRE* I 284; Keil 1907b: 23 n., 78, 92

Favorinus: 2nd c. AD; philosopher and sophist. See *Philostratus I. 8; *RE* VI 2078–84, Suppl. VI 65–70, s.v. Favorinus; *PIR²* F 123: 16 n.

Fortunatianus: Latin rhetorician, probably of the 4th c. AD. See *RE* VII 44–55; *PLRE* I 369; Gloeckner 1901, 109–11. Text and commentary: L. Calboli Montefusco (Bologna 1979); cited by page and line in *RLM* 81–134: 10 n., 82

Georgius: Probably 5th c. AD; commentator on *Hermogenes. See *PLRE* II 503; Schilling 1903, 667–93; Rabe 1908: 89, 92

Harpocration: Probably 3rd c. AD; one of the main sources used by the *Anon. Seguerianus. See *RE* VII 2411 f., s.v. Harpokration (3) and (4); *PIR²* A 186; Schilling 1903, 742 f.; Kennedy 1972, 618 f.: 92, 107, 123

Hermagoras of Temnos: 2nd c. BC; the most important Hellenistic rhetorical theorist, who made a particularly significant contribution to the theory of issues. His work is known only through testimonia and sparse fragments, and the detailed reconstruction of his doctrine is a complex and controversial task. Since Roman rhetorical writings of the 1st c. BC (*Cicero, *Rhet. ad Herennium*) attest both to the great influence which his theoretical work had, and also to continuing vigorous discussion and modification of his views, it is perhaps not surprising that the testimonia conflict on many points; the possibility (Quintilian 3. 5. 14) that texts were falsely attributed to him adds to the difficulties. See *RE* VIII 692–5, s.v. Hermagoras (5); Matthes 1958; Nadeau 1959; Barwick 1961, 1964, 1965; Kennedy 1963, 303–21; Heath 1994*b*, 116–21. Testimonia and fragments: D. Matthes (Teubner 1962): 7 n., 10 n., 12 n., 13 n., 19, 73, 76, 79, 110, 135

Matthes's edition also contains the fragments of two later rhetoricians of the same name. One was a pupil of *Theodorus of Gadara; the other dates probably to the first half of the 2nd c. AD (contemporary with *Lollianus), and taught a system of seven issues. See *RE* V/z 695 f., s.v. Hermagoras (6)-(7); Gloeckner 1901, 54; Matthes 1958, 79 f.: 20

Hermogenes of Tarsus: AD *c*.160–225. On the biographical tradition see Rabe 1907, with the more cautious comments in Radermacher's *RE* article. The only genuine source seems to be *Philostratus 2. 7, where he is presented as an exceptionally talented declaimer in his youth (he performed before the emperor Marcus Aurelius at the age of 15) whose talents inexplicably deserted him as he grew older. A later extrapolation of this image of Hermogenes as youthful prodigy also made his theoretical treatises the products of his youth; but there is no reason to believe this (Philostratus tells us that he died at an advanced age). Two genuine works survive, on issues and on types of style. See *RE* VIII 865–72, s.v. Hermogenes (22); *PIR²* H 149; Gloeckner 1901; Kennedy 1983, 73–103; Russell 1983, 40–73; Rutherford 1986; Patillon 1988. Text: ed. H. Rabe (Teubner 1913), cited by page and line. The treatise on types of style has been translated by Wootten (1987): 2, 7 n., 19 n., 20 n., 22 n., 24–7, 61–160, 175–8, 180 f., 194 f., 197, 209, 210 n., 213, 223, 224 f.

Hermogenes refers to other works, including one *On Invention*. However, the four-book treatise transmitted in the Hermogenean corpus under that title is not his; nor are the shorter works on preliminary exercises and method. These texts are included in Rabe's edition; the pseudo-Hermogenean treatise on preliminary exercises is translated in Baldwin 1928, 23–8: 9 n., 13 n., 14 n., 27, 82, 87, 91, 104, 121 f., 127, 132 f. 157 n.

Hermogenes' influence grew in later antiquity, and he attracted a large body of commentary; for a lucid overview see Hunger 1978, 79–84. The scholia to *On Issues* printed in Walz's *Rhetores Graeci* comprise two main bodies of material. *RG* 4 contains a composite work, based largely on *Sopater, *Marcellinus, and *Syrianus (see Rabe 1909); a different recension of Sopater's work is also to be found in *RG* 5. Of these only Syrianus has since appeared in a more satisfactory edition. *RG* 7 contains an anonymous compilation (on the date and sources see Keil 1907*a*, Gloeckner 1921). This can be supplemented by the unedited commentaries of *Georgius, *Nilus, and *Christophorus; the excerpts from these commentaries published by Rabe (1895, 1908), Gloeckner (1901), Schilling (1903), and Rychlewska (1940–7) contain much valuable information.

Himerius: 4th c. AD; sophist; his works include speeches and declamations, mostly preserved in fragmentary form. See Eunapius 494; *RE* III 1622–35, s.v. Himerios (1); *RE* Suppl. III 1151–3; Kennedy 1983, 141–9; Penella 1990, 97–9. Text: A. Colonna (Rome 1951): 23 n., 24 n., 118

Julius Victor: Latin rhetorician, probably of the 4th c. AD. See *RE* X/1, 872–9, s.v. Iulius (532); *PLRE* I 961. Text: R. Giomini and M. S. Celentano (Teubner 1980); cited by page and line in *RLM* 373–448: 83, 149

Libanius: AD 314–*c*.393. He taught rhetoric in his native Antioch, with great success (his pupils included *Aphthonius); he was also a prolific writer: his extensive works include speeches, declamations, preliminary exercises, hypotheses to the speeches of Demosthenes, and letters. See Eunapius 495 f.; *RE* XII/z 2485–51; *PLRE* I 505–7; Petit 1956 (on his pupils); Liebeschuetz 1972, 1–39; Kennedy 1983, 150–63; Fatouros and Krischer 1983 (a collection of articles, with bibliography); Penella 1990, 100–4; Berry and Heath (forthcoming) includes a rhetorical analysis of *Or.* 30, *In defence of the Temples.* Text: R. Foerster (Teubner 1903–23), cited by volume, page, and line. Translation: the declamations and preliminary exercises have not been translated; selected speeches can be found in A. F. Norman *Libanius: Selected Works* (Loeb 1969–77); see also Norman *Libanius: Autobiography and Selected Letters* (Loeb 1992). The autobiography (= *Or.* 1) is also translated, with an excellent introduction and commentary, in Norman 1965: 6 f., 12 n., 14 n., 16, 64, 89, 91, 137, 139, 156–75, 194–208, 222 n.

Lollianus of Ephesus (P. Hordeonius Lollianus): Distinguished Athenian sophist in the first half of the 2nd c. AD; in addition to teaching rhetoric he was active in Athenian public life (holding the office of general, with responsibility for the management of the city's food-supply). His varied skills are reflected in an honorific inscription (*IG* ii/iii² 4211) erected by the Athenian council and assembly, paying tribute to his ability both as a forensic orator and as a declaimer, and in a satirical epigram (*AP* 11. 274) plausibly attributed to *Lucian, which envisages Lollianus' ghost giving lectures on rhetoric to Hermes as the god conducts him down to the underworld. See *Philostratus 1.23; *RE* XIII/2 1373–5, s.v. Lollianos (15); *PIR*² H 203; Gloeckner 1901, 50–4; Keil 1953, 7–12; Heath 1994*b*, 123–5. Fragments and commentary: Schissel 1926/7: 20, 23 n., 108, 112, 120 f., 128

Lucian of Samosata: 2nd c. AD. His large and varied corpus contains several declamations: *Phalaris*, the *Tyrannicide*, and the *Disinherited son*. In *Phalaris* (a theme also treated by Hadrian of Tyre, according to his Suda entry) the infamous tyrant of Acragas proposes to dedicate his Bull at Delphi; Lucian gives a speech by Acragantine ambassadors presenting Phalaris' self-justification, and a speech by a Delphian in support of the proposal; see Keil 1913. The *Tyrannicide* is included in this volume; for an analysis of the *Disinherited son* see Berry and Heath (forthcoming). More generally, see *RE* XIII/2 1725–77; *PIR*² L 370; Bompaire 1958; Bowersock 1969, 114–16; Reardon 1971, 155–80; Kennedy 1972, 585–90; Baldwin 1973; Robinson 1979; Anderson 1982; Jones 1986. Text: M. D. Macleod (OCT 1972–87). Translation: A. M. Harmon *et al.* (Loeb 1913–67): 68, 75, 84, 103, 107, 175–89

Marcellinus: Commentator (of uncertain date, perhaps 5th c.) on *Hermogenes; one of the three main sources of the composite commentary in *RG* 4 (see Rabe 1909). See *RE* XIV/2 1487 f., s.v. Marcellinus (50); *PLRE* II 710 (Marcellinus 8); Kennedy 1983, 112–15. Text: *RG* 4: 92

Marcomannus: Latin rhetorician, probably of the 4th c. AD; his commentary on *Cicero's *On Invention* is lost, but was used by *Fortunatianus, *Julius Victor, and *Sulpicius Victor. See *RE* XIV/z 1637–42; *PLRE* I 557; Gloeckner 1901, 103–9: 137

Menander of Laodicea: Late 3rd c. AD; author of commentaries on *Hermogenes and the preliminary exercises of *Minucianus, which have not survived, and of other rhetorical works. See *RE* XV/1 762–4, s.v. Menandros (16); *PLRE* I 595; Nitsche 1883; Schilling 1903, 744–7; Soffel 1974, 90–105. He appears in this book in two capacities:

(i) as the author of an important commentary on Demosthenes, which can be shown (as I shall argue elsewhere) to have been a major source for the surviving Demosthenic scholia. Text: M. R. Dilts (Teubner 1983–6), 22 n., 87–9, 92, 99 f., 129.

(ii) as putative author of two influential treatises on epideictic transmitted under Menander's name. The authorship of these treatises is a matter of dispute; I incline to the view (Nitsche 1883) that the second is by the Demosthenes-commentator, while the first is from another hand (perhaps Genethlius of Petra). Text, translation, and commentary: Russell and Wilson 1981: 19 n.

Metrophanes of Eucarpia: 3rd c. AD; Neoplatonist commentator on *Hermogenes. See *RE* XV/2 1491, s.v. Metrophanes (5); *PLRE* I 601; Schilling 1903, 709–14, 747–53: 76, 78, 93, 110, 123, 131, 135

Minucianus: 2nd c. AD; the most influential rhetorical theorist of his time, and the target of some of *Hermogenes' polemical passages; ancient sources identify him as the earliest exponent of the system of thirteen issues (but see Heath 1994*a*). His work was eclipsed in later antiquity by that of *Hermogenes, so that his treatise on issues is known mainly through citations in the Hermogenes-scholia. See *RE* XV/2 1975–86, s.v. Minukianos (1); Gloeckner 1901, 22–50, 111–13; Schilling 1903, 753–9; Schissel 1927 (family); Kennedy 1983, 76 f.; Heath 1994*b*, 125 f: 10 n., 20, 64–8, 70, 73, 76, 79, 86, 92–4, 101, 105 f., 108, 110, 115, 120, 123, 127 f., 135, 141, 149, 152

The treatise on argument transmitted under the name of Minucianus may be the work of his homonymous great-grandson (3rd c.). See *RE* XV/2 1986–8, s.v. Minukianos (2). Text: Spengel-Hammer 340–51. Translation: Meador 1964: 9 n.

Neocles: 1st c. AD; one of main sources used by the *Anonymus Seguerianus. See *RE* XVI/2 2416–22, s.v. Neokles (6): 9 n.

Nicetes of Smyrna: Late 1st–early 2nd c. AD; sophist. See *Philostratus I. 19; *RE* XVII/1 319–21, s.v. Niketes (6); *PIR*² N 83; Kennedy 1972, 556–65: 12 n.

Nicolaus of Myra: 5th c. AD; author of an extant treatise on preliminary exercises. See *RE* XVII/2 424–57, s.v. Nikolaos (21); *PLRE* II 783; Kennedy 1983, 66–9. Text: J. Felten (Teubner 1913), cited by page and line. The preface only is translated in Matsen 1990, 264 f.: 4 n., 13 n., 91

Nilus: Commentator on *Hermogenes; probably Nilus of Rossano (d. 1005). See Gloeckner 1901, 3–10; Kennedy 1983, 313 f.; Romano 1989: 105 f., 108, 120, 149, 152

Philostratus: Early 3rd c. AD; his *Lives of the Sophists* is our main source of information about second-century sophists. See *RE* XX/1 136–74, s.v. Philostratos (10); Bowersock 1969, 1–16; Reardon 1971, 115–19; Kennedy 1972, 555–65; Anderson 1986; Swain 1991. Text and translation: W. C. Wright (Loeb 1922), cited by Olearius' pagination or by book and chapter: 12 n., 17 n., 18 n., 23 n., 66, 68, 121, 212

Phoenix of Thessaly: 2nd c. AD; sophist. See *Philostratus 2.22; *RE* XX/1 424 f., s.v. Phoinix (7): 23 n.

Polemo (Antonius Polemo): AD *c.*88–144; one of the most distinguished sophists of his time, he played a prominent role in the civic life of Smyrna as well as enjoying brilliant success as a declaimer (of which Philostratus gives a vivid account). Two declamations are preserved under his name, in which the fathers of Cynegirus and Callimachus (cf. Herodotus 6. 114) lay competing claim to the right (as father of the most heroic of the dead) to deliver the funeral speech for the Athenians who died at Marathon (cf. Syrianus 2. 164. 21–4; for this as a stock sophistic theme see Lucian *Jup. Trag.* 32 etc.). See *Philostratus 1. 25; *RE* XX/2 1320–57, s.v. Polemon (10); *PIR*² A 862; Reardon 1971, 107–13. Text: H. Hinck (Teubner 1873): 12 n., 121

Porphyry: AD *c.*232–305; Neoplatonist philosopher, whose works included a commentary on *Minucianus. See *RE* XXII/1 275–317, s.v. Porphyrios (2); Gloeckner 1901, 76 f.; Kennedy 1983, 77 f: 87, 97

Prohaeresius: AD 276–367/8; sophist, teacher of *Eunapius, who gives an extensive account of him. See Eunapius 485–93; *RE* XXIII/1 30–2, s.v. Proairesios (1); *PLRE* I 731; Kennedy 1983, 138–41; Buck 1987; Penella 1990, 83–94: 12

Ptolemy of Naucratis: 2nd c. AD; sophist. See *Philostratus 2. 15; *RE* XXIII/2 1861, s.v. Ptolemaios (76): 12 n., 66

Quintilian: AD *c.*35–100; a leading Roman teacher of rhetoric, whose *Institutio Oratoria* is the fullest sytematic exposition of rhetorical theory surviving from antiquity. There is a survey of theories of issue in 3. 6, with additional technical material in 3. 10 f. (for commentary see Adamietz 1966; cf. Holtsmark 1968; Heath 1994*b*, 121–3), and a discussion of the handling of each issue in 7. 2–10. In general see *RE* VI 1845–64, s.v. Fabius (137); Kennedy 1972, 487–514; Adamietz 1986. Text: Winterbottom (with notes in Winterbottom 1970). Translation: H. E. Butler (Loeb 1920–2): 3 n., 4 n., 5 n., 7 n., 8 n., 9 n., 10 n., 12 n., 13 n., 15 n., 17 n., 19 f., 22 n., 23 n., 61, 69 f., 73, 76, 82, 87 f., 91, 95, 103 f., 108, 111, 122, 127, 133, 143, 149, 151 f., 195 n., 212

Two sets of declamations are transmitted under Quintilian's name (see Håkanson 1986):

(i) In the *Minor Declamations* (which may show the influence of Quintilian's teaching) advice on the handling of each theme is interspersed with model declamations and passages for pupils to imitate (the combination of precept and example in the teaching of beginners is recommended in Quintilian 2. 6). Text and commentary: M. Winterbottom (Berlin 1984); see also Dingel 1988: 83, 88, 104, 118, 127, 138, 195 n.

(ii) The *Major Declamations* is a collection of nineteen complete declamations of uncertain date. Text: L. Håkanson (Teubner 1982). Translation: L. A. Sussman (Frankfurt 1987).

Rhetorica ad Alexandrum: Anonymous rhetorical treatise of the 4th c. BC, sometimes attributed to Anaximenes of Lampsacus. See *RE* I 2086–98, s.v. Anaximenes (3); Kennedy 1963, 114–24. Text: M. Fuhrmann (Teubner 1966). Translation: H. Rackham (Loeb 1937): 15 n., 19 n.

Rhetorica ad Herennium: Anonymous Latin treatise of the 1st c. BC, usually dated to *c.*85, although the evidence is not conclusive (Douglas 1960 argues that there is no obstacle to a date as late as 50 BC, and in one respect its treatment of issue-theory agrees with views which *Cicero advocated in the late 50s: Heath 1994*b*, 118). See *RE* IV 1605–23, s.v. Cornificius (1); Kennedy 1972, 126–38. Text and translation: H. Caplan (Loeb 1954); G. Achard (Budé 1989). Commentary: G. Calboli (Bologna 1969): 10 n., 14 n. 15 n., 19, 22 n, 76, 79, 88, 116, 145

Scopelian: Early 2nd c. AD; sophist. See *Philostratus 1. 21; *RE* IIIA 580 f., s.v. Skopelianos: 12 n.

Seneca the Elder: *c.*55 BC–AD 40; his collection of declamation themes includes anecdotes about leading declaimers of the early empire, as well as highlights from their work (choice epigrams, outlines, and lines of argument). See Sussman 1974, 1978; Fairweather 1981. Text and translation: Winterbottom (Loeb 1974): 18 n., 17 n., 67, 83, 104, 108, 118, 127, 149 f., 194, 195 n.

Sopater: Two rhetoricians of this name are cited in this book (they are often identified with each other, but differences in doctrine such as those pointed out on Hermogenes *55. 17–56. 3 and *60. 15–18 make the identification improbable):

(i) Probably 4th c. AD; his *Division of Questions* is a collection of declamation themes classified according to their issue, with more or less extensive outlines of the recommended treatment. Text: *RG* 8. 1–385; Innes and Winterbottom 1988 gives a brief introduction to the *Division of Questions*, with indispensable (though cryptic) textual and technical notes: 20, 24, 62, 69 ff., 76, 84, 89, 94–7, 99, 103, 106, 109, 111 f., 114, 116, 118, 120 f., 123, 127–9, 131, 136–40, 143, 150, 157, 159, 180 f., 189 f., 195 n., 208–11, 223–30

(ii) Commentator on *Hermogenes, of uncertain date; his work was one of the three main sources of the composite commentary in *RG* 4 (see Rabe 1909), and is also presented in abbreviated form in *RG* 5. Text: *RG* 4, 5. 1–211: 77 f., 81, 92, 95, 106

See *RE* IIIA/1 1002–6, s.v. Sopatros (10); *PLRE* II 1020; Gloeckner 1901, 71–6; Kennedy 1983, 104–9 (mainly on the commentator).

Sulpicius Victor: Latin rhetorician probably of 4th c. AD; he identifies as the main authority for his treatise the Greek rhetor *Zeno, but also makes use of *Marcomannus. See *RE* IVA 873–8, s.v. Sulpicius (106); *PLRE* I 961. Text: *RLM* 313–52: 10 n., 20, 79, 137

Syrianus: 5th c. AD; philosopher, head of the Neoplatonist school in Athens from 431/2. He wrote commentaries on both the genuine works of *Hermogenes, using *Evagoras and *Aquila as his main sources; his work on issues in turn became one of the three main sources of the composite commentary in *RG* 4 (see Rabe 1909). See *RE* IVA 1728–75, s.v. Syrianos (1); *PLRE* II 1051; Gloeckner 1901, 71–6; Schilling 1903, 693–714; Kennedy 1983, 109–12; Heath 1994*b*, 128 f. Text: the text in *RE* 4 is superseded by that of H. Rabe (Teubner 1892–3), cited by volume, page, and line: 10 n., 20 n., 23 n., 68, 70, 73, 77–9, 81 f., 84–8, 90–2, 94, 99, 103, 105–9, 112–15, 118–20, 122, 125 f., 129–32, 135 f., 138, 140 f., 145, 149, 152 f., 157 n., 158, 177, 181, 191–4, 212

Telephus of Pergamum: 2nd c. AD; grammarian; among his works was a book on rhetoric in Homer, which included issue-theory. See *RE* VA/1 369–71, s.v. Telephos (2), rightly cautioning against the exaggerated speculations in Schrader 1902 (see also Heath 1993, 360 n. 10): 61

Theodectes: 4th c. BC; rhetorician and tragedian. See *RE* VA/2 1722–34, s.v. Theodektes (1); Kennedy 1963, 114–24: 10 n.

Theodorus of Gadara: Late 1st c. BC; tutor to the emperor Tiberius; by contrast with *Apollodorus, his school stressed the adaptability of rhetorical principles to circumstance. See *RE* VA/2 1847–92, s.v. Theodoros (39); Grube 1959; Kennedy 1972, 340 f. Testimonia and fragments: Granatelli 1991: 22 n., 73

Theodotus (Julius Theodotus): 2nd c. AD; sophist. See *Philostratus 2. 2; *RE* X/1 841 f., s.v. Iulius (508); *PIR²* I 599: 12 n.

Theon: 1st c. AD; author of an extant handbook on preliminary exercises. See *RE* VA/2 2037–54, s.v. Theon (5); *PIR²* A 270 (Aelius Theon); Kennedy 1972, 615 f. Text: Spengel ii 59–130, cited by page and line; the preface only is translated in Matsen 1990, 254–62: 13 n., 133, 153

Troilus: Late 4th/early 5th c. AD; probably the author of the prolegomena to rhetoric transmitted under that name. See *RE* VIIA/1 615 f., s.v. Troilos (3); *PLRE* II 1128. Text: *PS* 44–58: 84, 157 n.

Tyrannus: Late 4th/early 5th c. AD; author of treatises, now lost, on issues (in one book) and division (in ten). See *RE* VIIA/2, 1843–7, s.v. Tyrannos (2); *PLRE* II 1134; Gloeckner 1901, 89 f.; Schilling 1903, 759–63; Heath 1994*b*, 128 f.: 92, 95

Zeno: The main source used by *Sulpicius Victor; probably to be identified with a Greek rhetorician known to have written various rhetorical works (including a treatise on issues and a commentary on Demosthenes) in the 2nd c. AD. Since Sulpicius explicitly signals departures from his source, he provides good evidence for the structure and contents of another 2nd c. treatise on issue-theory in addition to those of *Minucianus and *Hermogenes. There is some reason to believe that Zeno was the earliest of the three, antedating Minucianus (or at least preserving an older form of the thirteen-issue system): (i) there is no trace of the controversy on incomplete simple conjectures (see on *31. 6–11, *54. 9–55. 8), and no attempt is made to correlate the distinctions between complete and incomplete questions and simple and double questions; (ii) the issue of objection is not divided, as it seems to have been in Minucianus (Syrianus 2. 55. 5–8); the documentary species is classified under letter and intent (339. 1 f.). Zeno's treatise had a structure similar to that of *Minucianus (but rejected by Hermogenes: *34. 16–35. 14), with more general prolegomena preceding a treatment of the issues; but, like Hermogenes (*36. 7–9), he eliminated some traditional concepts from the prolegomena. See *RE* XA, 140–2, s.v. Zenon (9); Gloeckner 1901, 103–8; Heath 1994*a* and 1994*b*, 127. Text: all references to Zeno in this book are to the text of Sulpicius Victor in *RLM* 313–52: 7 n., 10 n., 11 n., 17 n., 20, 22 n., 68, 70, 73, 75 f., 79, 82–4, 86, 88, 93–5, 97–100, 103–6, 109, 111–15, 119 f., 125–8, 135 f., 143, 150, 157, 176 n., 194

Glossary

Act (πρᾶγμα):

(*a*) One of the six elements of *circumstance: 13, 37

(*b*) The events stated or implied in a *hypothesis; one of the two bases from which arguments can be derived (cf. *person): 25, 28–30, 32, 36, 41 f., 61, 63–6, 68, 80 f., 92–5, 192

Advantage (συμφέρον): One of the *heads of purpose: 28, 40, 52 f., 62, 74, 130, 133 f., 213, 230

Alternative intent (ἑτέρα διάνοια):

(*a*) In *counterpositions, the head in which the prosecutor offers a less credible account of the underlying intent of the defendant's actions than that given by the defendant in *intent and in the counterposition proper: 22, 50, 126, 143

(*b*) In *conflict of law, the head in which the first speaker appeals to the intent (as distinct from the letter) of the *verbal instrument on which the second speaker's case rests: 56 f., 147

Alternative presentation (ἑτέρα προβολή): Head putting forward the second *verbal instrument (in *conflict of law) or the second interpretation of an ambiguous verbal instrument (in *ambiguity): 56 f., 59 f., 147, 154

Ambiguity (ἀμφιβολία): *Legal issue turning on a dispute about the literal construction of a *verbal instrument: 34 f., 59 f., 72, 77 f., 131, 152–5

Ambiguous (ἀμφίδοξος): A *mode in which the scandalous nature of the act is balanced by a reputable person, or *vice versa*: 68

Amplification (αὔξησις): Techniques for increasing the perceived importance of some fact that is taken as given, used especially in certain heads of argument (*sequence of events, *presentation, *importance, *relative importance) and in the *epilogue: 15, 24 n., 49 f., 83 f., 88–91, 102 f., 105, 107, 111 f., 119 f., 123–5, 139 f., 143, 145, 151 f., 157, 176, 178 f., 181, 191 f., 225

Analysis (νόησις): According to some rhetoricians *invention is preceded by a preliminary analysis, in which the *class, *mode, and issue of the theme are identified: 11, 70

Anecdote (χρεία): *Preliminary exercise in which a wise saying (or other meaningful act) attributed to a named individual is prescribed as the basis for a moral essay: 13 f.

Arguments (ἀγῶνες): The part of a speech (normally placed between *narrative and *epilogue) in which a speaker tries to confirm his position by successive heads of argument: 9, 84, 110, 112, 158, 177, 196, 209, 212

Assimilation (συλλογισμός):

(*a*) Head which maintains that a looser *counterdefinition is effectively equivalent to a strict *definition: 43 f., 47, 54–8, 104, 107, 111 f., 119, 123, 140, 144, 147, 151, 177, 180 f., 190, 192

(*b*) *Legal issue in which assimilation is the crucial head, with the result that the application of a law is extended to cases which it does not explicitly cover: 34, 58 f. 72, 149–52, 224 f., 227–30

Capacity (δύναμις): Head of *conjecture in which it is disputed whether the accused was able to commit the crime alleged, and/or whether his ability to do so is significant; usually paired with *motive: 36 f., 41 f., 83, 92, 94 f., 109, 133, 158 f., 179, 180, 191

Character (ἦθος): One of the three means of persuasion (see also *emotion). A theme is based on character (ἠθικός) if it invites a treatment emphasizing this means of persuasion: 9 f., 64, 70

Characterization (ἠθοποιία): *Preliminary exercise in which the student is required to express what a specified individual would say in a given situation: 16, 176 f., 180, 190

Circumstance (περίστασις): The six elements of circumstance (περιστατικά) are the basic components of a situation or event (i.e. *person, *act, time, place, manner, and cause): 13, 17, 35, 37, 54, 79 f., 83, 85 f., 103, 109, 139 f., 158, 181, 190–2

Class (εἶδος): A way of classifying themes according to the dominant means of persuasion (see *practical, *emotional, *character, *mixed): 10, 31, 51, 69

Co-confirmatory (συγκατασκευαζόμενος): A species of *conjunct *conjecture, in which disputed claims are mutually supporting; ancient sources give conflicting accounts of its logical structure: 42 f., 83, 97–100

Combination (συμπλοκή): Opp. *distinction: a *counterplea is double by combination when two acts, neither of which could sustain a prosecution independently, are included in a single charge: 49, 122

Common quality (κοινὴ ποιότης): Part of the *epilogue which elaborates on the characteristics attributed to an individual person in generalizing terms (e.g. by means of a *common topic) for purposes of *amplification: 36, 40, 44, 90 f., 109–11, 121, 128, 141, 145, 149, 152, 155

Common topic (κοινὸς τόπος): *Preliminary exercise in which the student develops generalizations applicable to any instance of a given category (e.g. adulterers, tyrants); in speeches and declamations, a technique of *amplification used especially in the *epilogue: 15, 40, 50, 57, 60, 80, 90 f., 109, 111, 125 f., 154, 157, 181, 224, 227, 229

Comparison (σύγκρισις): *Preliminary exercise in which the student is required to compare the relative merits of two subjects: 16, 95

Complete (τέλειος): A *conjecture is complete if both *person and *act offer a basis for argument: 40 f., 92, 210

Complex (συμπεπλεγμένος): A case involving two distinct charges: 100

Confirmation (κατασκευή): *Preliminary exercise, in which the student is required to argue for the credibility of a specified narration: 15, 84

Conflict of law (ἀντινομία): *Legal issue arising when two legal instruments conflict when both are taken according to the letter: 34, 56–8, 72, 77, 145, 152, 154

Conjecture (στοχασμός): The issue which turns on a question of fact: 21, 32, 35, 36–44, 47, 52, 70 f., 73 f., 79, 80–101, 107–9, 116, 123, 128, 133, 136, 139, 152, 156–75, 179 f., 191, 195, 210

Conjunct (συνεζευγμένος): A species of *double *conjecture in which the question arising out of the charge is logically interlinked with a subsidiary conjectural question; see *incident, *pre-confirmatory, and *co-confirmatory: 42 f., 96–100

Consequence (ἐκβησόμενον): One of the *heads of purpose: 52 f., 134, 160, 181, 197, 213

Contingency (συμβεβηκός): A *counterplea is based on act and contingency when the act becomes subject to charge in the light of some consequence of it: 48, 116–18, 120–2, 159, 194, 197

Counter-representation (ἀντιπαράστασις): Opp. *refutation: a counterargument which allows the opponent's premises and seeks to show that they do not lead to the desired conclusion: 38, 47, 52, 87, 104, 109, 119 f., 127 f., 133, 179, 194, 196

Counteraccusation (ἀντέγκλημα):

   (*a*) Head (one of the *counterpositions) in which an acknowledged *prima facie* wrong is defended by a transfer of blame to the victim: 44, 50, 59, 120, 126, 140, 148, 154, 159, 194, 197, 224 f., 227, 229 f.

   (*b*) The issue in which counteraccusation is the crucial head: 33, 50, 72, 75 f., 125 f., 128

Counterdefinition (ἀνθορισμός): Head opposed to *definition: 43 f., 104, 106, 112, 119, 151, 177, 180, 190, 192

Counterdescriptive (ἀντονομάζων): Species of *definition in which the second speaker proposes an alternative description of the act: 44–6, 111, 113

Counterplea (ἀντίληψις):

   (*a*) Head (opposed to *objection) in which it is maintained that a given act is legitimate in itself: 24 n., 36, 38, 43 f., 46 f., 50 f., 54 f., 58, 78, 86 f., 90, 104, 108 f., 119 f., 125, 128 f., 137, 139 f., 145, 149, 151 f., 154, 156, 158 f., 176 n., 196, 225

   (*b*) The issue in which counterplea is the crucial head: 24 n., 33, 46–9, 51, 72, 75, 78, 115–21, 122 f., 129, 194–209

Counterposition (ἀντίθεσις):

(*a*) A head in which an acknowledged *prima facie* wrong is defended as justifiable or excusable in the circumstances: see *counterstatement, *counteraccusation, *transference, *mitigation: 43 f., 46–50, 54–60, 88 f., 107–9, 119 f., 125–7, 140, 145, 148, 151 f., 154, 159, 194, 197, 211, 225, 227

(*b*) The issue in which a counterposition is the crucial head: 33 f., 50–3, 72, 75 f., 83, 122–9, 143 f., 152, 157, 208–11

(*c*) A technique for introducing arguments for the opposition which the speaker wishes to refute; one may 'counterpose' an argument by attributing it to the opposing side, in order then to present a *solution: 17, 104, 177 f., 190, 209, 212 f. 224–30

Counterstatement (ἀντίστασις):

(*a*) Head (one of the *counterpositions) in which an acknowledged *prima facie* wrong is defended on the grounds of its beneficial consequences: 47, 50, 57, 88, 120, 126 f., 148

(*b*) The issue in which counterstatement is the crucial head: 33, 50, 72, 75, 126 f., 143

Custom (ἔθος): The *non-documentary counterpart to *legality: 132, 213

Definition (ὅρος):

(*a*) Head which maintains that a given act has been incorrectly categorized, since it does not satisfy a strict definition: 43 f., 46 f., 50 f., 54–8, 103 f., 106, 111 f., 114, 119, 123, 140, 144, 147, 151 f., 177–80, 190, 196, 209, 224, 226–9, 230

(*b*) The issue in which definition is the crucial head: 21, 33, 43–6, 70, 72, 74 f., 77, 101–15, 122 f., 136, 149–52, 175–94

Definitional exception (ὁρικὴ παραγραφή): Term used in some sources for the heads of *person and *definition in *counterplea: 119, 123, 128, 194, 209 f.

Deliberative (συμβουλευτικός): Oratory before a deliberative assembly, oriented to the future (opp. *judicial, *epideictic): 10 f., 17, 19, 21, 25, 28, 31, 70, 74, 129 f., 133, 212

Demand for evidence (ἐλέγχων ἀπαίτησις): Head of *conjecture in which the defence draws attention to the lack of witnesses for the prosecution or (if there are witnesses) seeks to undermine their credit: 36 f., 41, 82 f., 94 f., 158

Description (ἔκφρασις): *Preliminary exercise in which the student is supposed to place a scene vividly before the imagination: 16, 178, 192

Digression (παρέκβασις): Part of a speech (usually placed between the *arguments and *epilogue) in which considerations which go beyond the facts of the case in hand (e.g. about the defendant's previous life) are adduced to support the speaker's argument: 110, 112

Diminution (μείωσις): Techniques for minimizing the perceived importance of some fact that is taken as given; opp. *amplification: 49, 111, 193

Disposition (διάθεσις): The part of rhetoric concerned with the arrangement of material discovered through *invention: 7, 11 n.

Disreputable (ἄδοξος):
(a) Species of theme *lacking issue: 68 f., 86
(b) The *mode in which the person and/or act is disreputable: 10, 31, 67 f.

Distinction (διαίρεσις): Opp. *combination: a *counterplea is double by distinction when two acts, either of which could sustain a prosecution independently, are included in a single charge for purposes of *amplification: 49, 122

Division (διαίρεσις): The breaking down of an issue or theme into its component heads: 18–24, 28, 31 f., 47 f., 51, 53 f., 57, 61 f., 70, 121 f., 129, 133, 140, 147, 152

Documentary (ἔγγραφος): Opp. *non-documentary: making reference to a *verbal instrument. Both the *practical issue and *objection have documentary species: 35, 52, 54, 73, 78 f., 130 f., 134–7, 225

Double (διπλοῦς): Opp. *simple: a theme involving two questions: 41 f., 44–6, 48 f., 65 f., 94–100, 111–15, 122

Dual definition (δύο ὅροι): Species of *definition in which two persons make rival claims for a single description: 46, 114

Emotion (πάθος): One of the three means of persuasion (see also *character): 9, 15, 160, 178, 195, 197

Emotional (παθητικός):
(a) Opp. *practical: designates the parts of a speech (prologue and epilogue) primarily concerned with inciting emotion, as distinct from the parts primarily concerned with fact and argument (narrative and argument): 9
(b) *Class of themes inviting a treatment in which emotion is the dominant means of persuasion: 10, 70

Encomium (ἐγκώμιον): *Preliminary exercise in which the student is required to praise a given person (or other subject): 16, 29, 37, 44, 64, 83, 110, 118

Epideictic (ἐπιδεικτικός): Oratory other than *deliberative and *judicial: 10 f., 16, 19, 31, 70

Epilogue (ἐπίλογος): The concluding part of a speech, involving *recapitulation and elaborate *amplification: 9, 10 n., 15, 23 n., 40, 90 f., 109–12, 157, 160, 177–9, 191, 196 f., 211, 213, 227, 229 f.

Equivalent (ἰσάζων):
(a) *Person or *act offering no basis for different arguments on each side: 29 f., 42, 66, 95
(b) Species of theme *lacking issue, in which the arguments on each side are identical: 30, 67, 149

Exception (παραγραφικόν): Head which calls into question the validity of a prosecution: 36, 40, 54, 80–2, 86, 90, 97, 112, 116, 122 f., 135–7, 139, 158, 197, 224, 226, 228

Exclusion of further distinctions (τὸ μὴ προσδιωρίσθαι): Head which contests the validity of an appeal to the *intent of a legal instrument, as opposed to its *letter: 55–7, 144, 147

Fable (μῦθος): A *preliminary exercise: 13

Feasibility (δυνατόν): One of the *heads of purpose: 40, 52 f., 130, 133, 213

Figured (ἐσχηματισμένος): Having a covert aim in addition to or at variance with the speech's overt aim: 121 f., 138

Flawed in invention (κακόπλαστος): Species of theme which can be used as the basis for a declamation although technically flawed because of (e.g.) an anachronism or factual error: 31, 69

Forcible (βίαιος): Argument (distinct from *refutation and *counter-representation) which turns what appears to be a strong point in the opponent's position to one's own advantage. Also applied more generally to tendentious or strongly assertive arguments (including *refutation): 38, 126 f.

Forcible definition (βίαιος ὅρος): Head in which facts used by one party to characterize an action in one way are used paradoxically by the other to give an opposite characterization: 21 f., 40, 50 f., 55 f., 58 f., 89 f., 126–8, 145, 149, 151, 209–11, 225

Gloss (χρῶμα): *Transposition of cause: 30, 66, 87, 98, 107 f., 120, 152, 193, 210

Hard to follow (δυσπαρακόλουθος): *Mode in which the case is hard to understand: 10

Heads of purpose (τελικὰ κεφάλαια): A collective term for the standard topics used to evaluate a course of action (see *legality, *custom, *justice, *honour, *advantage, *feasibility, *consequence). They provide the *division of the *practical issue, and are also used in *epilogues: 15, 21, 40, 62, 91, 130–4, 157, 160, 181, 212 f.

Honour (ἔνδοξον): One of the *heads of purpose: 28, 39 f., 52 f., 62, 74, 133, 157, 160

Honourable (ἔνδοξος): *Mode in which both person and act are admirable: 10

Hypothesis (ὑπόθεσις): A circumstantially specific rhetorical theme (contrast *thesis): 17, 62

Ill-balanced (ἑτερορρεπής): Species of theme in which one side has a far stronger case than the other; although this comes close to being *one-sided (and therefore *lacking issue) it can be used (e.g.) as a demonstration of the declaimer's skill: 31, 60

Implausible (ἀπίθανος): Species of theme *lacking issue: 31, 67 f.

Importance (πηλικότης): Head which argues that something is important, for purposes of *amplification; cf. *relative importance: 43 f., 47, 58 f., 105, 107, 111 f., 119, 123–5, 139 f., 151, 178, 181, 190, 193, 224, 228–30

Impossible (ἀδύνατος): Species of theme *lacking issue: 31, 67, 149

Incident (ἐμπίπτων):
(*a*) A species of *conjunct *conjecture, in which the *transposition of cause presupposes a factually disputed claim: 42, 96, 99 f., 113 f.

(*b*) A species of *definition in which a second definition arises out of the defence to the main question: 46, 113 f.

(*c*) More generally, an incident question is one which arises in the course of the dispute over the main question arising out of a charge: 128, 209, 229

Inclusion (σύλληψις): Species of *definition in which the opponent's description of the act is accepted, and another description added to it: 45, 112

Inclusive and included (περιέχον καὶ περιεχόμενον): Head which argues that one of two conflicting legal instruments subsumes, but is not subsumed by, the other and should therefore take precedence: 56, 58–60, 148 f., 154, 192

Incomplete (ἀτελής): A *conjecture is incomplete if either *person or *act offers no basis for argument: 41 f., 63, 65 f., 88, 92–5, 180, 191

Insoluble (ἄπορος): Species of theme *lacking issue in which the question has no resolution in principle: 30 f., 67

Intent (διάνοια):

(*a*) In *counterposition, the head in which the defendant prepares for the counterposition proper by arguing that the underlying intent of his actions was innocent: 21, 50, 125, 143, 147, 209 f., 224, 226, 228

(*b*) In general, the meaning given to a *verbal instrument; more specifically, the verbal instrument interpreted according to its spirit (opp. *letter): 33, 77, 141, 145, 149, 224, 226, 228

(*c*) In *letter and intent, the head which argues that the underlying intent of the act in question is consistent with the intent (as distinct from the letter) of the *verbal instrument: 55 f., 55–7, 143, 147, 224, 226, 228

Intention (γνώμη): Head (paired with *quality) which relates the alleged intention of an act to the individual agent's character and behaviour in general: 43 f., 46 f., 50 f., 54–6, 58–60, 110, 121, 128, 141, 145, 149, 152, 155

Invective (ψόγος): *Preliminary exercise in which the student is required to attack a given person (or other subject): 16, 64

Invention (εὕρεσις): The part of rhetoric concerned with identifying the resources for persuasion which exist objectively in a given subject and situation. Some rhetoricians distinguished invention from a preliminary phase of *analysis and a subsequent phase of assessment and selection (*judgement): 7 f., 11 n., 23, 28, 53, 62

Issue (στάσις): A classification of rhetorical themes according to the different kinds of dispute they involve. The *division of an issue sets out the heads of argument which provide an effective strategy for handling each kind: 2, 11, 18–24, 31–5, 70–9

Judgement (κρίσις): The assessment and selection of material generated by *invention: 7, 53, 65, 80, 133

Judicial (δικανικός):

(*a*) Oratory before judges and/or a jury (opp. *deliberative, *epideictic): 9–11, 13, 16 f., 19, 21, 25, 28, 31, 70, 74 (*b*) A term used in some sources as equivalent to *practical: 10 n.

Juridical (δικαιολογικός): The sub-division of *quality concerned with the evaluation of a past act (opp. *practical): 33, 52, 72, 75

Justice (δίκαιον): One of the *heads of purpose: 28, 40, 52, 62, 74, 130, 133, 213

Lacking issue (ἀσύστατος): A theme which cannot sustain a rhetorical dispute lacks issue, and is therefore invalid: 30 f., 66–9, 73, 125, 149

Legal (νομικός): Opp. *logical: issues which turn on the interpretation of a *verbal instrument, as distinct from the evaluation of an act: 21 n., 33–5, 52, 54, 72, 74, 76 f., 130 f., 134–7, 141, 157, 223–30

Legality (νόμιμον): One of the *heads of purpose; the *documentary counterpart to *custom: 40, 52, 132

Legislator's intention (γνώμη νομοθέτου): Head in which the intended meaning of a legal instrument is disputed (sometimes also called legislator's intent, διάνοια νομοθέτου): 43 f., 47, 55–60, 104 f., 107, 112, 119, 140, 143 f., 147, 151, 154, 177, 180, 190

Letter (ῥητόν): The literal interpretation of a *verbal instrument: 58, 151

Letter and intent (ῥητὸν και διάνοια): *Legal issue in which an alleged implicit *intent is opposed to an interpretation of a *verbal instrument according to the *letter: 34 f., 38 f., 55 f., 72, 77, 79, 119 f., 131, 141–7, 149, 152, 157, 209, 211, 224

Logical (λογικός): Opp. *legal: issues which turn on the evaluation of an act, as distinct from the interpretation of a *verbal instrument: 21 n., 33 f., 54, 72, 74, 76 f., 130 f., 134, 136 f., 141, 153, 225

Maxim (γνώμη): *Preliminary exercise, similar to *anecdote except that the saying on which it is based is not explicitly attributed: 14 f., 224

Mitigation (συγγνώμη):
    (*a*) Head (one of the *counterpositions) in which an acknowledged *prima facie* wrong is excused as due to factors outside the defendant's control, and not capable of being brought to account (or, according to some, due to internal factors outside the defendant's control, such as emotion): 39 f., 50 f., 88, 113, 120, 122, 159, 197
    (*b*) The issue in which mitigation is the crucial head: 33 f., 50 f., 72, 76, 100, 126, 129

Mixed (μικτός): *Class of themes involving a balance of the three means of persuasion (i.e. *practical, *emotional, and based on *character): 10

Mode (τρόπος): A way of classifying themes according to the quality of the subject-matter (see *honourable, *disreputable, *ambiguous, *paradoxical, *hard to follow): 31, 51, 68 f.

Motive (βούλησις): Head of *conjecture in which it is disputed whether the defendant had a motive to commit the crime alleged; usually paired with *capacity: 36 f., 41 f., 84, 92, 95, 109, 133, 158 f., 179 f., 191

Narration (διήγημα): *Preliminary exercise: 13

Narrative (διήγησις):

(a) The part of a speech (normally placed between *prologue and *arguments) in which a speaker puts forward an account of events favourable to his own case: 9, 10 n., 84 f., 105 f., 157 f., 176 f., 208, 212, 227

(b) A 'plain' exposition of facts, opp. *statement: 84 f.

Non-documentary (ἄγραφος): Opp. *documentary: without reference to a *verbal instrument. In the non-documentary species of the *practical issue, no verbal instrument is cited at all; in non-documentary *objection a legal instrument is cited, but the dispute turns on the circumstances of the act: 35, 52, 54, 73, 78 f., 131 f., 134–7, 213

Non-technical proof (ἄτεχνος πίστις): A means of persuasion, such as the testimony of a witness, that is not dependent on technical devices of rhetoric (opp. *technical): 82

Objection (μετάληψις):

(a) Head (opposed to *counterplea) which concedes the legitimacy of an act in itself, but disputes its legitimacy in the given circumstances: 22, 38, 43 f., 46 f., 50, 54–60, 86 f., 104, 109, 120, 126, 140, 145, 148, 151, 154, 156, 177, 179, 192 f., 209, 211, 226–30

(b) The issue in which the validity of a charge is challenged on the basis of the explicit provisions of a legal instrument, and in which the dispute turns *either* on the interpretation of that legal instrument *or* on the circumstances of the act charged: 35 f., 54 f., 73, 78 f., 82, 115 f., 118, 134–41, 144, 223–20, 246 f.

One-sided (μονομερής): Species of theme *lacking issue, in which a case can be made on only one side: 30, 67

Paradoxical (παράδοξος):

(a) *Mode in which the case to be made is difficult to believe: 10

(b) Species of *conjecture in which normal expectations are reversed: 101

Part of right (μόριον τοῦ δικαίου): Head of *counterplea offering a preliminary formulation of the counterplea proper as an *exception: 24 n., 46, 116, 196

Person (πρόσωπον):

(a) One of the six elements of *circumstance: 13, 25, 35, 37, 79, 87, 116, 158, 192, 223, 229

(b) The persons stated or implied in a *hypothesis; one of the two bases from which arguments can be derived (cf. *act). When using person as a basis for argument, the speaker may consider the concomitants (παρακολουθοῦντα) of person, which are the topics of *encomium: 28–30, 32, 36 f., 41 f., 44, 53, 61, 63–5, 68, 74, 81, 83, 92–5, 118 f.

(c) Head of *counterplea (a *definitional exception) in which it is argued that the charge is in principle inapplicable to the person of the defendant: 46 f., 118 f., 196

Persuasive defence (πιθανὴ ἀπολογία): Head of *conjecture, in which it is argued that the events cited as indications that the defendant committed the crime imply his innocence: 36, 39, 41, 83, 86, 89 f., 93, 96, 159 f.

Practical (πραγματικός):

(a) The issue turning on a dispute about the evaluation of future acts (roughly co-extensive with *deliberative oratory) divided according to the *heads of purpose: 33, 52, 72, 74, 129‒34, 145, 149, 211‒23

(b) Opp. *verbal: the practical department (τόπος) of rhetoric is the part concerned with content, as distinct from its verbal expression, i.e. *invention and *disposition: 8

(c) Opp. *emotional: designates the parts of a speech (*narrative and *arguments) primarily concerned with fact and argument, as distinct from the more emotive parts (*prologue and *epilogue): 9

(d) *Class of themes inviting a treatment in which argument is the dominant means of persuasion: 10

Pre-confirmatory (προκατασκευαζόμενος): Species of *conjunct *conjecture, in which the charge presupposes a factually disputed claim: 42 f., 96‒9

Prejudiced (προειλημμένος τῇ κρίσει): Species of theme in which the jury's predisposition (rather than the strength of the case) makes the verdict a foregone conclusion: 31, 67

Preliminary confirmation (προκατασκευή): Part of a speech containing preparation for, or a preliminary outline of, the speaker's argument: 112

Preliminary exercise (γύμνασμα, προγύμνασμα): One of the practical exercises used in the early stages of rhetorical training: 13‒18, 22, 80, 82, 84, 88, 95, 105, 121, 133, 178, 224, 227

Preliminary narrative (προδιήγησις): *Preliminary statement: 157

Preliminary statement (προκατάστασις): Exposition of the background to events included in the *statement proper: 157 f., 176, 195

Presentation (προβολή): Head in which the events on which the case is based (or, in *legal issues, the relevant *verbal instrument) are briefly stated, usually with moderate *amplification: 43 f., 46, 50, 54‒6, 58‒60, 84, 102, 105 f., 116, 119, 123, 137, 139 f., 142, 145 f., 149‒51, 153 f., 177, 191 f., 196, 209

Procedural exception (παραγραφή):

(a) A challenge to the procedural validity of a prosecution: 35 f., 54, 71, 79, 82, 135 f., 139

(b) According to some rhetoricians, documentary *objection regarded as a distinct issue: 135 f.

Prologue (προοίμιον): The introductory part of a speech: 9, 10 n., 23 n., 40, 91, 112, 157 f., 160, 176, 178 f., 195, 212

Proposal of law (νόμου εἰσφορά): *Preliminary exercise, in which the student is required to speak for or against a legislative proposal, without reference to specific circumstances: 17, 105

Quality (ποιότης):

(a) Head (paired with *intention) which sets a particular act in the context of the agent's character and behaviour in general: 43 f., 46 f., 50 f., 54–6, 58–60, 91, 109 f., 121, 128, 141, 145, 149, 152, 155, 181, 197, 210

(b) The group of issues which turn on the evaluation of an act, there being no dispute about the fact (*conjecture) or about the description of the act (*definition): 21, 33, 71–4, 130, 136

Recapitulation (ἀνακεφαλαίωσις): A brief review of one's case included in the *epilogue: 40, 90 f., 160, 197

Refutation (ἀνασκευή): *Preliminary exercise, in which the student is required to argue against the credibility of a specified narration: 15, 84

Refutation (ἔνστασις): Opp. *counter-representation: outright denial of the opponent's position: 38, 47, 52, 87, 104, 119 f., 126–8, 133, 179, 194, 196

Relative importance (πρός τι): Head which argues that something is more important than the alternative, for purposes of *amplification; cf. *importance: 21 f., 43 f., 46 f., 50, 55–8, 105, 107, 111 f., 119, 123–6, 139 f., 145, 148, 151, 178, 190, 193, 230

Request for intention (γνώμης αἴτησις): Head which challenges the opponent to explain what intention an act could have had other than that proposed by the speaker: 107, 120, 152, 181, 193

Reversible (ἀντιστρέφων): Species of theme *lacking issue in which the arguments used by each side can also be used as arguments against the same side: 30, 67

Second intent (ἑτέρα διάνοια): Head which examines the consistency of the *exclusion of further distinctions with the intention of the legislator: 55–7, 144, 147

Second objection (ἑτέρα μετάληψις): The head of *objection on its second occurrence in a *division: 22, 46 f., 50 f., 54–6, 121, 127 f., 140, 145, 149, 227

Second speech (δευτορολογία): Speech concentrating on sustained *amplification in the manner of an *epilogue, the argumentative part of the case having been handled by a previous speaker: 40, 91

Sequence of events (τὰ ἀπ' ἀρχῆς ἄχρι τέλους): Head in which the events on which the case is based are subjected to step-by-step analysis and/or amplification: 36–9, 41, 47, 50, 82, 84, 88 f., 92, 102 f., 105, 107, 119 f., 123–6, 159, 178, 194, 209 f.

Simple (ἁπλοῦς): Opp. *double: theme involving a single question: 40 f., 44, 48, 65, 92–4, 97, 111, 114

Solution (λύσις): A speaker's response to an argument attributed to the opposing side by *counterposition: 17, 104, 127, 178, 191, 209 f., 213, 224, 228–30

Statement (κατάστασις): An exposition of facts slanted to the speaker's advantage, opp. *narrative: 84, 105 f., 112, 158, 176–8, 190, 195 f., 208–10, 226–8

Technical proof (ἔντεχνος πίστις): A means of persuasion dependent on technical devices of rhetoric (opp. *non-technical): 82 f.

Thesis (θέσις):

(*a*) *Preliminary exercise in which the student is required to argue for or against some general proposition; most (but not all) sources distinguish thesis from *hypothesis by the fact that there is no reference to particular circumstances: 16 f., 62, 82

(*b*) Head in which a general proposition is developed in support of a case being made about the particular circumstances of a given *hypothesis: 22, 39, 46 f., 50 f., 54–6, 58–60, 88 f., 120 f., 140, 145, 148, 154

Transference (μετάστασις):

(*a*) Head (one of the *counterpositions) in which an acknowledged *prima facie* wrong is defended by the transfer of blame to a third party (other than the victim or the defendant) who could be held to account (or, according to some, to any external factor outside the defendant's control): 21, 50 f., 120, 159, 194, 209

(*b*) The issue in which transference is the crucial head: 33 f., 50 f., 72, 76, 126, 128 f., 208–11

Transposition of cause (μετάθεσις τῆς αἰτίας): Head of *conjecture in which the defence offers an innocent explanation of the events cited by the prosecution as a sign of the crime; also known as *gloss: 36, 38–42, 66, 86–9, 93, 96, 98, 107, 114, 156, 159

Uncircumstantial (ἀπερίστατος): Species of theme *lacking issue, in which neither *person nor *act offers a basis for argument, and no question arises: 31, 67

Verbal (λεκτικός): Opp. *practical: the verbal department (τόπος) of rhetoric is the part concerned with expression, as distinct from content: 8

Verbal instrument (ῥητόν): Any utterance or written text cited in a dispute: 21 n., 33–6, 52, 55 f., 59 f., 77, 82, 129, 130 f., 139 f., 143, 150, 224–6, 229 f.

Greek–English Key

ἄγραφος non-documentary
ἀγῶνες arguments
ἄδοξος disreputable
ἀδύνατος impossible
ἀμφιβολία ambiguity
ἀμφίδοξος ambiguous
ἀμφισβήτησις dispute
ἀνακεφαλαίωσις recapitulation
ἀνασκευή refutation
ἀνθορισμός counterdefinition
ἀντέγκλημα counteraccusation
ἀντίθεσις counterposition
ἀντίληψις counterplea
ἀντινομία conflict of law
ἀντιπαράστασις counter-representation
ἀντίστασις counterstatement
ἀντιστρέφων reversible
ἀντονομάζων counterdescriptive
ἀπερίστατος uncircumstantial
ἀπίθανος implausible
ἁπλοῦς simple
ἄπορος insoluble
ἀρχῆς ἄχρι τέλους, τὰ ἀπ sequence of
  events
ἀσύστατος lacking issue
ἀτελής incomplete
ἄτεχνος non-technical
αὔξησις amplification

βαρύτης indignation
βίαιος forcible
βίαιος ὅρος forcible definition
βούλησις motive

γνώμη intention, maxim
γνώμη νομοθέτου legislator's intention
γνώμης αἴτησις request for intention
γύμνασμα exercise

δευτορολογία second speech
διάθεσις disposition

διαίρεσις division, distinction
διάνοια intent
διάνοια νομοθέτου legislator's intent
διήγημα narration
διήγησις narrative
δικαιολογικός juridical
δίκαιον justice
δικανικός judicial
διπλοῦς double
δύναμις capacity
δυνατόν feasibility
δύο ὅροι dual definition
δυσπαρακόλουθος hard to follow

ἔγγραφος documentary
ἐγκώμιον encomium
ἔθος custom
εἶδος class
ἐκβησόμενον consequence
ἔκθεσις exposition
ἔκφρασις description
ἐλέγχων ἀπαίτησις demand for evidence
ἐμπίπτων incident
ἔνδοξον honour
ἔνδοξος honourable
ἔνστασις refutation
ἔντεχνος technical
ἐπιδεικτικός epideictic
ἐπίλογος epilogue
ἐσχηματισμένος figured
ἑτέρα διάνοια alternative intent, second
  intent
ἑτέρα μετάληψις second objection
ἑτέρα προβολή alternative presentation
ἑτερορρεπής ill-balanced
εὕρεσις invention

ζήτημα question

ἠθικός characterizing, based on character
ἠθοποιία characterization

ἦθος character

θέσις thesis

ἰσάζων equivalent

κακόπλαστος flawed in invention
κατασκευή confirmation
κατάστασις statement
κεφάλαιον head
κοινὴ ποιότης common quality
κοινὸς τόπος common topic
κρινόμενον matter for judgement
κρίσις judgement

λεκτικός verbal
λογικός logical
λύσις solution

μείωσις diminution
μετάθεσις τῆς αἰτίας transposition of
    cause
μετάληψις objection
μεταξύ intermediate
μετάστασις transference
μικτός mixed
μονομερής one-sided
μόριον τοῦ δικαίου part of right
μῦθος fable

νόησις analysis
νομικός legal
νόμιμον legality
νόμου εἰσφορά proposal of law

οἰκονομία artificial order
ὁρικὴ παραγραφή definitional exception
ὅρος definition

παθητικός emotional
πάθος emotion
πανηγυρικός panegyric
παραγραφή procedural exception
παραγραφικόν exception
παράδοξος paradoxical
παρέκβασις digression
περιέχον καὶ περιεχόμενον inclusive and
    included
περίστασις circumstance
περιστατικά elements of circumstance

πηλικότης importance
πιθανὴ ἀπολογία persuasive defence
πίστις proof, means of persuasion
ποιότης quality
πολιτικὸν ζήτημα political question
πρᾶγμα act
πραγματικός practical
προβολή presentation
προγύμνασμα preliminary exercise
προδιήγησις preliminary narrative
προειλημμένος τῇ κρίσει prejudiced
προκατασκευαζόμενος pre-confirmatory
προκατασκευή preliminary confirmation
προκατάστασις preliminary statement
προοίμιον prologue
προσδιωρίσθαι, τὸ μὴ exclusion of further
    distinctions
πρός τι relative importance
πρόσωπον person

ῥητόν letter, verbal instrument
ῥητὸν καὶ διάνοια letter and intent

στάσις issue
στοχασμός conjecture
συγγνώμη mitigation
συγκατασκευαζόμενος co-confirmatory
σύγκρισις comparison
σύλληψις inclusion
συλλογισμός assimilation
συμβεβηκός contingency
συμβουλευτικός deliberative
συμπεπλεγμένος complex
συμπλοκή combination
συμφέρον advantage
συνεζευγμένος conjunct

τάξις natural order
τέλειος complete
τελικὰ κεφάλαια heads of purpose
τέχνη art
τόπος topic
τρόπος mode

ὑπόθεσις hypothesis

χρεία anecdote
χρῶμα gloss

ψόγος invective

Index of Passages Cited

General Index

DATE DUE